MIKE MEYERS' CERTIFICATION
Passport ★

CompTIA Security+
Certification Second Edition

T. J. SAMUELLE

McGraw Hill

New York · Chicago · San Francisco · Lisbon · London
Madrid · Mexico City · Milan · New Delhi · San Juan
Seoul · Singapore · Sydney · Toronto

Cataloging-in-Publication Data is on file with the Library of Congress

McGraw-Hill books are available at special quantity discounts to use as premiums and sales promotions, or for use in corporate training programs. To contact a special sales representative, please visit the Contact Us page at www.mhprofessional.com.

Mike Meyers' CompTIA Security+® Certification Passport, Second Edition

1234567890 FGR FGR 0198

ISBN: Book p/n 978-0-07-160125-2 and CD p/n 978-0-07-160126-9
of set 978-0-07-160123-8

MHID: Book p/n 0-07-160125-2 and CD p/n 0-07-160126-0
of set 0-07-160123-6

Sponsoring Editor Timothy Green	**Proofreader** John Gildersleeve
Editorial Supervisor Jody McKenzie	**Indexer** Karin Arrigoni
Project Editor Laura Stone	**Production Supervisor** James Kussow
Acquisitions Coordinator Jennifer Housh	**Composition** Apollo Publishing Services
Technical Editor Glen E. Clarke	**Cover Series Design** Ted Holladay
Copy Editor Lisa Theobold	**Art Director, Cover** Jeff Weeks

Dedication

This book is dedicated to all my family and friends, who have always given me their tremendous support throughout my writing career.

—T.J. Samuelle

Acknowledgments

First, I want to thank everyone at McGraw-Hill, especially Timothy Green, Jennifer Housh, Glen Clarke, and of course Mike Meyers. And a big thanks to all the people in the graphics and production departments!

I would like to thank my good friends and colleagues: Sandro Henriques, Les Lorincz and Paul Louro. I would also like to thank Joe P., Steve H., N.P.K, Jorge Alves, Steve Freedman, Juan Romero, Melissa Somerville, Tom Carter, Barry and Pauline Harrison, and Yngwie Malmsteen.

Contents

2   System Software Security 35

III Access Control 153

5 Access Control 155

Check-In

May I See Your Passport?

What do you mean, you don't have a passport? Why, it's sitting right in your hands, even as you read! This book is your passport to a very special place. You're about to begin a journey, my friend, a journey toward that magical place called *certification*! You don't need a ticket, you don't need a suitcase—just snuggle up and read this passport, because it's all you need to get there. Are you ready? Let's go!

Your Travel Agent: Mike Meyers

Hello! I'm Mike Meyers, president of Total Seminars and author of a number of popular certification books. On any given day, you'll find me replacing a hard drive, setting up a web site, or writing code. I love every aspect of this book you hold in your hands. It's part of a powerful book series called the Mike Meyers' Certification Passports. Every book in this series combines easy readability with a condensed format—in other words, it's the kind of book I always wanted when I went for my certifications. Putting a huge amount of information in an accessible format is an enormous challenge, but I think we have achieved our goal, and I am confident you'll agree.

I designed this series to do one thing and only one thing—to get you the information you need to achieve your certification. You won't find any fluff in here. T.J. and I packed every page with nothing but the real nitty gritty of the CompTIA Security+ certification exams. Every page has 100 percent pure concentrate of certification knowledge!

Your Destination: CompTIA Security+ Certification

This book is your passport to CompTIA's Security+ Certification, the vendor-neutral industry standard certification developed for foundation-level security professionals. Based on a worldwide job task analysis, the structure of the exam focuses on core competencies in systems security, network security, access control, assessments and audits, basic cryptography, and organizational security.

Whether the Security+ certification is your first step toward a career focus in security or an additional skill credential, this book is your passport to success on the Security+ Certification exam.

Your Guides: Mike Meyers and T.J. Samuelle

You get a pair of tour guides for this book, both me and T.J. Samuelle. I've written numerous computer certification books—including the best-selling *A+ Certification All-in-One Exam Guide* and the *Network+ Certification All-in-One Exam Guide*. More to the point, I've been working on PCs and teaching others how to make and fix them for a *very* long time, and I love it! When I'm not lecturing or writing about PCs, I'm working on PCs, naturally!

T.J. Samuelle is an Information Technology (IT) consultant from southwestern Ontario, Canada. To contact T.J., please email him at tjsamuelle@gmail.com.

About the Technical Editor

Glen E. Clarke (MCSE/MCSD/MCDBA/MCT/CEH/SCNP/CIWSA/A+/Security+) is an independent trainer and consultant, focusing on network security assessments and educating IT professionals on hacking countermeasures. Glen spends most of his time delivering certified courses on Windows Server 2003, SQL Server, Exchange Server, Visual Basic .NET, ASP.NET, ethical hacking, and security analysis. He has authored and been technical editor for a number of certification titles, including the *Network+ Certification Study Guide*, Third Edition. You can visit Glen online at www.gleneclarke.com, or contact him at glenclarke@accesswave.ca.

About LearnKey

LearnKey provides self-paced learning content and e-learning solutions to enhance personal skills and business productivity. LearnKey claims the largest library of streaming-media training content that engages learners in dynamic, media-rich instruction complete with video clips, audio, full-motion graphics, and animated illustrations. LearnKey can be found on the Web at www.LearnKey.com.

Why the Travel Theme?

The steps to gaining a certification parallel closely the steps to planning and taking a trip. All of the elements are the same: preparation, an itinerary, a route, even mishaps along the way. Let me show you how it all works.

This book is divided into 13 chapters. Each chapter begins with an *Itinerary* that lists the objectives covered in that chapter, and an *ETA* to give you an idea of the time involved in learning the skills in that chapter. Each chapter is broken down by the objectives, which are either those officially stated by the certifying body or our expert take on the best way to approach the topics.

Each chapter contains a number of helpful items to call out points of interest:

Exam Tip

Points out critical topics you're likely to see on the actual exam.

Local Lingo

Describes special terms, in detail and in a way you can easily understand.

Travel Advisory

Warns you of common pitfalls, misconceptions, and downright physical peril!

Travel Assistance

Directs you to additional sources, such as books and web sites, to give you more information.

The end of the chapter gives you two handy tools. The *Checkpoint* reviews each objective covered in the chapter with a handy synopsis—a great way to review quickly. The end-of-chapter *Review Questions* test your newly acquired skills.

But the fun doesn't stop there! After you've read the book, pull out the CD-ROM and take advantage of the free practice exam! Use the full practice exam to hone your skills, and keep the book handy to check answers. Appendix A explains how to use the CD-ROM.

When you reach the point that you're acing the practice questions, you're ready to take the exam. Go get certified!

The End of the Trail

The IT industry changes and grows constantly, *and so should you*. Finishing one certification is just a step in an ongoing process of gaining more and more certifications to match your constantly changing and growing skills. Read Appendix B, "Career Flight Path," to determine where this certification fits into your personal certification goals. Remember, in the IT business, if you're not moving forward, you're way behind!

Good luck on your certification! Stay in touch.

Mike Meyers
Series Editor
Mike Meyers' Certification Passport

PART

I

Systems Security

System Security Threats and Risks

	NEWBIE	SOME EXPERIENCE	EXPERT
ETA	3 hours	1.5 hours	0.5 hour

With the explosive growth of network access systems and removable media and peripherals, an increasing array of security risks and dangers threaten the security of an organization's servers and client computer systems. Malicious software such as viruses, worms, Trojan horse programs, and logic bombs can wreak havoc on an unsecured system, while coordinated attacks on a specific computer system from external threats such as a botnet can be equally damaging. Within the network, insecure passwords and accounts and access to removable media and devices and network attached devices cause additional concern for system security. System administrators must be aware of the numerous threats and risks to their server and client systems both from within an organization and from external sources.

This chapter explores various security threats and risks for systems, including software threats such as malicious programs (viruses, worms, Trojan horses, and so on), system peripherals, removable storage, account and password threats, and social-engineering hacking techniques.

Differentiate Among Various Systems Security Threats

Objective 1.01
CompTIA Security+
Objective 1.1

Systems security means not only securing sensitive data against unauthorized access, but also protecting the integrity and existence of that data from malicious users and software. Most companies use security resources, such as security guards and cameras, to prevent unauthorized physical access to their equipment and facilities. With the proliferation of networking and removable peripheral devices and media that are attached and connected to computers, organizations must also protect themselves from numerous technological pathways that can potentially provide unauthorized system access.

Damage from virus attacks or unauthorized access gained via back-door or Trojan horse types of programs can be catastrophic. A simple worm attached to an e-mail message can cause mail and network systems to grind to a halt. Other viruses contain payloads that destroy or damage information that might never be recovered if a backup plan is not in place.

System administrators must be aware of the numerous types of system software attacks, how these attacks gain entry into the system, and what can be done once they infect a system. First and foremost, proactive protection in the form of knowledge and user education is critical in dealing with these types of threats.

Viruses

Viruses are probably the most common and prevalent type of system attack. A *virus* is a computer program that replicates itself within the affected system, even if the virus program does not harm the system. Most computer viruses self-replicate without the knowledge of the computer user.

Like a human virus, computer viruses can be passed along from one system to another—via e-mail messages, instant messages, web site downloads, discs and removable media, and network connections. An enormous amount of expense and time can be required to clean up and restore operations after a virus attack. Some companies take many days, or even weeks, to get back to full operations after their systems have been infected with a virus. For certain time-sensitive businesses, a virus infection can be fatal to the entire computer system and company work.

Types of Viruses

Viruses come in a variety of forms, with different locations and methods of infection and severity of payload. The following sections outline some common virus types.

Boot Sector Viruses   *Boot sector* viruses infect the boot sector or partition table of a disk. The *boot sector* is used by the computer to determine what operating systems (OSs) are present on the system to boot. The most common way a boot sector virus finds its way into a system is through an infected disk or removable media device that is inserted into the computer. After infecting the boot sector, the virus will not allow the system to boot into the operating system, rendering the computer useless until the boot sector is repaired.

The best way to remove a boot-sector virus from a system is to boot the system using an anti-virus or similar emergency recovery boot disk or CD. This lets you start up the computer with basic start-up files, bypassing the boot sector, and then run the anti-virus program on the CD.

Companion Viruses   A *companion* virus disguises itself as a legitimate program, using the name of a legitimate program but with a different extension. For example, a virus might name itself *program.com* to emulate a file called *program.exe*. A .com file under the Windows/DOS operating systems is a higher priority than a standard .exe file with the same name, so the virus file program.com would run first. Typically, the virus runs the legitimate program immediately after installing the virus code, so it appears the system is performing normally. Some viruses replace the original legitimate file with their own version that performs the same tasks and includes new, malicious code to run with it.

File Infector Viruses *File-infector* viruses generally infect files that have the extensions .com or .exe. These viruses can be extremely destructive because they try to replicate and spread further by infecting other executable programs on the system with the same extensions. Sometimes, a file-infector virus destroys the program it infects by overwriting the original code.

Travel Advisory

If your computer is afflicted with a file-infector virus, do not attach it to a network or it could start infecting files on other workstations and file servers.

Macro Viruses A macro is an instruction that carries out program commands automatically within an application. Macros are typically used in popular office applications such as Microsoft Word and Excel. A *macro virus* uses the internal workings of the application to perform malicious operations when a file containing the macro is opened, such as deleting files or opening other virus-executable programs. Sometimes these viruses also infect program templates that are loaded automatically by the applications. Every time the user creates a file using the default template, the macro virus is copied to the new file.

Memory Resident Viruses When a system is infected by a virus that stays resident in the system memory, the *memory-resident* virus will continue to stay in memory and infect other files that are run at the same time. For a memory-resident virus to spread, the user has to run an infected program that, once activated, inserts the virus into system memory, where the virus examines each new program as it is run and, if the program is not already infected, infects it.

Polymorphic Viruses *Polymorphic* viruses change themselves with each infection. These types of viruses were created to confuse virus-scanning programs. These viruses are difficult to detect by scanning because each copy of the virus looks different from the previous copies.

Metamorphic Viruses A *metamorphic* virus is capable of recompiling itself into a new form, and the code keeps changing from generation to generation. A metamorphic virus is similar to a polymorphic virus because both can modify their forms. A metamorphic virus does not decrypt itself to a single constant virus body in memory, though, as a polymorphic virus does. A metamorphic virus can also change its virus body code.

Stealth Viruses　A *stealth* virus hides itself from virus protection software by encrypting its code. Stealth viruses attempt to cover their trail as they infect their way through a computer. When a stealth virus infects, it takes over the system function that reads files or system sectors. When something or someone attempts to access the corrupted file, the stealth virus reports that the original file is there. In reality, however, the original information is gone and the stealth virus has taken its place.

Local Lingo
encryption　The transformation of readable data into some unreadable form.

File Types That Commonly Carry Viruses

Some types of files are susceptible to virus infections because they are common to certain types of computer systems and applications. The following are a few of the most popular types of program files targeted by viruses:

- **.bat**　An MS-DOS batch file contains a series of commands for the OS that are executed automatically in sequence.
- **.com**　MS-DOS command files usually execute within a command shell interface, or they can be by executed from a user interface such as Windows. Most early computer viruses were created as .com files because the main DOS program files were in this form.
- **.doc**　This file extension is associated with Microsoft Word. Along with Microsoft Access and Excel files, .doc file extensions are susceptible to macro virus infection.
- **.dll**　A dynamic-link library (DLL) is a library of executable functions or data that can be used by a Windows application. Typically, a DLL provides one or more particular functions and a program accesses these functions.
- **.exe**　An executable file is most commonly found on MS-DOS and Windows OSs.
- **.html**　The .html or .htm extension is used for a document written in HTML coding that can be opened by web browsers.
- **.mdb**　This file extension is associated with a Microsoft Access database. As with Word and Excel files, the .mdb file is susceptible to macro virus infection.

- **.scr**   This is the default file extension for Microsoft Windows screensavers. As screensavers are popular items to copy to other users, .scr files are typically easy targets for viruses.

- **.vbs**   Files with the .vbs extension are for Microsoft Visual Basic Scripting, a subset of the Visual Basic programming language. This powerful language can create scripts that can perform a wide variety of functions such as control applications and manipulate the file system. VB Script is powerful and can be used to create malicious code.

- **.xls**   This file extension is associated with a Microsoft Excel spreadsheet. As with Word and Access files, .xls files are susceptible to macro virus infection.

- **.zip**   This extension is used for a compressed file that contains one or more other files. Zip files are compressed to save space and to make grouping files for transport and copying faster and easier. Zip files must also be checked by anti-virus software to ensure that the files in the archive are not infected.

Exam Tip
Recognize which types of files are most likely to carry a virus.

Trojan Horses

Trojan horse programs are named from the ancient myth in which Greek warriors invaded the gated city of Troy by hiding inside a gigantic wooden horse. Once inside the city gates, the warriors leapt from inside the horse and attacked the surprised inhabitants, winning a decisive battle.

A Trojan horse program hides on your computer system until called upon to perform a certain task. A Trojan is usually downloaded through e-mail attachments or from Internet web sites and instant messages. Trojans are usually disguised as popular programs such as games, pictures, or music. When the program is run, it usually appears to the victim user as if nothing has happened, but the Trojan has secretly installed itself on the user's computer. The Trojan horse runs a service on the victim's computer and opens a port (such as TCP/IP port 12345 in the case of NetBus) on the system to which the attacker can be connected when he runs the control application from a remote location. Once connected, the attacker has full access to the infected system. Popular Trojan horse programs used by attackers include NetBus, Sub7, and Back Orifice, which enable the attacker to take control of a user's computer once the Trojan horse file is installed.

Travel Advisory

A firewall can detect suspicious incoming and outgoing network traffic from your computer. If you do not recognize a program, it could be a Trojan horse communicating out to the network.

Logic Bombs

Although it can be running on a system for a long time, a *logic bomb* program will not activate until a specific trigger, such as reaching a specific date or starting a program a specific number of times, is set off. Logic bombs can be highly destructive depending on their payload. The damage done by a logic bomb can range from changing bytes of data on the victim's hard disk to rendering the user's entire hard drive unreadable.

Logic bombs are distributed primarily via worms and viruses; however, cases of malicious programmers inserting code into a trusted application that will trigger at a later time have been documented. Logic bombs can be difficult to detect because after the initial installation, there may be no indication for hours, days, months, and even years that the logic bomb is present before it is scheduled to release its malicious payload.

Most anti-virus software is able to detect the most common types of logic bombs; however, if a logic bomb is hidden within a trusted application, it may be difficult to detect its presence until it is too late. For software development companies, all code must be peer-reviewed before the application is released to ensure that a single malicious programmer cannot insert hidden logic bomb code.

Worms

A computer *worm* is a self-contained program or set of programs that can spread full copies or smaller segments of itself to other computer systems via network connections, e-mail attachments, or instant messages. Worms are most common in various types of networking application servers such as e-mail servers, web servers, and database servers.

The explosive increase in worms within e-mail attachments and instant messages has caused anti-virus program companies and e-mail software companies to reevaluate the functionality of their applications to prevent the spread of messaging-based worms. A user receives an attachment to an e-mail that contains a malicious worm. When the attachment is opened, the worm infects the user's computer and then replicates itself by sending copies of the same e-mail to everyone in the user's address book. Each user, in turn, sees the e-mail arrive from someone familiar and automatically opens the attachment, thinking it is safe. These types of worm infections can spread quickly and can bring down an e-mail server in a matter of minutes.

Application server vendors have taken steps to prevent these types of worms from spreading by patching their applications to prevent malicious attachment code from executing.

Adware and Spyware

Adware (advertising software) and *spyware* are potential software threats that are not always considered security risks. Many free or low-cost software programs are often supported financially by embedding advertising content within the applications themselves. Although this provides a modest revenue stream for the software developers, it also opens the door to potential security threats such as compromised private and personal data. Even software as simple as a downloadable screensaver may contain adware or spyware that installs code to deliver advertising to the user and/or collect personal information for use in targeted advertising.

In addition to the nuisance of the advertising (which is not easily disabled) is the threat that the program itself is sending the user's personal information back to the advertiser. This information can include web surfing habits, key logging, online purchases, and personal contact information such as e-mail address, home address, and credit card details. This personal information can be used directly by the advertiser or sold to other companies that will also use or distribute the personal information.

Spyware is not necessarily involved with advertising, and it can be installed by any type of software application, even trusted, popular application and entertainment software. Spyware typically tracks the user's habits while using an application such as a music player that relays the user's musical preferences back to the application vendor. This information can then be compiled by the vendor and sold to third parties such as record companies.

Many types of anti-virus software can detect and clean software designated as adware and spyware. It is critical that end users run some type of anti-virus software on their computers and regularly scan their hard drives for evidence of adware and spyware programs that are secretly sending personal data from the computers to advertisers. User education is also important to advise users not to download non–work-oriented software that may contain adware or spyware, such as games, entertainment, or social networking software, to a networked company computer.

Rootkits

A *rootkit* is a type of back-door program that is inserted into application software and allows a remote user *root* access (administrator access) to the system on which the software is installed, without the permission or knowledge of the user. This access potentially results in full control over the target system. Although rootkits are usually related to malware and Trojan horse types of malicious software, they are also becoming more common in trusted applications that are potentially used by millions of users.

For example, a well-known entertainment company was found to be distributing rootkits on its music CDs. This software was installed on a user's computer while the music CD was played on the system. This software installation was not disclosed to the user, and the software (primarily used for digital rights management of music copyright) allowed root access and control of the computer system for anyone aware that the software was installed. After the issue was widely publicized on the Internet, the company quickly intervened to ensure that this software was no longer distributed with its music CDs.

Rootkits are not always installed by application software. They can be distributed via firmware updates for a hardware device, embedded into the primary operating system kernel (kernel rootkits), and included on application software libraries such as DLL files. Rootkits do not spread like a worm or virus; they typically infect one system only. However, rootkits themselves are typically spread as the payload of replicating worms and viruses.

Several types of rootkits exist, including the following:

- **Firmware rootkits** The rootkit is embedded within the firmware of a device, such as a computer peripheral or network device. The rootkit is always available as it is embedded within the firmware of the system and is always activated when the device is running.

- **Kernel rootkits** The rootkit is embedded within the operating system core itself. This effectively hides the rootkit, as it runs as a hidden process and can rarely be spotted by checking active processes on the system.

- **Persistent rootkits** The rootkit is enabled when the system starts and will not turn off unless the system is shut down. This type of rootkit is often installed and activated within the Windows Registry and is run each time the system boots.

- **Application rootkits**   The rootkit is activated and run in current system memory only when a specific application is launched and is not persisted when the system is shut down and restarted.
- **Library rootkits**   In software applications that use code library files, such as Windows DLLs, the rootkit can intercept specific system and API calls and replace them with its own code.

Most anti-virus software applications are able to detect the presence of rootkits; however, they may be difficult to clean from a system, especially if they are embedded in the kernel or boot sectors of an OS. In such cases, it is often the safest and most secure practice to reinstall the system to ensure that any rootkit code is deleted.

Botnets

Botnet is short for *robot network*. A *bot* is typically any type of computer system that is attached to a network whose security has been compromised and that runs malicious software completely unknown to the system users. Botnets (often called "zombie" computers) are typically used for *distributed denial-of-service (DDoS)* attacks in which hundreds or even tens of thousands of computers are overtaken and programmed to send network attacks to a single target site. Botnets can also be used to send out large amounts of spam, adware, spyware, and malware.

An infected computer (which is typically infected by a worm, virus, or Trojan horse) that is made part of the botnet might not show any initial effects. It is only after the computer is remotely "turned on" to start its attack on another computer that the compromise becomes apparent. Typical symptoms include slow responsiveness and large amounts of network packets being sent from the infected system.

Because compromised servers are controlled by the botnets and are typically not under local control, and because of servers' distributed nature, which means the affected servers could be located anywhere in the world, it can be difficult to mitigate the effects of these types of coordinated attacks. It is also very difficult to plan for future attacks. Although the originating addresses of the systems in the botnet can be blocked, other compromised systems can be easily added to the botnet to continue the attack from different addresses. Nevertheless, regular investigations of system activity and frequent anti-virus scans can help prevent a system from becoming infected with a virus or worm and becoming a bot within a larger botnet.

Privilege Escalation

Many software applications contain bugs that create security vulnerabilities. A *software bug* is a term used to describe an error in a program that hinders or alters its ability to function properly. In a *privilege escalation*, an unauthorized user exploits these "bugs" within the software to gain more privileged access to a computer system by taking advantage of the bug exploit to bypass the application and perform commands with escalated privileged access.

Vulnerabilities that typically lead to privilege escalation scenarios are most often found in web site code, where scripting and other types of running programs can potentially reveal exploits for malicious users to take control of a system. These are often buffer overflow attacks, in which conditions and boundaries are not properly set on user-entered fields in an application or web site and allow malicious users to crash the program or allow highly privileged command execution.

Protection against privilege escalation requires that programmers be diligent about testing their code for bugs and exploits before releasing software. In the event that a documented exploit is found after software is released, it is critical that a patch be quickly made available to fix the bug to prevent proof-of-concept exploits from turning into real security threats. Systems administrators must be diligent in ensuring that any software they run is using the latest patch level to ensure that all known bug fixes are currently deployed.

Local Lingo

proof-of-concept exploit   A situation when a potential threat due to a vulnerability in an application or operating system has become known to the general public, enabling malicious hackers to create code to exploit the vulnerability.

Software and Operating System Exploitation

Bugs in software can provide security holes that can be compromised by malicious hackers. At risk are not only the applications and programs that run on the computer, but the computer's operating system as well.

Application Software

Application program bugs affect the programs a user accesses daily, such as e-mail applications, word processing applications, and Internet access applications. Security vulnerabilities in these applications can be exploited to allow a malicious user to spread viruses more easily into the user's system and the systems of others on a network. Office productivity programs are especially vulnerable to macro-type viruses, which allow an attacker to use macro commands to perform malicious activities.

For example, e-mail programs can inadvertently spread viruses and worms to anyone in a user's address book with only a few lines of macro code. Internet surfing with an insecure web browser can result in the spread of viruses and a loss of privacy, because personal information can be sent through the web browser to another user. To avoid such activity, the application software should be current and running the latest security patches and updates. These updates typically fix security vulnerabilities and bugs so they cannot be compromised by malicious users. The most recent version of software, plus any service packs and security patches, should be available from the software vendor's web site.

Operating Systems

Operating system vulnerabilities can be dangerous if not appropriately addressed. As the OS is the brains behind the entire system, if security vulnerabilities exist in its most critical components, an unauthorized user could exploit them to gain access and cause serious damage to the operating system and sensitive data. Keep the OS current with the latest patches and service packs, especially those that fix security vulnerabilities and software bugs from previous versions.

Travel Advisory

In an effort to increase application functionality, some OS vendors closely tie their applications, such as a web browsers or media players, with the OS itself. This can cause a number of serious security vulnerabilities to occur, because the application has privileges to OS services and functions. Be aware of the capabilities of your applications and keep them current with the most recent versions and software patches.

System User Accounts and Password Threats

Although the most common form of system authentication is a login and password procedure, this is also considered one of the weakest security mechanisms available. Users' passwords tend to be weak because users use common dictionary words or personal information that can be easily guessed by an unauthorized user. Often a user's password is the name of a spouse or pet, or a birth date. Or the user may reveal passwords to others or write them down in conspicuous locations, such as a note taped to the computer monitor.

Unauthorized users can resort to *social engineering* (discussed later in the chapter), the act of using everyday conversation to gather clues about someone's personal information, which can be helpful in an attempt at guessing a user's password. Enforcing the use of strong passwords, which are not based on dictionary words or personal information but include the use of alphanumeric and uppercase and lowercase letters, greatly diminishes an unauthorized user's ability to guess a password. To ensure the usefulness and efficiency of a login and password procedure, account and password policies, such as enforced password expiry and rotation after a specific period of time, must be created and strictly followed.

Administrative Accounts

Most operating systems come with a default administrative account called *admin, administrator*, or another obvious name that points to this account as being necessary to manage and administer the system. For Unix-based systems, the *root* account is still the primary account that's been used for decades for full access to a Unix system. Most malicious users and attackers look for the admin or root account of a system or device as the first account to be compromised.

It is a best practice for network administrators either to disable or rename the admin account, or, if that is not possible, to create an alternative administrative account with equal access rights and name it something inconspicuous. This ensures that a malicious user cannot automatically try to log in using the well-known account names for the admin user. It is a regular practice to use separate logins for each administrator to ensure that any admin account actions can be properly logged and audited. Generally, network administrators should never name accounts after their job function, such as *admin, backup, databaseadmin*, and so on.

Password Security

Most user account vulnerabilities are caused by insecure or easy-to-guess passwords. Insecure passwords are susceptible to a number of password-cracking techniques that use dictionary names or even personal information in an attempt to guess the password of a login account.

As mentioned, passwords to any system should have a minimum length of between six and eight characters and should contain both uppercase and lowercase letters, as well as numbers and symbols. Any word that can be found in the dictionary should not be used, because password-cracking programs can easily find your password by trying every word in the entire dictionary in a short time. Personal information—such as birth dates or names of family members and pets—should never be used, because anyone who knows your personal information can use this information to try to guess your password.

The following sections outline some of the methods used by a person to attempt to compromise a user account and password.

Brute-force Attacks   A *brute-force* attack is an attempt to break a password or encryption scheme through simple repetition of attempts. A wide variety of utilities, such as LC4 and Cain & Abel, can be used to automate these attacks. These modern hacking utilities can cycle through millions of combinations of letters and numbers to guess a password. The simplest and most efficient way to prevent brute-force attacks on user accounts is to set limits on login attempts. For example, if the amount of login attempts is limited to five, the brute-force attack method will have only five chances to guess the password before the account is locked and further login attempts are denied.

Dictionary Attack   By capturing an encrypted password file that contains all the login names and their corresponding passwords, an unauthorized user can run special programs that compare the file with a list of common, dictionary-based passwords. Most users tend to use simple, easy passwords, which correspond to everyday words in the dictionary. By running a comparison of the encrypted password file with the hashed values of the common passwords, many user login accounts can be unlocked with the revealed passwords. This type of attack is much faster to operate than a simple brute-force attack that uses random password characters, because it uses common dictionary words that are more likely to be used as a password. However, a dictionary attack may not be as efficient as a brute-force attack, as it uses a finite number of words and the password must be present in the dictionary in order to be cracked.

Hybrid Attack   A *hybrid attack* is a combination dictionary and brute-force attack that utilizes a dictionary of commonly used words (like a dictionary attack) but also checks for variations on these words to increase the efficiency of password cracking. A hybrid attack takes much longer to complete than a basic dictionary attack, but it is more effective because it includes misspellings and adds digits to the words (users often add their birth dates or other personally identifiable digits to their passwords).

Shoulder Surfing   Users must be aware of their environments and the people in their surroundings while entering login names and passwords or accessing sensitive data. An unauthorized person can easily cast a casual glance over the shoulder of an employee who is concentrating on her work and watch her enter login names and passwords. The person who is "shoulder surfing" can see the keys the employee is typing on her keyboard and can take note of the login name and password to attempt to access that account at a later time. Other sensitive and confidential data, such as personnel records, can also be gathered surreptitiously, even while other employees are present. An unauthorized person can watch the computer monitor of an unsuspecting employee as such data is accessed or entered.

Office workers should examine their surroundings before entering or viewing confidential data. Those working in a private office should be sure that their computer monitor is not easily seen from a distance via a hallway or window. A desk can be oriented to ensure that the computer monitor is always facing the worker and the back of the office. Special privacy monitor screen covers can also block prying eyes. In open office spaces, it is up to the users to ensure that no one is standing behind them or viewing over their shoulders while they are entering and working on sensitive data.

Social Engineering   *Social engineering* uses nontechnical methods to attempt to gain unauthorized access to a system or network; these attackers use and manipulate people to obtain information. A user can be tricked into bypassing normal security measures to reveal a password or providing personal information that might reveal his password. The malicious hacker acts like a con man who tries to manipulate a person's basic human nature to uncover sensitive information. For example, an unauthorized user might call a legitimate user on the phone, pretend to be from another department, and ask for the user's password to retrieve a file. The user, thinking he knows the person on the other end, might give the unauthorized user the password without authenticating the caller's identity or learning why the information is needed. Or the caller might make small talk with the user and trick him into revealing names of family members or a birth date, so the malicious user can try out this information as a password to the user's account.

Another typical example of this type of security breach occurs when an unauthorized user calls the help desk, asking for a password to be reset. After learning the name of an important manager in the company, the unauthorized user pretends to be this impatient, high-level manager who needs access into his account immediately. The help desk operator, if not trained properly, gives this user a new password, without properly identifying the caller. The attacker can log in to the system using the manager's account password. Plenty of other examples of this type of attack could also be mentioned, such as a person posing as a support tech from a company that provides network equipment and questioning a network administrator for IP address information of critical equipment, such as firewalls and routers.

The only way to protect against security abuses from social engineering is to educate users, emphasizing the need to follow security procedures at all times, even when dealing with people they know within the company. Users should never write down passwords, never give out their passwords to anyone, always log off their system before leaving it unattended, and never let people without proper security access credentials into a secured area of the workplace. Such procedures must be strictly followed by users and especially network and system administrators, who are often the targets of social engineering techniques because of the access privileges they possess.

Phishing E-mail Scams   A *phishing* scam is an e-mail or web security scam that tricks an unsuspecting user into visiting a web site or replying to an e-mail with confidential personal information, such as the user's name and address, login and password, and banking or credit card details. Phishing e-mails often contain logos, messages, and links to what appears to be well-known trusted sites, such as a genuine bank or credit card companies. In reality, if the user clicks a link in the message, she is redirected to the web site of the phishing scam operator. Such web sites are usually designed to look just like a real bank or credit card site, where the user enters her login and password information and personal details; unfortunately, the user is unknowingly entering this information into the database of the phishing web site operator. This activity is commonly related to identify theft, in which the unauthorized user is able to collect enough personal information about the victim to perform forged credit card and banking transactions using the victim's financial and personal details.

To help protect users, many web browsers, e-mail clients, and anti-virus software applications can detect behavior that might indicate the presence of a phishing e-mail or web site. This is typically accomplished by the software parsing the URL links in a message and comparing them to lists of known phishing web sites.

User education and awareness again are the most important tools for protecting against phishing attacks. Users must be aware that financial institutions will never ask for personal details, especially bank account numbers and credit card details, in an e-mail. If a suspicious e-mail is received, the user should check the destination of any clickable links within the message to see where they lead. If the destination site is not recognized, it is most likely a phishing attempt.

Explain System Hardware and Peripheral Risks

Device and media security often centers around the physical protection of a company's computing assets, such as servers, desktops, and laptops. Although property theft is a big security concern, it is overshadowed by the possibility of someone using these devices to access the company's network and cause damage or steal valuable data.

Media security involves protecting the ways in which information is stored and transferred. The price of lost data, whether due to damage or corporate espionage, can ultimately put a company out of business. The media used to store information, such as Universal Serial Bus (USB) drives and keys, memory cards, hard drives, CDs and DVDs, and backup tapes, must also be protected from damage, theft, and unauthorized access, just like any other aspect of your systems. A company must implement security policies to cover its computer system and network devices and media and prevent unauthorized access to the company's computer resources and the valuable data they contain.

Servers and Clients

The server systems are at the heart of network operations, as they provide most of the centralized processing power and storage. Servers need to be protected from both external and internal users to prevent the main network resources from being compromised. Server security issues include access from the Internet, open service ports, physical access to the server, and authenticating and granting access to server resources.

Workstation and laptop computers in your organization enable employees to perform their daily work and to connect to the resources and services offered by company servers. Protecting these client systems from unauthorized use is another extremely critical aspect of network security. Anyone who can gain access to an unsecured client system can try to access the resources of the entire network. Client security issues include Internet access, remote access to clients, application and workstation privileges, and the security and data protection of mobile devices.

Servers

Network servers provide access to data and services required by all the users on the network. They are the central resources on the network, and a high level of security must be maintained to protect the valuable data and services from getting into the hands of unauthorized users. The following sections outline server security concerns.

Physical Access   Access to servers should be restricted to authorized individuals, such as the network administrator. Servers should be stored in a locked room or, at the least, locked in some type of cage or rack to prevent passersby from being able to access the console or the server equipment itself. The server console should be password-protected, so only authenticated users can physically access the server or attempt access through a network connection.

Internet Servers   Servers on your network that connect to or are accessed by the Internet are prime candidates for malicious attacks. You should install a firewall to increase security and protect a private network from publicly accessible Internet servers. Internet servers, such as Hypertext Transfer Protocol (HTTP) web servers and File Transfer Protocol (FTP) systems, should be running on their own network (such as a DMZ, or demilitarized zone) off the firewall. If an unauthorized user breaks into your FTP server and it is part of your internal private local area network (LAN), the attacker might be able to access any system on the network. With the firewall in place, the attacker can see only the servers on the Internet portion of the firewall, which effectively hides the internal network from external users.

All the latest OS and application software patches should be installed on Internet servers to ensure that existing security vulnerabilities are closed and the servers are not exposed to existing threats.

Services and Ports   Many server OSs are installed by default with a number of different Internet services, such as HTTP, Telnet, and FTP, which enable outside users to access the server remotely. These services can contain security vulnerabilities that can be exploited by unauthorized users to gain access to the system. Network ports operating without your knowledge can also provide access to your server.

To ensure that the system is running only the services the server needs, you can examine the services and open network ports on the system and disable any that are not in use. This is especially necessary for Internet servers, which can be accessed by anyone on the network or Internet and are vulnerable to network scanners that look for and exploit open ports. Some of the most common programs installed by default on an Internet server include HTTP server software, FTP, Simple Mail Transport Protocol (SMTP), and Telnet. These services should be turned off if they are not in use.

> ### Exam Tip
> Auditing your system regularly and removing access to services and ports that are no longer in use are critical to mitigating potential risks and threats.

Clients

The *clients* of a company are the desktop and laptop computers and mobile devices that are used to perform daily job functions. A mid-size to large company can have hundreds or thousands of computer clients connected on a network. Trying to control the security of all these computers can be a huge task, but a well-planned network can make the job easier.

When networking client workstations, properly structuring the network is important; for example, user data should be stored on centralized file servers or network attached storage devices. This enables you to control access to these resources easily through the use of authentication and file access permissions. Each person should be required to authenticate to the network with a user name and password before being granted access to any network resources. The following sections outline security concerns for workstation and mobile device users.

Internet Access   In today's corporate networks, most users have access to the Internet to send and receive e-mail and instant messages, and to access information they need to do their work. Although most networks are secured from outside intrusion through the use of routers and firewalls, several security vulnerabilities can be created by users inside the network.

At the office, users often download and install applications that should not be operating on the company network, such as chat, file sharing, and music-swapping programs. Unfortunately, these applications can contain security vulnerabilities that allow access to unauthorized users outside the company via unique service ports that the company firewall might not be blocking. On top of the security vulnerabilities, in-house user interaction with outside Internet users can result in viruses or Trojan horse programs being downloaded, which allow back-door access to the user's computer. To protect against the use of these programs, the network administrator should block the service ports accessed by these programs on the firewall so they cannot communicate with the Internet. The administrator can also assign access rights to users on their computers that deny them the ability to install any type of software that is not already loaded on their system.

Some users also download questionable content from the Internet, such as pornographic materials or other objectionable content, onto their office computer. This presents a legal problem for the company, as many companies have been sued for allowing such access. To prevent this activity, network administrators can install special web filter programs that block access to these sites. These filters use a list of known objectionable sites that is compared to the web sites users try to access through their web browsers. These lists can also contain web sites of well-known phishing, spyware, and malware sites, which can also be blocked accordingly.

Remote Access   Remote access tools, virtual private network (VPN) software, and modems can be installed on a user's work computer to make it available for access from home or other locations. This creates many security vulnerabilities, however, because, for example, a modem line creates a direct connection to the company network if an unauthorized user tries to connect to that system using a phone line. If the user did not set up proper authentication schemes, a malicious hacker can simply call that modem with her own computer and instantly access the corporate network. Installing remote access software creates an even worse security situation, because if the user didn't set up proper authentication, anyone managing to connect to that computer remotely can access the company network.

Network administrators must be aware of all remote access devices connected to the computers on the company network. These devices should be removed unless they are legitimately critical to the work. If a user must use a modem or needs remote access to a computer, the administrator should ensure that proper authentication and encryption schemes are set up on the system and computer to protect the line of communication from unauthorized users.

Locking the Workstation   When a workstation is left unattended for a lunch break or at the end of the work day, the user should log off and lock the computer with a password. This prevents passersby from being able to access the systems of others and gaining access to restricted network resources.

Software Access and Privileges   All software on the workstation should be kept current with the most recent patches and upgrades to remove security vulnerabilities from previous versions. The administrator should ensure that users have only the access privileges they need to perform their job functions. For example, any system functions that enable changes to be made to the network address of a computer—or any other type of system change—should be off limits to a regular user and accessible only to the administrator. Regular users should not be able to access any application or configuration programs other than what are required for their jobs. The most efficient way of preventing certain system functions from user abuse is to enact network-wide security policies that are automatically set for each workstation on the network. This can save considerable time over an administrator having to visit each workstation and block out items one by one.

BIOS Security

The Basic Input and Output System (BIOS) of a computer system contains the program code and instructions for starting a computer and loading the OS. BIOS software can be updated when new hardware support and device drivers are required. BIOS software updates may also contain bug fixes and security enhancements that prevent problems in the BIOS code from being exploited and causing a system to be compromised; the BIOS of servers and clients should be updated to the latest version.

Most BIOS programs also contain a basic password feature that allows the network administrator to assign a password to the BIOS system that must be entered before any BIOS changes or updates can occur. This provides an additional layer of security to prevent unauthorized access to the BIOS software or the primary system settings.

Administrators should be aware that unauthorized users can also boot a system (if they have physical access to it) using a CD that can boot its own OS and bypass the actual BIOS and OS of the computer. Often called a LiveCD, the disc contains complete OS software and does not boot any code from the system hard disk. From the LiveCD OS environment, an attacker can access the system and the hard disk. The most popular LiveCDs often run the Linux operating system, which involves a small number of files that get the base OS up and running.

Mobile Devices

Mobile computing devices include laptops as well as cellular phones, personal organizers, personal digital assistants (PDAs), and other types of wireless devices. Security concerns for mobile devices derive from the nature of their portability, which makes them susceptible to theft, vandalism, and unauthorized access.

The portable nature of mobile devices makes them easy to steal without observation. A PDA lying on a desk can be tucked into a coat pocket in seconds, but even unattended laptops can disappear quickly off a user's desk, even during office hours. Mobile devices should never be left unattended, and small items, such as cell phones and PDAs, should be safely secured in a pocket, purse, or belt holster. Larger items, such as laptops, can be secured to a desk or workstation by using a special lockable cable.

If a mobile device is stolen, a simple authentication scheme can deter the unauthorized user from accessing any sensitive information on the device. The thief may simply want the hardware rather than the data that resides within, but any device that contains confidential information can be stolen for its valuable content, such as company data or personal identity information. A login and password can be used to protect everything stored on the computer—from the OS, to a single file or directory, to the unit itself.

Travel Advisory

A password can be set on the hard drive or basic input/output system (BIOS) of a laptop system. With this authentication, the unit will turn on but will not load the OS until the correct password is entered.

Beyond authentication, critical data can be protected through the use of encryption. By encrypting the contents of a flash card or hard drive, the corresponding encryption key is required before any user can read any data: no key, no access. This is useful for password files that users sometimes keep on their PDAs, flash memory cards, and other mobile devices.

Many OSs now come with encryptable file systems, such as BitLocker for Windows and FileVault for Apple Macintosh. Users can selectively encrypt partitions or entire hard drives that require a password key for access. The files are encrypted and decrypted "on-the-fly" as the authorized user accesses them. The drive encryption typically employs Advanced Encryption Standard (AES) 128- or 256-bit encryption technology. This encryption slows down performance but provides excellent security for laptops and prevents an unauthorized user from accessing any contents of the hard drive.

Almost everyone owns a personal and/or company cell phone these days. Cell phones are now used for more than telephone conversations and often offer a combination of features—such as a music player, PDA, camera, and data storage device.

In high-security environments, camera cell phones are often banned because they can be concealed and used to take high-resolution images that can be instantly transferred offsite via the cell phone network. In unprotected environments, it can be easy for an unauthorized user to connect a cell phone or other type of mobile device to a computer and copy data to the device for later use.

Many cell phone companies offer Bluetooth service, a mobile device wireless protocol that allows cell phones to communicate with other Bluetooth-enabled computers and devices to transfer information back and forth wirelessly. Several vulnerabilities in vendor implementations of Bluetooth have allowed unauthorized access to personal data on cell phones and computer devices. Many Bluetooth phones and devices have a "discovery" mode that allows them to automatically detect and connect to other Bluetooth devices, much like a wireless

LAN. Without proper authentication, an unauthorized user can connect to an unprotected Bluetooth device and download any data to it. This practice is often called *bluesnarfing*: An unauthorized user leaves a device in discovery mode and connects to unprotected Bluetooth devices in the vicinity.

Cell phones are considered vital communications devices, and it can be difficult to justify the temporary confiscation of a camera cell phone. But in high-security environments, doing so protects the confidentiality and security of data.

Network Attached Storage

Network attached storage (NAS) is a type of storage subsystem device that can be attached to a network for sharing and storing files. The NAS device is typically a set of hard drives (usually in some sort of redundancy configuration) that is shared on the network. Although the system is not a server in the traditional sense, it does contain OS code or firmware that controls the device, including its security and access privileges.

NAS devices have gradually replaced traditional file server systems, especially in large network environments, yet they retain the same security concerns regarding authentication, access permissions and rights, policies, physical security, protection from network-based attacks, and, in high-security environments, encryption of data.

Local Lingo

firmware   Software that is embedded into a hardware device to provide its initial operating system instructions when booting and operating the device.

Media Security

Media in a computer network can be described as a device on which information is stored and transferred from one point to another. Media can be a CD or DVD that stores data transferred from a desktop computer hard drive to another device, the actual hard drive itself, a digital camera's memory card that stores image files to download to a laptop, or tape media that is used to perform backup and storage of critical network data. Media can be part of a computer system itself or a portable version of the same media type that can be connected to another system.

The ability to transfer information easily from one computer device to another has been made easier with the introduction of several types of removable media. Technologies such as removable hard drives, USB keys, flash cards, and smart cards give users flexibility in moving data from one system to another. These technologies also provide ways to transfer data to and from small devices, such as digital cameras, PDAs, MP3 music players, and video game console systems.

Computer media can contain critical and confidential data that must be protected from unauthorized access and physical damage or destruction. The portable nature of many types of computer media means more opportunities for an unauthorized user to obtain or damage the information they contain. Security must be a priority to protect the confidentially and integrity of data, especially when this information is being physically moved from one place to another. This involves the use of encryption and authentication to secure access to the data, as well as physical and environmental protection of the removable media itself.

The following sections discuss the most common types of system and removable media as well as their security concerns and how to protect them.

USB Devices

With continuing enhancements in flash memory and memory card technology, gigabytes of data can be stored on small USB keys or other portable storage devices. USB keys provide an efficient way to transfer very large files from one computer system to another: For example, a user can copy several files from a work computer onto a USB device and take the device home to copy the files from the device to a home computer.

Because of the greater risk of theft or loss of these small devices, users should be discouraged from keeping confidential files on removable media such as USB keys. If private, confidential data is to be transported this way, several security options can be used to encrypt and/or password-protect files on a USB key or other type of memory card. Due to their small size and portability, USB keys can also be used to hold special token security codes that allow computer systems to be accessed only when the USB key is attached to the system and another secondary form of authentication is entered, such as a password or personal identification number (PIN).

USB hard drives and other types of removable storage have also become smaller in physical size while being able to store hundreds of gigabytes of data. The same security concerns apply to any other type of removable storage device, including authentication and data encryption of contents.

CDs and DVDs

CDs and DVDs are still popular for storing and backing up information and for transferring data between devices. CDs and DVDs use optical technology to record information on a disc that can hold 700MB of data for CDs, 4.7GB for

DVDs, and 8.5GB for dual-layer DVDs. CDs and DVDs are adequate sizes for personal home use but impractical for large companies that need to back up terabytes of data.

Although resistant to many kinds of physical abuse such as dropping, CDs and DVDs can be damaged by scratches on the surface of the media. Some have argued that the chemical composition of CDs and DVDs can break down over time, estimated to be from 20 to 100 years, depending on the type of media. Because of these disadvantages, CD or DVD technology is suitable for short-term data backups or archives, but for increased protection and longevity, other media such as tape should be considered.

Before disposing of CDs and DVDs, a good security practice is to break the disc or damage its surface to prevent someone from retrieving the discarded disc and accessing the information stored on it.

> **Travel Advisory**
>
> A simple way to make CD-ROMs or DVDs unreadable is to use a sharp object to scratch part of the reflective layer of the CD.

Hard Drives

Desktop, laptop, and server hard drives are the most common form of general magnetic storage for information. While desktops and laptops typically have only one hard drive per machine, servers can use several hard drives to provide a large amount of storage space and fault redundancy.

> **Local Lingo**
>
> **fault redundancy**   Ensuring that, in the event a hardware device fails, an additional device in the system can automatically take over to avoid any down time.

Removable hard drives have grown dramatically in storage capacity with a corresponding decrease in physical size. By installing a special removable drive bay in your computer, the hard drive can be removed from the computer and installed in a removable drive bay on another system. This technology, however, doesn't offer hot-swap technology, which is offered by Small Computer System Interface (SCSI)–based RAID storage systems, so the system must be shut down before a removable hard drive can be removed. To protect the information on this type of hard drive, it should be encrypted. When not in use, a removable hard drive should be stored in a secured or locked area.

> ### Local Lingo
>
> **RAID** (Redundant Array of Inexpensive Disks) A method of using multiple hard disks to improve redundancy and reliability in the event one of the disks fails.
> **hot swapping** A technology that enables system devices such as hard drives to be removed and added while the system is still operating.

Hard drives aren't considered safe for data integrity and longtime storage because of their mechanical and magnetic nature. Hard drives are susceptible to magnetic interference or physical shock because of the sensitivity of the magnetic heads that read the data. Simply dropping a hard drive on the floor can render it useless. Hard drives are also more prone to failure than other storage media because the constant heating and cooling of the components causes expansion and contraction, which shortens their life span.

Hard drives cannot be easily write-protected, and a simple error within a command can delete the entire contents of the hard drive. If you do not have a current backup of the data on your hard drive and you suffer from a mechanical or user error that deletes or corrupts the data, you might not be able to recover that data. Or you might have to send the device to a special data-recovery lab, which can attempt to extract the information from the damaged hard drive, sometimes at significant cost.

Simply erasing or reformatting a hard drive does not overwrite the data on the drive; instead, data is erased from the hard-drive directory sector, while the data remains in place until it is overwritten. That means that the data is still present, and still potentially accessible. To wipe a hard drive clear of any data it contains and prevent someone from examining the contents of a hard drive, special "shredder" type programs exist that can write "garbage" data to the drive to overwrite the previous data. To prevent any sort of data recovery from a hard drive, the data should be overwritten many times using a shredder application.

Flash Memory Cards

A *flash memory card* is a popular device that can be used for a variety of applications, including console game systems, MP3 music players, and digital video and image cameras. The flash card contains information in its memory and does not provide any sort of processing ability, as provided in smart cards (discussed next). Flash memory is similar to RAM on a personal computer, except the information is stored in flash memory indefinitely, until the information is updated or deleted by a user and replaced with new information.

Data can be extracted from a device or computer onto the flash card, which can then be connected to another device onto which the information can be transferred. For example, a user can use the flash card to save the current state of a game being played on a console system; he can take the card to another user's house to transfer the information to the other system and continue playing. Digital cameras can save images on the card, which can then be attached to a desktop computer where the user can access images to manipulate or print them. PDA users can save confidential information from the PDA onto a flash card, such as login and password information they use frequently.

Unfortunately, many types of flash cards do not contain inherent security mechanisms, and the information is usually unencrypted and easily accessible. Encryption software programs can be used to encrypt the contents of flash cards. Because these small cards can easily be lost or stolen, security is an important consideration if the information stored on them is confidential.

Travel Advisory
Do not store confidential information on devices that are not encrypted.

Smart Cards

A *smart card* is a small device about the size of a credit card that contains its own memory and computer processing unit (CPU). A smart card is similar to a memory or a flash card, but it provides even more functionality because of its ability to process information like a computer. The amount of memory available on a smart card is just enough to retain information and run programs. The smart card can store a wide variety of information, such as authentication data and personal financial or biometric data.

To use the smart card, the user swipes or inserts the card into a card reader. Typically, to access the information on the smart card, the user must enter a PIN before the card reader will authenticate. This allows a *dual authentication* security mechanism, in which the user must be authenticated as the owner of the card while the card reader authenticates the credentials on the card itself. Many cards also contain embedded encryption techniques for protecting the data stored on them. These security protections greatly reduce the risk of someone gaining unauthorized access with a stolen card or trying to access the information stored on a smart card.

Tape Media

Tape media is the most popular media for network backup use among large and small companies alike. Tape media provides a large storage capacity for an inexpensive price. Tapes can hold hundreds of gigabytes of data and provide an excellent way to back up data on large file or database servers.

Tape media, like any other magnetic type of media, is susceptible to magnetic interference, which can corrupt or delete the data stored on the tape. Tapes must be properly and carefully labeled so that important information is not overwritten. Tapes have write-protect mechanisms that can be enabled to prevent someone from overwriting critical data.

Tapes are also prone to wear and tear, so the media supply must be refreshed regularly with new tapes. Continued use of a tape slowly wears down the integrity of its recordable areas. The best practice is to pull tapes out of rotation after about a year or after about 50 uses.

Many companies send backup tapes to an offsite storage facility that protects the data in case a disaster destroys the main company site. Any storage facility should have proper environmental controls in place, because tapes can be damaged from prolonged exposure to extreme temperatures or humidity.

To ensure completely secure data integrity, backups should be tested regularly by performing weekly restores. Even though a backup program will state when a backup is successful, mechanical problems such as a misaligned head can cause corrupted data to be written to the tapes. Only by regularly testing the restore process can you ensure that backups are storing data properly.

Travel Advisory

If tapes are stored for long periods of time, make sure that the backup application software used to write the data to the tapes is always available and usable. Many companies upgrade their backup software periodically or switch to a different software vendor. Many new or different applications can't read data stored by another application, and if you do not have the original backup application, the data stored on the tape may be unreadable.

CHECKPOINT

✔**Objective 1.01: Differentiate Among Various Systems Security Threats**
Numerous threat vectors across multiple access points and communications channels create security risks for computer systems, including physical hardware access, software exploits, viruses, malicious code, network communications, and social engineering. Security administrators must be aware of every possible way that computer systems and users can be exposed to security threats that endanger the integrity, confidentiality, and existence of sensitive data.

✔**Objective 1.02: Explain System Hardware and Peripheral Risks** From physical security to firmware and software updates, the network administrator must maintain an awareness of security with regard to laptops, removable media, storage media, cell phones, and other portable devices. The network administrators must ensure that not only basic system security is maintained, but that any other types of access points to a system, either via removable USB keys or other types of devices, are scrutinized for security risks.

REVIEW QUESTIONS

1. You suspect that your server has been compromised and become part of a botnet. Which of the following characteristics is evidence of bot-like behavior?

    A. The system is not running the latest operating system updates.

    B. Adware has been found on the system.

    C. The system is under a distributed denial-of-service attack.

    D. Slow responsiveness and large amounts of network data are being sent out.

2. What is the best method for protecting against software exploitation and privilege escalation types of software-based threats?

    A. Reinstall the application software.

    B. Install the latest updates and patches for the software application.

    C. Install the latest operating system updates.

    D. Install anti-virus software.

3. A computer system is suspected of carrying a rootkit. What is the most efficient method of removing the rootkit?

    A. Install anti-spyware software.

    B. Disable the BIOS of the computer system and reboot.

    C. Install the latest operating system update patch.

    D. Reinstall the operating system.

4. Which of the following is the best method for protecting the privacy of data on a USB key?

    A. Keep the key physically with you on your person when it's not in use.

    B. Encryption

    C. Access controls

    D. Keep the key plugged into the computer system.

5. Which of the following is the best way to protect against security vulnerabilities within OS software?

 A. Install the latest service pack.

 B. Reinstall the OS on a regular basis.

 C. Back up the system regularly.

 D. Shut down the system when it is not in use.

6. Which of the following passwords would be the most difficult for a hacker to crack?

 A. password83

 B. reception

 C. !$aLtNb83

 D. LaT3r

7. A user has brought a virus-infected laptop into the facility. It contains no anti-virus protection software and hasn't been hooked up to the network yet. What's the best way to fix the laptop?

 A. Get the laptop on the network and download anti-virus software from a server.

 B. Boot the laptop with an anti-virus disc.

 C. Get the laptop on the network and download anti-virus software from the Internet.

 D. Connect the laptop to another PC and clean it up from there.

8. Which of the following files is most likely to contain a virus?

 A. database.dat

 B. bigpic.jpeg

 C. note.txt

 D. picture.gif.exe

9. What type of malicious code can be installed with no effect, until a certain trigger activates it?

 A. Worm

 B. Trojan horse

 C. Logic bomb

 D. Stealth virus

10. During an audit of a server system log, which of the following entries would be considered a possible security threat?

A. Five failed login attempts on an admin account

B. Two successful logins with the backup account

C. A 500K print job sent to a printer

D. Three new files saved in the accounting folder by user *finance*

REVIEW ANSWERS

1. **D**   If your system has been infected with a worm or virus and has become part of a botnet, at certain times it may take part in distributed denial-of-service attacks on another system on the Internet and may exhibit slow responsiveness and a large amount of network data being sent out of the system.

2. **B**   The most recent software updates and patches for an application will contain the latest bug and exploit fixes. This prevents known bugs and weakness in the application code from being exploited.

3. **D**   The most effective way to remove a rootkit is to reinstall the operating system. Simply running anti-virus or anti-spyware software might not remove embedded rootkit files that may be hidden from application software.

4. **B**   Encryption is the best way to protect the contents of a USB key. If the key is lost or stolen, the contents can be easily read by another person if the contents are not encrypted.

5. **A**   To ensure that bugs and security vulnerabilities from previous versions of your OS have been fixed, the latest service packs and patches for your release should be obtained and installed.

6. **C**   The best type of password is one with a minimum of six characters that contains a variety of uppercase and lowercase letters, symbols, and numbers.

7. **B**   If a computer is infected with a virus, do not connect it to a network or you run the risk of the virus infecting other computers and servers. Use an anti-virus program on disc to clean the virus off the laptop before connecting it to the network.

8. **D**   Executable files can contain compiled code for a virus or other malicious program. In this case, an image file is disguised with the.exe extension, so someone might think it is an image and open the file.

9. **C**   After installation, a logic bomb does nothing until a trigger, such as a specific date, activates it or the program has been opened a certain amount of times.

10. **A**   Experiencing a large amount of unsuccessful logins for one user, especially the admin user, is unusual. Either the user has forgotten his or her password or someone is trying to guess the password to hack into the account.

System Software Security

	NEWBIE	SOME EXPERIENCE	EXPERT
ETA	3 hours	2 hours	1 hour

With the abundance and variety of software threats, vulnerabilities, and risks, it is critical that the servers and workstations in your environment be protected and continuously monitored to make sure that vulnerabilities in their operating system and application software cannot be exploited.

Network and system administrators must check that all the servers and workstations in their environment are not running outdated versions of the operating system or software applications that may leave them open to security vulnerabilities. To help with this process, organizations should create security baselines and security policy templates that are applied to all systems in the organization. This creates a common security baseline from which the administrator can protect resources from the most common types of software vulnerabilities and exploits. In addition, several additional security applications such as personal firewalls, anti-virus software, anti-spam software, and software virtualization technology provide more layers of security to servers and workstations.

This chapter examines the procedures necessary to harden and lock down operating systems and software applications to prevent security risks from being exploited. Administrators must be aware of the types of security risks and know which preventive steps to take to protect a network and systems from software-based attacks.

| Objective 2.01 |
| CompTIA Security+ |
| Objective 1.3 |

Implement OS Hardening Practices and Procedures

The following sections describe the procedures an administrator should take when securing server and workstation operating systems and applications and creating and deploying a security policy across all systems in the network.

Travel Assistance

See Chapter 3, "Network Security," for details on hardening and protecting network devices.

Software Security Baselines and Templates

A *security baseline* is a minimum standard that each system and application must meet to supply the absolute minimum standard of protection against security vulnerabilities and to mitigate threats and risks. Security baselines are created to provide assurance that all aspects of operating system and software applications are running at a specified base level of security.

To establish initial baselines, specific security requirements of your environment and a history of past security vulnerabilities in your systems and applications should be compiled. You can also gather information from industry security standards, associations, and organizations of systems administrators. This information helps ensure that your operating systems and applications are all running the latest software updates, patches, and hotfixes that minimize the risks of known software exploits. After these baselines have been compiled and configured specifically for your environment, they must be implemented across the network and updated regularly to ensure maximum security efficiency for all systems in your organization.

Security templates and *policies* provide a documented minimum configuration baseline for all of your server and workstation operating systems and applications. When a server or workstation is first installed, the template must be applied so that the system meets the minimal version and security update policies as outlined by the organization.

Organizations typically have separate security *group policies* that cover different organizational groups such as development, sales, human resources, IT, and so on. This ensures that the security issues that are specific to a certain organizational department are treated in separate policies. For example, a server in a human resources department may have much stricter security policies and baselines than a server in the sales department. The human resources server contains confidential data about employees and therefore causes greater security concerns for the privacy and security of the data than a file server containing sales and marketing information.

Operating System Hardening

The operating system (OS) is the primary software that controls how your system works and how it interoperates with your hardware. The OS is the most critical part of your computer system. *Operating system hardening* refers to keeping the OS and any software patches up to date and removing unnecessary software services from the system.

Despite having been tested before being released, every OS experiences some software bugs and security vulnerabilities that crop up after release. New versions of the software or bug fixes and patches are released to correct these issues, and you should make sure that these are installed on the system as soon as possible. In addition to software updates, many other areas of your OS need to be examined for security vulnerabilities, including setting configuration options, examining available running services, and securing file systems.

Operating System Updates

Your OS software should be operating at the latest release version with the most recent security patches applied. OS vendors regularly release software updates, which are often rolled into larger software packages called *service packs* or *updates*. Smaller bug fixes or patches that fix critical security vulnerabilities are usually released quickly (often called a *hotfix*), so administrators can patch their systems before hackers can take advantage of the vulnerability. Vendors usually provide these patches and service packs as downloads from their web sites. Some OSs have automatic system update functions that can periodically connect to the vendor's web site and download the latest versions of software components. Some vendors release CDs and DVDs every few months that contain all the latest patches and bug fixes since the last version.

It is especially important that you perform this software update procedure just after a new system has been installed. The OS installed on a computer is often the original version that shipped with the hardware; since that time, a number of service packs and patches have probably been released.

Travel Advisory

Even if you just installed a service pack for your OS, you need to install any security patches released after that service pack to be fully protected and current.

Server and Workstation Patch Management

In organizations with hundreds and often thousands of workstations, it can be a logistical nightmare to keep all the operating systems and application software up-to-date. In most cases, automatic operating system updates can be enabled on workstations that allow them to be automatically updated via the network. However, administrators must have a clear security policy and baseline plan to ensure that all workstations are running a certain minimum level of software versions.

Before installing any update or patch onto networked systems, they should first be installed on a server in a lab environment. In some cases, software updates have been known to fix one problem but cause another. If no lab system is available, you can patch a server after business hours, constantly monitoring that server and having a backout plan in place to remove the update if something should go wrong.

Services and OS Configuration

After you've installed an OS, configuring a number of administrative and security-related options can increase your system security. Other options might make your system more vulnerable to attack—that's why installing or enabling only the necessary options for a particular system is critical. By enabling unnec-essary options, you create potential vulnerabilities for unauthorized users to ex-ploit.

The system should also be investigated for services installed by default that are not required, and this is especially important when you are enabling services to be run on your system. Examples of services that might not be needed, but could be running, are file- and print-sharing services and Internet services such as Hypertext Transfer Protocol (HTTP), File Transfer Protocol (FTP), Simple Mail Transfer Protocol (SMTP), Domain Name System (DNS), and Dynamic Host Configuration Protocol (DHCP). If the system you are configuring does not need to share files, the server service should be disabled so no one on the network can connect to a network share on that system. Enabled Internet ser-vices can cause a variety of security vulnerabilities by opening network ports on your system to which unauthorized users can connect. For example, enabling web server services on your system enables hackers to connect to your system by issuing HTTP requests to the server, where they can attempt a variety of attacks to gain access or to disrupt communications.

Travel Advisory

Services that are not required by the system should be disabled or removed, while existing services should be configured to provide maximum security.

File System Security

For file servers that share files with other users and computer systems, the file system in use must properly address security concerns for locking down file sharing. Older types of disk file systems, such as file allocation table (FAT), do not provide the same security as NTFS on Microsoft systems or ext3 on Linux. Newer file system formats allow for greater access controls, such as specific secu-rity permissions for files and directories. Some file systems also provide encryp-tion capabilities, so no one can read the contents of a system without the proper encryption key.

Another aspect of file system security is how access permissions are config-ured for files on the server. Without proper access control, users can read or modify files that could be confidential in nature. Protection is critical for OS files that contain administrative programs and sensitive configuration pro-grams. Access to system files should be granted only to system administrators, and user files should be stored on a separate disk or partition to ensure these sys-tem files are not accidentally accessed or removed.

Users should each have a separate home directory, to which only that user has access. Group or department directories should be set up for files that must be shared among groups.

Server Application Hardening

The next step in securing your systems and services is analyzing your software applications for security vulnerabilities. A poorly designed application can provide as many critical security flaws and unauthorized access points as a network or OS vulnerability. If an unauthorized user can penetrate the security of an application, he can move on to other aspects of the system, such as the OS itself. Because of the variety of software applications that run on your network, it is vital that you are aware of the security vulnerabilities that could occur while running a certain type of service. For example, running an SMTP server to allow users to send e-mail without proper security precautions could allow users from outside the network to send unauthorized e-mail containing spam, or worse, through your server.

The following sections deal with hardening the security of your applications and services to prevent unauthorized users from exploiting vulnerabilities in those programs.

Application Updates

Application software can contain a variety of bugs and security vulnerabilities that can be exploited by malicious users. For internal application software, such as word processing, spreadsheets, or custom-built applications, bugs are usually annoying at most and might not provide real security threats. The usual effect of software bugs is simply interruption or corruption of services that affect performance, productivity, and data integrity. Software applications specifically made for the Internet, however, can provide more than simple annoyances, because security vulnerabilities created in the software can allow an unauthorized user to access your internal network through the faulty application or service.

To protect yourself from inherent bug or security vulnerabilities, all application software should be upgraded to the latest versions and the latest service and security patches installed. In the most recent version of the software, known problems have been corrected. This does not, however, protect you from any problems that might have arisen since the most recent version was distributed. Continuing product research and testing, plus the proliferation of compromised security incidents, might require the software vendor to release an interim update or patch (typically called a *security patch* or *hotfix*) for the affected program.

Vendor web sites should be checked regularly for software updates for any applications running on your systems. Many vendors can automatically notify you through e-mail updates if you registered the software for technical support, or the software itself could contain a procedure that checks for the latest versions of its components automatically. Other companies might send out CDs and DVDs containing all the latest updates since the last major release of the product.

Server Types

Servers on the Internet can provide services such as file transfer, e-mail, and database transactions. The nature of the Internet means these servers are wide open to abuse from external users. Each type of server has its own way of providing information and services and could contain a number of security vulnerabilities that might allow them to be compromised by unauthorized users. The following sections outline popular Internet servers and identify which security vulnerabilities they could contain.

Exam Tip

Be aware of the different types of security vulnerabilities inherent with each type of Internet server and know how to prevent them from being exploited.

Web Servers   Internet web servers accept HTTP port 80 requests from client web browsers, and they send back the requested information to the client. Web servers are the most common forms of servers on the Internet and, as a result, they are the most often attacked. An attack can occur in a variety of ways. Some attacks disrupt users from accessing the information on a web site. Other attacks spread worms and viruses over the Internet. Some attacks vandalize web sites and deface information on web pages or replace it with false information. Most of these attacks take advantage of security vulnerabilities in the web server. The most popular types of exploits include malformed requests, buffer overflow attacks, worms, and denial-of-service (DoS) attacks.

- **Malformed Request**   A request that contains some type or sequence of information that causes the web server to malfunction. This type of attack is caused by bugs in the web server software that cause certain input coming from a web browser to have adverse effects on the system.
- **Buffer Overflow**   This type of attack is caused by sending a parameter that is outside the bounds of the system's programs. The system's data buffer can overflow with information, causing it to crash or even provide administrative access to the system.
- **Worm**   Worms are malicious code transmitted through normal HTTP communications. A web site can be infected by the worm from an infected client. The worm then tries to replicate itself to other servers

and clients, by scanning the Internet for servers using the HTTP service port 80. Clients can be infected simply by connecting to the affected web server.

- **DoS**   This type of attack is used to prevent other users from accessing the web site. This is accomplished by flooding the web server with requests, so it can't process legitimate requests. These attacks can occur from one system or a coordinated attack from a number of systems over the Internet via a distributed denial-of-service (DDoS) attack.

All these attack types can be prevented by installing current web server and browser software and applying the most recent security patches.

E-mail Servers   An *e-mail server* can store messages and enable users to send and retrieve e-mail. Other types of e-mail servers are used as message transfer agents (MTAs), whose purpose is to relay mail from site to site. Security for e-mail systems is a great concern because e-mail is one of the most common targets for viruses and worms that can infect users' computers. Unsecured e-mail servers can be secretly used by malicious users to send out spam e-mail to thousands of unsuspecting users, while protecting the identity of the original sender. As with other applications, e-mail software should be current with the latest revisions and service patches. Specific e-mail threats are discussed in detail in the next objective.

FTP Servers   *FTP servers* are used to transfer files from one system to another across the Internet. A server hosting the files will be running an FTP server service that awaits file transfer requests originating from clients using FTP client software. Many FTP server sites on the Internet are public in nature and allow anonymous users to log in and download or upload files to their system. Other companies use authenticated FTP servers to enable clients to download engineering or technical support files. To access the server, the client needs to authenticate using a login and password. Basic types of FTP communications are not encrypted, so any login and password information is sent over the network in clear text and can be easily intercepted by a malicious hacker. Secure FTP (SFTP) software uses encrypted communications to prevent interception by unauthorized users.

Exam Tip

Remember that basic FTP communications, including login and password authentication, are transmitted in clear text. SFTP should be used to encrypt the session utilizing SSH.

FTP servers are a widely used resource on the Internet and one of the most popular servers for hacking attempts and abuse. FTP server software can be vulnerable to attacks because of inherent bugs in its programming. Software bugs in FTP programs allow unauthorized individuals to gain administrative access to the machine on which the FTP service resides. The malicious hacker can then use that machine as a starting point for other activities, such as performing DoS attacks or hacking attempts on other machines. Because of bugs, any FTP server software you use should be the latest version, with the most recent security patches installed.

Another problem with FTP servers is they are usually installed by default with some kind of anonymous account. This account enables users to access the FTP server without having to authenticate. If the FTP server is a private server containing confidential data that should be accessed only by authorized users, this anonymous account and any anonymous access should be disabled.

DNS Servers   Domain Name System (DNS) servers provide a way to translate Internet domain names into IP addresses. For example, the web site *www.server.net* can be translated to an IP address of *192.168.1.12*. This allows network applications and services to refer to Internet domains by their fully qualified domain name (FQDN) rather than their IP address, which can be difficult to remember and can often change. If a company changes its system's IP address, it can simply update the DNS tables to reflect this. External users will not see a difference because they will still be connecting to it by name.

DNS servers perform an extremely valuable function on the Internet, and wide-scale communication interruptions can occur if a network DNS server is disabled. Most client machines use DNS each time they try to connect to a network host. The client's DNS server is configured using its network settings, which can be set manually or automatically through services such as DHCP. Each time a client tries to access a host, such as a web site, the local DNS server is queried for the IP address of the domain name. The DNS server translates the name into an IP address, which the client uses to initiate its connection.

DNS servers can suffer from DoS and malformed request attacks. In a DoS attack, the DNS server is inundated with DNS or ping requests. The load becomes so much that the DNS server cannot respond to legitimate DNS queries. DNS queries to servers can also be manipulated to include malformed input that could crash the server. Ensure that your DNS software is the latest version, with the most recent security patches installed, to prevent these types of attacks.

File and Print Servers   File and print servers are used for the majority of most users' daily operations. *File servers* are used to store the user's data, including personal work files, and departmental or company-wide information. *Print* *servers* are used to administer print services and print queues, where a user's print jobs are organized and sent to the appropriate printer.

Security concerns with file and print servers center around authentication and access permissions. File servers should be configured so no one can access the server through the network without first being authenticated using a user name and a password. Beyond that, various directories and files, depending on their ownership and confidentiality, need to be secured with access permissions.

Most files servers have their directories set up as a hierarchy, typically split into user and departmental or group directories. For example, each user would have her own personal user directory, where only she has access rights to create, delete, and modify the files and directories within. Other users are prevented from accessing her files by use of a required login name and password. Typically, a company will set up other directories as departmental or group directories that provide an area in which an entire department can store files; everyone in that department would have access to that directory. For example, each person in the finance group can access the confidential accounting files in the finance group directory. The access permissions would be set so no other user or department could access that directory.

Other directories can be set up to allow only read-only permissions, such as a directory of the company policy and benefit files, which all employees need to access for reference, but should not be allowed to modify or delete.

This same methodology should be used for printing services. Most printers are set up so anyone can send print jobs to them. For more confidential printers, such as a human resources department printer where employment or termination notices might be created, the printer should have its access permissions set so only members of the human resources department can print to that printer. More granular security-access permissions can be set, so users cannot modify or delete jobs after they have been sent to the printer. Most of these controls, however, are usually the administrator's responsibility, so he or she can control the flow of print queues.

Exam Tip

Remember that when new file and print resources on the network are created, their default permissions must be modified to ensure that they are secure.

DHCP Servers   A DHCP server is used to allocate IP addresses and other network information on a network automatically, such as DNS and Windows Internet Naming Service (WINS) information, to clients as they access the network. DHCP servers can be configured instead of having to configure each client on the network manually with specific information. This greatly reduces administrative overhead—the use of static manual addressing means if something changes on the network, such as the address of a DNS server, you'd have to change the information manually on every client.

The main vulnerability with DHCP servers is the lack of an authentication mechanism to allow or disallow clients. Any client system that accesses the network and is configured for DHCP will be allocated network information, so it can communicate with the network. This means any unauthorized user can plug his system into a network and be automatically configured for access. A malicious user can also attack a DHCP server using DoS methods to overload it or by trying to use up all the available IP addresses in the DHCP address pool. Then, no new clients can be assigned an address to communicate with the network.

Local Lingo

DHCP address pool   A range of IP addresses that have been set aside by the DHCP server to assign to new clients as they access the network.

As a countermeasure to some attacks, DHCP servers can be configured to communicate only with clients with specific Media Access Control (MAC) addresses. The list of MAC addresses should contain only computers and devices on your *internal* network. This way, when a DHCP server sees a configuration request from an unknown host, it will ignore the request. You should also keep the DHCP server up to date with service packs and security hotfixes.

Another security concern is the ability for an unauthorized user to set up her own DHCP server on the network. If the server manages to answer a client's request for configuration information before the real DHCP server does so, the client might be configured with bogus information that could cause the user's communications to be redirected to other servers under the control of the attacker. The only way to prevent this type of scenario is to scan your network regularly for rogue servers running these services and to control physical access to the facility.

Directory Services   *Directory services* are a repository of information regarding the users and resources of a network. Directory service software applications and protocols are often left open and unprotected because the information they contain sometimes isn't considered important, compared to file server or database server information. Depending on the level of information they provide however, directory services can be an excellent resource for unauthorized users and attackers to gain knowledge of the workings of the network and the resources and user accounts they contain.

A simple Lightweight Directory Access Protocol (LDAP) service that contains user names, e-mail addresses, phone numbers, and locations can be a resource for unauthorized users looking for an accounting user or an engineering user, if a malicious hacker is performing corporate espionage. Other types of directory services, such as Microsoft Active Directory, can contain more critical network and user information, such as network addresses, user account logins and passwords, and access information for servers.

At the bare minimum, users who query directory services should be authenticated via a login ID and password. This will at least prevent casual unauthorized users from accessing the data on the network's directory services through queries. This is especially important when protecting more critical network-wide directory services, such as Microsoft Active Directory. Only the administrators of the network should have access to read and change the highest levels of the directory hierarchy, while common users should be allowed only to look up information for basic information, such as the e-mail address of another user. To increase security, directory services should be used in conjunction with secured, encrypted communications protocols, such as Secure Sockets Layer (SSL) or Transport Layer Security (TLS).

Database Servers   *Database servers* typically contain relational data used as a back-end repository of information for front-end applications and web services. The most popular forms of database software are Oracle, Microsoft SQL, and MySQL.

The front-end application that accesses the database usually sends commands as a set of procedures for the database to run on the data and so that it can return the required results. A malicious user can insert her own code into these procedures to run some query on the database that can reveal or damage confidential data. This is called a *SQL injection* attack and is similar to buffer overflow and invalid data types of attacks that can be performed from a web browser by passing certain parameters of input that transcend the boundaries of the software's thresholds. If the database software or query function is not configured or programmed correctly, the parameters could bypass built-in security to reveal confidential data or destroy thousands of data records. By keeping your database and application software current, and properly validating input, these security vulnerabilities can be avoided.

> ### Exam Tip
> Remember that SQL injection attacks harm database servers by inserting SQL commands into input fields of the application that provides the front end to the database. The commands are then run against the database, providing the unauthorized user with escalated privileges to harm the data stored there.

To protect data privacy and integrity, the use of authentication and access permissions should be configured for a database server. This creates a layered security model that first authenticates the user before he can use the database, and then restricts the user's access through the use of permissions and access control lists (ACLs). For example, for certain types of data, you might want most users to have read-only access. Other users who need more access can be granted permission to add, delete, and modify records.

When creating user accounts and logins, employ the same type of care used for general network authentication, such as requiring minimum lengths and types of secure passwords. Ensure that the default database accounts, such as the supervisor or administrator account, or any other type of database service account, have changed their default passwords to something more secure.

Objective 2.02
CompTIA Security+
Objective 1.4

Establish Application Security

Users in your organization can access several Internet communications applications, including web browsers and e-mail. In some cases, users may also be running instant messaging (IM) and Peer-To-Peer (P2P) types of applications that should not be running on a corporate network and typically serve no purpose in a work environment. The following sections describe IM, P2P, and other types of applications and procedures to help you make sure these applications are running in a secure manner.

Web Application Vulnerabilities

As programmers add increased functionality to web sites and web browsers, the potential for security vulnerabilities increases. The biggest danger is the tendency toward integrating the web browser functionality with other computer applications and even the OS itself. This means if a web-browser security vulnerability is exploited, an unauthorized user has access to the core system files and data of an authorized user's computer. The following sections outline some of the more popular web application components and the security vulnerabilities they might create.

JavaScript

JavaScript is a scripting language created by Netscape, but it is unrelated to the Java programming language. JavaScript's code is not compiled; instead, it is *interpreted* by the web browser. JavaScript can interact with HTML source code, enabling web authors to create web sites with dynamic content.

Since the introduction of JavaScript, the language has been plagued with security issues. The problems originate from the nature of JavaScript, which allows executable content to be embedded into web pages. These vulnerabilities include the ability for hackers to read files on a user's hard drive and to monitor and intercept a user's web activities. Security precautions are required to prevent malicious code from entering, executing, and retrieving data from the underlying system.

The insecurities of web browsers that implement JavaScript, rather than the JavaScript language itself, are the source of the vulnerabilities. Most security problems discovered in JavaScript implementations require the installation of software patches from the web browser vendor. JavaScript can also be disabled on your web browser. Check the browser's options to disable or enable the use of JavaScript for web sites accessed by users.

Java

Java is an object-oriented, platform-independent programming language created by Sun Microsystems. Java is typically used on Internet web sites to provide small programs, called *applets*, that can be downloaded to a user's web browser. Because Java is platform-independent and can run on any type of machine or OS, it requires the use of a Java Virtual Machine (JVM) to convert the program to the code understood by the local machine or OS. Java programs run in their own special area, called a *sandbox*, which restricts the applet's access to certain parts of the computer system. This prevents malicious or buggy software from accessing critical parts of your system. Hackers, however, are able to program applets that can bypass the security features of the sandbox and access the data on a user's hard drives. For added security, most web browsers can be configured to allow only certain access privileges to Java programs.

Signed Applets

Signed Java applets are programs that are authenticated through the use of a digital signature that provides information on where the applet originated. The web browser reads this signature and checks to determine whether it comes from a known, trusted source. This allows an applet to have fewer restrictions applied to its operations than those of a normal unsigned applet. An authenticated signed applet is usually given more access over OS functions to perform operations.

ActiveX

ActiveX is a technology created by Microsoft to create reusable components across Windows and web applications. This includes increasing the functionality of Internet applications. Similar to components created with Java, ActiveX components can be downloaded to the computer through the web browser. Unlike Java, which has software controls that allow programs to run only in a certain area of memory and influence, ActiveX functions are controlled by the users themselves. This requires the need for greater security controls because a malicious ActiveX component can be downloaded that could compromise the security of your system. Users must be careful when configuring their web browsers to control ActiveX programs.

Exam Tip

Know that ActiveX controls run with the same permissions as those used by the user currently logged in.

For web browsing security, ActiveX uses a form of authentication control based on security levels. The user's web browser can be configured to set a certain security level at which ActiveX controls can operate. The lowest level allows all ActiveX components to be downloaded automatically. Increased levels provide warning dialog boxes to alert the user of an ActiveX element and enable the user to download it or not do so. ActiveX relies on digital certificates and trusting certificate authorities to authenticate the origin of ActiveX controls.

As always, your web browser should be updated to the latest version, so the most recent security controls are in place and any previous security vulnerabilities are removed.

> **Travel Advisory**
>
> Many people, in the interest of higher security, disable some of the advanced web browser functions, such as downloading ActiveX and running Java applets. Unfortunately, many web sites require these to perform even the most basic functions, and if you disable these functions, you might be unable to access the site. Try to maintain a balance between convenience and security.

Input Validation

Input validation refers to the process of coding applications to accept only certain valid input for user-entered fields. For example, many web sites allow users to fill in a web form with their name, address, comments, and other information. If proper input validation code has not been included in these types of web forms, in certain cases a malicious user can enter invalid input into a field that may cause the application to crash, corrupt data, or provide the user additional unauthorized system access. Invalid input often leads to buffer overflow types of errors that can be easily exploited.

Encoding proper input validation within an application reduces the risk of a user inadvertently or intentionally entering input that can crash the system or cause some other type of security concern.

Buffer Overflows

Buffer overflow is a programming term used to describe when input data exceeds the limits recognized by a program. For example, a program might be expecting only a certain amount of characters in an input dialog box. If the amount of characters exceeds this limit, the added information might also be processed. This extra code could be malicious in nature and cause the program or even the entire system to crash. Buffer overflow attacks typically result in command shell access in which the attacker has administrative privileges.

> **Travel Advisory**
>
> A number of Denial of Service (DoS) attacks are in the form of buffer overflows.

For Internet web applications, the buffer overflow vulnerability is a common security concern for web servers and web browsers. A malicious web server set up by a hacker can crash the systems of the users connecting to that web site by sending various HTTP buffer overflow data streams to the client. Similarly, a malicious hacker using a simple web browser can send certain HTTP data to a web server that overflows its software buffers and crashes the web site.

Buffer overflows are caused mainly by bad programming that allows illegal data to be entered into the application. Buffer overflows are typically fixed by patches issued by the software company, so you should ensure that all your software is current with the latest software patches and service packs to prevent these types of errors. Patches can be downloaded from the software vendor's web site and installed on your computer to fix the application.

Travel Advisory
Buffer overflows have been a thorn in the side of companies that create web server and web browser software. These vulnerabilities are easy to exploit and can significantly affect the performance of a system, which includes crashing it. The only way to protect a system is to ensure the latest versions and patches have been installed for the software you are using.

CGI Scripts

Common Gateway Interface (CGI) scripts are programs designed to accept and return data that conforms to the CGI specification. CGI programs are typically written in scripting languages, such as PERL, and are the most common way for web servers to interact dynamically with users. Web pages that contain forms typically use a CGI program to process the form's data once it's submitted.

Each time a CGI script is executed, a new process is started. For some web sites, multiple CGI requests can noticeably slow the server. CGI scripts also are vulnerable to programming bugs, so they should be written with the same care and attention as any software application. Poorly programmed CGI scripts can intentionally or unintentionally provide information about the host system that can aid malicious hackers in accessing the web server. Scripts that utilize user input from web forms can be used against the client machine. For example, on a server system, a subverted CGI script can be used to run malicious code as a privileged user and provide unauthorized access to any part of the system, including sensitive user data as well as logins and passwords. Another concern of CGI scripting is the ability of the user to input data that can be used to attack the web server through buffer overflows and malformed requests.

Cross-site Scripting

Cross-site scripting (XSS) is a type of web site application vulnerability that allows malicious users to inject malicious code into dynamic web sites that rely on user input. An example of this would be a search engine web site or user message forums that utilize user input. The malicious user can input a script or series of commands, such as JavaScript, within a legitimate input request that can permit the attacker additional administrative access to hack user accounts and embed malicious code with cookies and other web site code that can be downloaded by end users. An unsuspecting user can click a link that downloads a malicious script that collects data on the user's web browser cookies and transmits it back to the web site.

Cross-site scripting can be prevented by careful web programming and strong input validation that does not permit additional code to be included in dynamic input and is effectively ignored by the application.

E-mail Security

The ability to send electronic mail from one computer to another over a network is one of the original primary uses of the Internet. Even today, e-mail is the most important communications tool used by corporate institutions and the public.

Security has become increasingly important regarding e-mail communications. The most publicized abuse of e-mail is the use of spam, malicious viruses, and worms that can quickly spread from user to user and affect hundreds of networks in a matter of minutes. These viruses take advantage of security weaknesses within e-mail programs to spread malicious program code instantly to a large number of people.

Other security concerns include the use of *spoofing* e-mail addresses, where someone replaces the original FROM field of the e-mail with a different source address. This technique is most often used by *spammers,* who send unsolicited advertisements to users while hiding behind a fake originating e-mail address.

E-mail security can be increased through the use of encryption to protect information from being stolen by unauthorized users. The user must also be educated on the proper ways of sending and receiving e-mail attachments. Finally, a good anti-virus program should be installed on every computer to scan e-mails and their attachments for viruses and other malicious code.

E-mail Encryption

As a default setting, the mail server usually does not encrypt e-mail messages. This means anyone who might have captured network traffic with a packet sniffer or who has hacked the system can read your private e-mail messages. E-mail messages, once sent, can relay among a large number of e-mail servers until they arrive at their destination. If any one of these servers is insecure, your e-mail could be captured and viewed. Users can protect themselves by using encryption products, such as *Pretty Good Privacy (PGP)*, or through the use of digital certificates. Once the e-mail is encrypted, an unauthorized user cannot view the contents of the e-mail. The destination user must also have the matching encryption key so she can unlock the message when it arrives.

> **Local Lingo**
>
> **PGP**   Pretty Good Privacy, a tool for encrypting messages, is one of the most common ways of protecting messages on the Internet because it's both easy to use and effective. PGP uses a public-key encryption method with two keys: One is a public key you give to anyone you share messages with, and the other is a private key you use to decrypt messages you receive.

E-mail Attachments

E-mail messages themselves typically consist of only text characters, which can do little to harm your computer. The attachments sent along with e-mails, however, can potentially cause damage if they contain malicious program code or viruses. The following sections outline some of the tools and protocols used when sending and receiving attachments.

MIME   *Multipurpose Internet Mail Extension (MIME)* is a specification for transferring multimedia and attachments through e-mail. This specification creates the standard for all mail clients and mail transfer systems for handling certain types of attachments. For example, if a user sends an audio clip to another user through e-mail, the MIME header will include information on the attachment. When the audio clip reaches the destination user, her computer will understand what type of file it is and what application can be used to open it.

The uses of MIME, however, extend beyond e-mail. For example, when a user downloads an image from a web site, the header for the request usually contains information on what type of file it is, such as a GIF format image. When the file is saved on the user's computer, it can easily identify what type of file it is and automatically open the corresponding application to use it.

S/MIME   *Secure MIME (S/MIME)* is an extension of the MIME standard and is used for digitally signing and encrypting e-mail. S/MIME is used for sending confidential e-mails that need to be secured so other users cannot capture the message and read its contents. S/MIME utilizes certificates and encryption key services to encrypt the e-mail, so that an unauthorized user will be unable to decipher the contents of the e-mail and its attachments along its path to its destination.

E-mail Anti-virus Protection

E-mail attachments can potentially contain harmful viruses, worms, or Trojan horse programs that can allow an unauthorized user access to your computer. The first rule is never to click or activate an attachment from a source of which you are unsure. Many e-mail worms and viruses can infect your e-mail application itself, however, and will forward malicious programs to users in your address book, whether or not you open an attachment. Because the user recognizes your name, he might feel safe opening the attachment. The virus then goes through that person's address book, sending out infected e-mail, and so on.

> **Travel Advisory**
>
> Some types of e-mail worm viruses spread so fast that e-mail servers can be overloaded within minutes as the virus automatically propagates itself to people in the e-mail program's address book.

Many users have been tricked into activating a virus-infected file or running a malicious program, often disguised as an anti-virus product or software update, which can give an unauthorized user access to another's computer. A user might receive a seemingly innocent file, such as a JPG image file, but the extension .*exe* has been appended to the file name, making this an application file. Assuming that image files cannot carry viruses, the user opens the file, and the malicious executable program is started.

To protect computers from e-mail viruses, install an anti-virus program that supports scanning e-mail attachments. As an e-mail is downloaded into an inbox, the anti-virus scanner examines it for any known viruses and then quarantines or deletes the attachment before it can be activated. All virus signature files must be kept current so any new viruses can be detected.

Some e-mail applications, such as Microsoft Outlook, inform the user if another program is trying to access your address book or attempting to send you an e-mail.

Spam and Hoaxes

Spam and hoaxes are two of the most annoying e-mail problems. *Spam* is a deliberate attempt to mass e-mail a large number of users with unsolicited advertisements. Any time you enter your e-mail address on a public web site or a newsgroup, you open yourself to the possibility of having your e-mail address added to spam mailing lists. These mailing lists are shared among Internet spam advertisers and, sometimes, you can receive multiple junk e-mails every day. This annoys not only users but also networking administrators because of the amount of space and bandwidth these mass mailings can consume. Many Internet service providers (ISPs) and corporate networks use anti-spam mail filters that block incoming spam e-mail from reaching users' inboxes.

Hoaxes can be just as annoying as spam, but they are usually caused by social engineering rather than maliciousness. A hoax is typically some kind of "urban legend" that users pass on to others because they think it is of interest to them. The most common types of these e-mails usually tell the user to forward the e-mail to 10 of their friends to bring the users good luck or inform them of some danger. Others claim to be collecting e-mails to benefit a sick person. Of course, all this does is consume network and computer resources because the number of e-mails grows exponentially as users send them to all their friends, and so on. The only fix for the spreading of hoax e-mails is user education.

Exam Tip	
Know how to spot an e-mail hoax and how to handle it properly. The best solution is to delete it immediately and do nothing more at all.	

Authentication

Most e-mail servers are configured to protect user inboxes by requiring users to authenticate to the account. If the user login or password is not valid, the user won't be able to access the contents of the inbox.

Post Office Protocol 3 (POP3) is an Internet protocol that provides a way for users to retrieve mail from their inboxes using a POP enabled client such as Outlook Express or Eudora. The e-mail messages are stored on the server until the user connects to it and downloads messages to the e-mail client using POP. Most POP accounts are set to delete the messages after they've been retrieved.

Internet Message Access Protocol (IMAP) is similar to POP in that it's used to provide a mechanism for receiving messages from a user's inbox. IMAP has more functionality than POP, however, because it gives the user more control over what messages they download and how it stores them online.

Both basic POP3 and IMAP send credentials in clear text when authenticating. To protect the transfer of credentials from packet sniffers, you should use Secure POP or the Secure IMAP services that utilize Secure Sockets Layer (SSL) to encrypt the login and passwords.

Exam Tip	
POP uses TCP port 110 and IMAP uses TCP port 143. Secure POP uses TCP port 995 and Secure IMAP uses TCP port 993.	

For sending e-mail via SMTP, the capability to send e-mail from a mail server is often not protected at all. This enables any user to send an e-mail that originates from that mail server. This is most often exploited by spammers who use unprotected e-mail servers to send junk e-mail. The receiver will see that the source of the e-mail was the server, even though the e-mail did not originate from that company or institution. Authenticating the sending process ensures that only authorized users are allowed to send mail from that server.

SMTP Relay

SMTP is the e-mail message-exchange standard of the Internet. While POP and IMAP are the Internet protocols used to read e-mail, SMTP is the Internet protocol for delivering e-mail. SMTP operates on the main networking protocol—TCP/IP—to navigate an e-mail to its destination server. Mail servers that run SMTP have a *relay agent* that sends a message from one mail server to another. Because mail servers, as per their function, need to accept and send data through an organization's routers and firewalls, this relay agent can be abused by unauthorized users who relay mail through that server. These e-mails are usually sent by spammers sending out unsolicited e-mails and advertisements, while hiding the original sending location of the e-mails. The need for e-mail server security becomes even more important when these users send malicious e-mails with attachments that contain computer viruses.

To protect the mail server from this type of abuse, the SMTP relay agent should be configured to send only mail originating from its own network domain. SMTP authentication should also be enabled to allow only authenticated clients to relay through the SMTP server to send mail.

Exam Tip

SMTP uses TCP port 25 for communication, although many ISPs have started to use alternative ports to prevent connections from spammers' relays. It is a security best practice to disable SMTP relay on your SMTP server.

Instant Messaging

One of the most popular Internet services is *instant messaging (IM)*, which allows users to send real-time messages to each other via their PCs. Unlike e-mail, in which a delay occurs between the time a user sends an e-mail message and when another user receives that e-mail, IMs are received immediately. For IM to work, both users must be online at the same time and using the same type of IM software. Both parties must be willing to accept instant messages. An attempt to send a message to someone who is not online or who rejects the message results in a notification that the message could not be sent. On the recipient's computer, a window and sound will indicate a message has arrived and the recipient can choose to accept or reject the incoming message. Web links, files, and other types of multimedia can also be exchanged between IM users.

Unlike e-mail, which can be protected by authentication and encryption tools, IM applications reside on a user's hard drive and are usually not protected by a firewall by default. This is even more critical in corporate environments, where IM programs used by employees make the corporate network vulnerable to attack because these programs are often not part of a company's traditional network security plan. To prevent users from using IM in the workplace, the administrator can configure the firewall to block specific IM ports. In certain cases, it may be necessary to allow IM within the company network, but not allow it to connect to clients outside of the network. The following sections outline some of the security vulnerabilities specific to IM programs.

File Transfer Vulnerabilities

As with any Internet-based service or application, vulnerabilities occur that make running IM programs a security risk to your computer. Like e-mail, IM can be used to send files to another user, and the same risks associated with attachments exist, such as receiving virus-infected files.

When receiving a message with an option to download the file, the user must always establish the identity of the sender before replying or downloading the file. The best practice is simply to ignore the message unless the user has no doubt about its origin. Some IM programs enable the user to create a list of users whose messages will be automatically rejected. This is helpful if the unknown user continues to send a user messages even after being ignored the first time. Of course, an anti-virus scanner should always be running on the system to protect against any type of virus, spyware, or malware in downloaded files.

Packet Sniffing

Like e-mail, instant messages must travel from a source to the destination user and along the way might travel through a number of servers and network equipment. An effective hacking technology that's been used to capture data along these routes is packet sniffing. *Packet sniffing* refers to using a hardware device or software program to tap into a network connection and record the network packet information that passes through. Most IM programs send their data unencrypted, so if a user sends sensitive data such as logins, passwords, or banking information, it could be recorded by the packet sniffer and used by a malicious hacker.

Some IM programs allow the user to encrypt communications. This option should be used if the user is transferring confidential messages, conducting business conferences, or transferring files with the IM program. The packet sniffer will still record the data, but the hacker will not be able to read it because the data is encrypted.

Privacy

When using IM programs, the user must not communicate personal information, especially to strangers. If the user does not recognize another person and that person asks for personal details, such as addresses, phone numbers, or credit card information, the user should end the connection immediately.

IM runs using the Internet networking protocol TCP/IP. This means messages are transferred back and forth using the IP addresses of the source and destination computers. If a malicious user knows your IP address, she can run all kinds of special hacking software that probes your computer for vulnerabilities, and then exploit them. Some IM programs can hide your IP address, so it cannot be discovered by the person you are messaging. When this option is available, you should activate it.

Travel Advisory

Many hacking tools can now reveal your IP address, even though you have this disabled within the messaging system itself. To protect your computer fully, you should use a personal firewall program that can block scans and attacks against your IP address.

IM programs can store information about you that can be used as part of a messaging directory (much like a telephone book). Carefully check these settings to be sure you are not revealing private information, such as addresses or phone numbers.

P2P Applications

Internet file-sharing is much like sharing files on a local area network (LAN). For example, in a corporate network, users might access file servers with network shares from their own computers. In Internet file sharing, most connections use P2P.

Local Lingo

Peer-to-Peer (P2P)   As opposed to a client/server architecture—where many clients connect to a central server for their services and applications—P2P networking involves two computers connecting to each other directly, rather than through an intermediary server.

The most popular application using P2P Internet file sharing is the trading (often illegally) of music, movies, and videos. Unfortunately, many of these P2P programs can contain a number of security vulnerabilities that can give unauthorized users access to your system. The P2P application enables you to configure a specific directory on your hard drive that can be accessed by other users. The P2P servers can scan the contents of these directories to create a centralized master database that can be searched by users of the service. Once the user finds the file he is looking for, he connects directly to your computer to download the file. Insecure P2P software may put your system at risk by opening it up to network attacks and the possibility that other remote users can gain access to your non-shared files.

The biggest issue with P2P sharing is that the files you download may be disguised viruses or Trojan horse programs. The open nature of this type of networking and file sharing means little trust and control exists over what files are offered for download. When using these types of file-sharing programs, you must ensure your computer is fully protected with a current anti-virus program and a personal firewall to protect against network attacks.

In general, P2P applications have no place on a corporate network, and any P2P protocols and ports should be closed off at the firewall to prevent these applications from operating on the network.

Exam Tip

Know the various ways of transferring files over the Internet and how to protect these communications properly.

Objective 2.03
CompTIA Security+
Objective 1.5

Implement Security Applications

A wide variety of security software can be installed on your system to protect it against various types of security threats such as viruses, spyware, malware, e-mail spam, access intrusion, network attacks, and web browsing threats. The following sections describe some of the types of system security software that can be installed to protect your system.

Travel Assistance

See Chapter 7, "Risk and Vulnerability Assessment," for details on other software programs that can aid you in finding security issues on your systems and networks.

Anti-Virus Software

To protect your systems from being infected by viruses and other types of malicious code, anti-virus systems should be installed in all aspects of the network—from desktop computers to servers and firewalls. Because viruses can enter a company network in a variety of ways, such as from a user bringing in a USB key from home, from e-mail attachments, and from Internet downloads, anti-virus protection should be set up for all these different types of access points.

Anti-virus protection should be set up on every desktop and laptop in the system and should include scheduled updates of virus signature files from a central server. This can protect both the computers and the networks to which they connect, as well as provide a first level of defense from the user level to prevent viruses from spreading to the network.

Protecting just the end user systems is not enough, however. All servers should be protected to prevent viruses transmitted from a desktop system from spreading to any of the server systems. The reverse situation is also a great concern: If a common file on a server is used by all company systems, they can also be infected simply by accessing the infected server file.

Most viruses enter a system from e-mail attachments and Internet downloads that come from outside the company. E-mail servers that send and receive mail should be protected with special anti-virus software that can scan incoming e-mail for attachments with viruses. The virus is either cleaned or quarantined, or the message is deleted, and notification e-mails are sent to the source and recipient to warn about the existence of the virus.

Travel Advisory
When installing anti-virus software on an e-mail server, be certain you install the version of the software that examines incoming mail and attachments. Normal anti-virus protection only prevents viruses in normal program files outside the e-mail system.

Many types of network firewalls or other types of network-perimeter devices can be set up with virus-protection software that can scan files being downloaded from the Internet. With the amount of traffic that goes through a firewall, this type of protection can slow down the network considerably, so be aware and evaluate your system needs carefully.

Virus Signature Files

Anti-virus software companies update their software regularly to add code that protects against new threats that are created every day. Having to update the entire software package on every user's computer in a company would be extremely expensive and impractical. Anti-virus software companies use a virus pattern or signature file to patch users' systems conveniently and quickly.

Each computer virus contains or creates a specific binary code that can be used as a unique identifier. From these binary signatures produced by the virus, the anti-virus engineers create a signature file that can be used to identify the viruses when scanning with the anti-virus scan engine program. These signature files can contain thousands of known virus types. They can even include special algorithms for detecting common virus-like behavior that can indicate a new virus. When the virus is identified, the anti-virus software can use that information to quarantine the file or attempt to remove the virus from the file.

To make use of these signature files, a user/administrator must be diligent in regularly updating the system with the latest virus definition file. This usually involves connecting to the anti-virus vendor's web site and downloading and installing the latest signature file. Some anti-virus programs can be set up to automate this process, checking for a new signature file on a schedule and automatically updating the file without user intervention.

Anti-spam Software

One of the most annoying e-mail problems, *spam,* is a deliberate attempt by an advertiser or business to mass e-mail a large number of users with unsolicited advertisements. Any time you enter your e-mail address on a public web site or a newsgroup, you open yourself to the possibility of having your e-mail address added to spam mailing lists. These mailing lists are shared among Internet spam advertisers and, sometimes, you can receive multiple junk e-mails every day. This annoys not only users, but also network administrators because of the amount of space and bandwidth these mass mailings can consume. Many ISPs and corporate networks use anti-spam mail filters that block incoming spam e-mail from reaching users' inboxes.

E-mail spam continues to be one of the prime nuisances and security issues affecting organizations. Spam has evolved from the early years of simple text adverts to full HTML messages with clickable links, images, and even spam messages hidden in attached images and document files. The links in spam messages are often redirected to malicious sites containing spyware, malware, and phishing activities.

Local Lingo

phishing   An attempt at fraud by luring an unsuspecting user into exposing personal or financial information such as passwords or credit card details. Spam messages often contain links to phishing web sites that are disguised to look like trusted, legitimate sites.

Server Anti-spam Software

Your first line of defense against spam is to install anti-spam software on your e-mail server or on a separate appliance that sits inline between your system's Internet connection and your e-mail servers, and filters out spam messages. Stopping spam at the server level means that users will never see any spam messages because they are filtered out before they reach the users' inboxes on the server. A wide variety of anti-spam filters and technologies generally work the same as anti-virus software, which checks for certain characteristics that have been noted in previous virus outbreaks. Anti-spam software scans incoming messages for patterns of previous spam messages, including specific words, phrases, images, and other aspects. The links in spam messages are also scanned to see where they lead. If a link in a message redirects to a known spammer or malicious software site, the message is flagged as spam.

Anti-spam software often uses a graded approach to identify and act on spam messages. Messages with high spam scores are typically rejected or deleted immediately, while those with lower spam scores (which may indicate it might or might not be spam) are usually quarantined for review by the end user, who will make the final decision on whether the message is spam or not. This helps protect against false positives—legitimate e-mail that was mistakenly classified as spam. It is a good policy to quarantine only suspicious e-mail messages with medium level spam scores to ensure that the user has a chance to see the message before it is deleted or quarantined. Many anti-spam software programs need to be "trained" so that they can differentiate legitimate e-mail from spam messages, but most applications come with a strong default set of spam characteristics that were experienced in past spam campaigns.

Client Anti-spam Software

Anti-spam software is widely available for client systems. Most e-mail clients now include spam-blocking applications that filter e-mail as it is downloaded from the mail server. Utilizing spam training identification, mail clients can automatically detect spam messages and move them to a special junk or spam e-mail folder. This keeps the spam and junk mail distinct from regular e-mail messages that are passed directly to the mail client inbox.

These types of spam blockers are normally not as efficient as server-level spam blockers; however, they do provide an additional layer of protection for any spam messages that happen to make it to the client from the server. Users can typically add friends and co-workers to a trusted list that will bypass the spam scanner to ensure that these e-mails are never blocked.

Host-based Intrusion Detection System

A *host-based intrusion detection system (HIDS)* differs from a network-based system because it monitors a specific host or device for suspicious behavior that could indicate someone is trying to break into the system. An HIDS monitors inbound and outbound network activity, networking service ports, system log files, and time stamps and content of data and configuration files to ensure they have not been changed.

A host-based system needs to be installed on a specific system or device. This differs from networking intrusion detection, which needs to install monitors only at certain access points on the network. The host-based system can only monitor the system on which it is installed and is typically used for critical server systems rather than user workstations.

A host-based system can detect attacks that occur from a malicious user who is physically accessing the system console, rather that over the network. The unauthorized user may be trying to access an administrator account or trying to copy files to or from the system, for example. The intrusion detection system (IDS) is able to alert the administrator if someone has tried to log in to an account unsuccessfully too many times.

Active Detection

An HIDS using active methods of detection can take immediate steps to halt an intrusion. This is the most preferable method, because it prevents the suspicious activity from continuing. Passive methods merely log the incident or send an e-mail to the administrator, who might not see the message for many hours before she can take action. An *active detection* system can terminate network connections from clients who are performing some type of suspicious activity. The system can prevent any further connection from that particular network address. Another method of preventing an intrusion is shutting down the network service that is under attack. For example, a web server can immediately stop accepting HTTP requests to prevent the attack from continuing.

If the intrusion is detected as originating at the system console, the system can shut down and disable that user account or automatically log out the user. Locking accounts is a form of detection used by most network operating systems that disable accounts if a predefined number of unsuccessful logins occurs.

The disadvantage of active detection is the case of a false positive detection, in which the system automatically shuts down services when no attack is occurring; this can cause unnecessary and often costly downtime.

Passive Detection

Passive detection methods do not take active steps to prevent an intrusion from continuing if it is detected. Passive methods typically include logging events to a system log, which can be viewed by an administrator at a later time, or, if configured to do so, to forward the log entries through a pager or e-mail systems. The latter method is preferable because it enables the administrator to be notified as the intrusion is happening. This gives the administrator a chance to catch the unauthorized user in the act and to prevent damage or data theft. If the administrator is not immediately notified, he must be sure to audit system log files regularly for critical warnings and errors that indicate suspicious activity.

Exam Tip
Remember that active intrusion detection takes steps to mitigate an intrusion, while a passive system typically logs the event or generates alarms.

Personal Software Firewalls

Most organizations have firewall servers or appliances that protect the perimeters of their network from Internet attacks and hide the details of the internal network. Home computer users who connect directly to an Internet connection rarely have any type of hardware-based firewall. Software-based firewall applications, however, have become an absolute necessity for a user connecting directly to the Internet from home or work directly using a cable modem, digital subscriber line (DSL), or dial-up methods.

A software firewall application performs several critical functions to protect a user's computer:

- **Blocks incoming network connections** The primary purpose of the personal firewall is to block incoming network connections from the Internet. It can hide your system from port-scanning attacks whereby malicious hackers probe network-connected computers for open network ports and vulnerabilities. The firewall software effectively makes your computer invisible to those on the Internet, and it will not reply to any network probes or diagnostic utilities such as ping or traceroute. Worms and other malware threats that are spread through the Internet will be stopped in their tracks by the firewall software as they will not be able to see your system to connect to it.

- **Watches for suspicious outbound activity**   A personal firewall application monitors outbound activity and allows the user complete control over what applications are allowed or blocked access to the Internet. For example, when your anti-virus software periodically retrieves the latest virus signature file from an Internet site, your personal firewall will alert you that the application is trying to access the Internet. In this case, the activity is acceptable, and you can allow the software to pass through the firewall and to do so automatically on subsequent accesses so you will not receive an alert each time. This type of protection is extremely important to protect against Trojan horse and spyware applications that may be running on your computer and sending private information back to a malicious user. The personal firewall will detect the suspicious outbound activity and alert you. You can block the application if you do not recognize it and then attempt to remove it with your anti-virus or anti-spyware software.

- **Provides ability to block/allow programs**   All applications that potentially try to communicate out to the Internet can have their access controlled by the personal firewall. The personal firewall allows you to control which applications can send data to the Internet and which cannot. Some applications need to communicate to other servers to work properly, and care must be taken not to block critical system or application services. In addition, trusted applications can occasionally visit an Internet site to check for new updates to the software, and this can be considered acceptable activity. Other applications, however, may be secretly sending information out to the Internet, such as personal identification information or data about your activities on your computer, such as lists of web sites you have visited.

- **Warns of unpatched software and outdated anti-virus files**   Many personal firewalls can scan your computer to make sure that your OS and application software are running the latest versions, and they will alert you if your software seems to be out of date. Most personal firewalls will alert you if your anti-virus signature files are out of date and will prompt you to run the updated software to get the latest files.

- **Provides web browser security**   Personal firewall software can also strengthen the security and privacy of your web browsing sessions. The software can block pop-up and banner ads to prevent you from accessing known phishing or spyware sites and to ensure that your web browsing cookies and web cache are not causing security and privacy issues. Many firewalls will also block web sites that run scripting, which is a primary source for browser exploits and security risks. However, scripting and cookies are often necessary for certain web sites such as online banking, and it will be necessary to adjust your firewall settings as appropriate to protect your web browsing sessions without impacting functionality.

- **Provides e-mail security** Some personal firewalls monitor your inbound and outbound e-mail and can quarantine suspicious attachments to help prevent the spread of viruses, worms, and Trojan horse software. In some cases, if you are infected by a worm and your e-mail application is attempting to mail the worm to everyone in your address book, the personal firewall can detect this activity and block outbound mail from being sent out from your computer and prevent you from accidentally infecting other computers.

Local Lingo

cookie A small file placed on a user's computer by an external web site. This file is sent back to the web server each the time the client accesses the web site and contains information that the user has entered on the site, such as a login name. Cookies can also contain session tracking information and often contain personal data on web browsing history.

Web Browser Security

As web browsers are the most widely used Internet applications, security is of the utmost importance. Web browser vulnerabilities and misuse can open a computer system to a vast array of security risks and threats, including viruses, worms, malware, spyware, and identity theft.

Security Modes and Trusted Sites

Many popular web browsers such as Internet Explorer, Firefox, and Safari come with enhanced security settings that allow users to run their web browser in specific security modes such as high, medium, or low. Each security mode offers a level of security that is contrasted with ease of use. For example, high security modes typically disable many web site features that cause security concerns such as scripting, ActiveX and JavaScript controls, and installation of third-party software and other potentially malicious software. Unfortunately, many legitimate web sites use these technologies, and users can be frustrated with the number of warnings that occur when accessing these web sites. Many popular web sites also require scripting and pop-up windows and will not work properly if they are disabled. Lower security modes tend to allow certain levels of scripting, while disabling the most obvious web site security risks. Users must select a security mode that offers the highest security possible. It is much safer to start with a strong security mode and to add exceptions to that mode rather than start with a weak security mode.

> **Exam Tip**
>
> Administrators must lock down operating systems and applications with a strong security mode, and then add exceptions to that mode rather than starting with a weak security mode and strengthening as they go.

Users can add lists of trusted sites to their web browser security modes to ensure that these legitimate sites bypass any high-security controls. For example, a user may add an online banking web site to the list of trusted sites to allow cookies, scripting, and pop-up windows to be used, while blocking all other web sites with these functions.

Pop-up Blockers

Several popular add-ons and extensions to web browsers allow certain types of *pop-up advertising* to be blocked before it appears on the user's monitor. These *pop up ads*, typically generated by JavaScript or other type of web scripting language, can be a nuisance when web browsing as the ad will open up a new browser window in front of the one you are currently viewing. The ad will link to another site for advertising purposes and will direct you to a new web site if clicked. In many cases, closing the pop-up ad may cause another ad to pop up in its place. The web site may also open up several pop-up windows, and often it may be difficult to close them without having to shut down and restart the web browser.

Pop-up ads can be a security issue if they link back to spyware and malware sites or download malicious scripts and applications to the browser. Many pop-up ads contain a link or control to close the window, but the control is actually a link to another web site or a control to download malicious software. For the user, it is sometimes difficult knowing how to close the pop-up ad properly to prevent others from appearing.

Most modern web browsers contain some type of pop-up ad-blocking capabilities, ensuring that when you visit a web site containing pop-up ads, the primary web site will appear, but all pop-up ads will be blocked and will not appear on your monitor. Some third-party ad-blocking software goes further by blocking banners ads within the primary web site itself.

In some cases, pop-up windows are used for legitimate purposes, such as help windows with additional information or the installation of legitimate software. Most web browsers give you control on whether to block or allow pop-up ads and windows, and you can allow certain trusted sites to display pop-ups if you are aware of their content.

Cookies

Cookies are small files that are saved on your computer and store data for a specific web site you have visited. Cookies can contain all types of data specific to that web site, such as information to track unique visitors to the web site, login information for the user, and information on other web sites you have visited. Some cookies are cleared after your session on a specific web site ends, other cookies expire over a certain period or time, and still other cookies do not expire at all and stay on your system (until you delete them).

Due to the often sensitive information they contain, cookies can often be a security and privacy risk in the event a cookie with your credentials for a specific web site is accessed by a malicious user. Many web users also have privacy concerns with web site cookies that track previous web sites they have visited.

Most web browsers have a configuration option that lets you examine each cookie on your system. You can keep or delete cookies, or clear all the current cookies off of your system. Cookies can also be expired after a certain amount of time has passed. When you start web surfing again, new cookies will appear in your cookie directory.

> **Travel Advisory**
>
> To protect your privacy even more and to avoid sending demographic information to web sites, most web browsers allow you to disable cookies and to delete any existing ones on exiting the program. Unfortunately, many web sites require cookies to be enabled to function properly.

Private Web Browsing Data

As you use your web browser, it collects data on the web sites you visit, the site addresses, and any downloads you make from the web site; caches certain types of content such as frequently loaded images; and stores cookies with personal identifying data for a specific web site. Most of this data is helpful to store—for example, your browsing history will contain all the sites you have visited, and you may need to access the history to remember a specific web site if you want to return there. Cookies remember information about a specific web site, such as login credentials, and fill them in for you the next time you visit that web site.

Privacy concerns for your personally identifiable information and web surfing habits will increase as this data collects over time, and is important to clear this data periodically. All web browsers offer some type of functionality to clear the information manually or automatically after a certain period of time. Most web browsers also offer anti-phishing protection to prevent your personal data from being revealed to phishing fraud sites.

Objective 2.04
CompTIA Security+
Objective 1.6

Explain Virtualization Technology

V*irtualization technology* allows computer desktops or servers to host and run additional *virtual computers*. Using virtualization technology, a computer can host multiple instances of an operating system environment all running from the same computer on the same hardware. These virtualized environments run as if they were a separate system and can run applications, be networked, run remotely, and perform almost any type of function that a single computer running a single operating system can perform. Virtualized systems are popular for cross–operating system and application testing that allows software to be run and tested on several different types of operating systems, all on the same server.

High-powered servers can run several virtualized systems simultaneously, and this helps reduce costs of purchasing additional hardware and power resources. In addition, virtual systems provide improved security, high availability, and disaster recovery by running as separate processes on the same hardware.

Virtualization works by emulating a complete computer system environment by sharing a single system's processors, memory, and hard disks for several individualized OS environments. Each virtual machine runs its own separate OS and its own separate applications. Several different OS types, such as Linux, Windows, Mac, and Unix, can all run together on one computer in separate virtualized environments, yet they share the same hardware resources. Any software crashes or security issues in one virtual machine will not affect another virtual machine running on the same computer.

The advantage of virtualization is that the number of physical systems running in the environment can be consolidated on several high-end servers, allowing several virtualized environments to be running on each server. In large-scale data centers, this can greatly reduce the amount of hardware required, the space required by the hardware, and the amount of infrastructure resources required, such as power and environment controls. Virtualization can significantly reduce overall operating costs. In terms of desktop computing environments, administrators can deploy several secure desktop environments that can be accessed remotely without the need for separate keyboards, monitors, and input devices; this reduces the number of access points that create security risks.

Virtual machines each run in a separate and isolated area on the system as if it were on a separate physical machine. This increases security, as any issues arising in one virtual machine will not affect another virtual system. Therefore, if a virtual OS environment suddenly crashes because of a software issue, the other virtual machines will not be affected. Many virtual machines offer the ability to save a current snapshot of the system that is saved to disk. If the virtual machine were to be infected by a virus, you could revert to the system snapshot that existed before the virus infection.

CHECKPOINT

✔ **Objective 2.01: Implement OS Hardening Practices and Procedures**
Network and system administrators must ensure that all the servers and workstations in their environment are not running outdated versions of operating system or software applications that may leave them open to security vulnerabilities. To help with this process, organizations should create security baselines and policy templates that are applied to all systems in the organization. This creates a common security baseline from which the administrator is assured that the systems are protected from the most common types of software vulnerabilities and exploits.

✔ **Objective 2.02: Establish Application Security** Users in the organization access several Internet communications applications every day, including web browsers and e-mail. In some cases, users can also be running IM and P2P types of applications that should not be running on a corporate network and typically have no value in a work environment. These sorts of applications, when not necessary for work, should be blocked from use.

✔ **Objective 2.03: Implement Security Applications** Administrators must be aware of the wide variety of security software that can be installed on the system to protect it against various types of security threats, including viruses, spyware, malware, e-mail spam, access intrusion, network attacks, and web browsing threats.

✔ **Objective 2.04: Explain Virtualization Technology** Virtualization allows several virtual machines to run on a single hardware platform. Each virtual machine can run separate operating systems and applications. This allows an organization to consolidate and reduce the amount of hardware it maintains, and it improves security by reducing the number of access points to specific virtualized environments. The integrity of each virtualized environment is maintained, and security or software issues will not affect other virtual machines running on the same hardware.

REVIEW QUESTIONS

1. You suspect that a system is infected with a Trojan Horse program and is sending data outbound from the system. Which of the following can be used to detect this activity?

   A. Anti-spam software

   B. Pop-up blocker

   C. HIDS

   D. Personal firewall

2. Which of the following is an advantage of using virtual machines?

   A. Reduces the need to install OS software updates

   B. Allows an OS to run in its own separate, secure area on a system

   C. Helps secure the hardware from unauthorized access

   D. Anti-virus software has to be installed only once

3. Which of the following is the term used to describe when a malicious user inserts his own code into a database query that can reveal or damage confidential data?

   A. SQL injection

   B. LDAP insert attack

   C. Buffer overflow

   D. Denial-of-service

4. To protect the privacy of web surfing habits, which of the following should be deleted on a regular basis?

   A. Download history

   B. SSL certificates

   C. Cookies

   D. Plug-ins

5. A user wants to encrypt a sensitive e-mail message before sending it to an HR manager. What of the following types of encryption can be used for e-mail?

   A. SSL

   B. S/MIME

   C. DES

   D. AES-128

6. A security patch for your OS was released about a week after you applied the latest service pack. What should you do?

    A. Wait until the release of the next full service pack.

    B. Download the patch only if you experience problems with the OS.

    C. Do nothing—the security patch was probably included with the service pack.

    D. Download and install the security patch.

7. Some kind of HTTP worm is trying to infect a file server, which also seems to be running an HTTP web server on port 80. The server does not need any type of web services. What should be done?

    A. Install anti-virus software.

    B. Change the web server to use a different port.

    C. Disable the web server.

    D. Update your firewall software to the latest version.

8. As a network administrator, you need to set up a file transfer service for customers so they can retrieve confidential files from your servers. What service should you set up?

    A. SFTP

    B. FTP

    C. Windows File Sharing

    D. P2P sharing

9. Why should SMTP relay be disabled or restricted on an e-mail server?

    A. SMTP is used only for file transfer.

    B. You don't need it if you run anti-virus software.

    C. SMTP prevents unauthorized users from checking their e-mail.

    D. SMTP prevents unauthorized users from sending e-mail through your server.

10. You receive an e-mail stating that it should be forwarded to 20 of your friends or else you will receive a virus that will damage your system. What should you do?

    A. Check the e-mail's MIME type.

    B. Forward it to 10 of your friends to see the result.

    C. Delete the e-mail—it is a hoax.

    D. Forward the e-mail to 20 friends to be safe.

REVIEW ANSWERS

1. **D**   In addition to monitoring and protecting your system from inbound activity, a personal firewall software application will monitor outbound activity and notify the user of suspicious activity. This type of protection is extremely important to protect against Trojan horse and spyware applications that may be running on your computer and sending private information back to a malicious user.

2. **B**   Virtual machines all run in their own separate and isolated areas on the system as if each were running on a separate physical machine. This greatly increases security, as any issues arising in one virtual machine will not affect another virtual system.

3. **A**   A SQL injection attack occurs when arbitrary code is inserted into a SQL database query that can reveal or damage information in the database.

4. **C**   Certain cookies can contain information on the last web page you have visited and communicate this information to the web server that placed the cookie on your system. Cookies should be routinely cleaned from your system to ensure they are not collecting too much information over time.

5. **B**   To ensure that sensitive e-mail attachments are encrypted before being sent to their destination, they can be encrypted using S/MIME (Secure MIME).

6. **D**   Even though you just installed the latest service pack, a security vulnerability might have recently been discovered, requiring that you install a new security patch. You will not be protected from the vulnerability if you do not install the security patch, and it might be too dangerous to wait for it to be included in the next service pack. Also remember to verify that the update does not cause problems with existing software by installing it on a test system first.

7. **C**   Any application or service that is not needed by the server should be disabled or uninstalled. This is known as *system hardening*. Leaving services enabled, such as a web server, could make the server vulnerable to web server attacks such as viruses and worms.

8. **A**   By using Secure FTP, you provide a way to transfer files over an encrypted communications channel. SFTP uses Secure Shell (SSH) to provide this function, while using an FTP service sends information in an unencrypted format, allowing hackers to use a sniffer to capture the traffic.

9. **D**   If your SMTP relay agent is left wide open, users from other
    networks can send e-mail through your server. This is most often used
    by spam advertisers who want to hide the identity of the source of the
    e-mail. By disabling or restricting the SMTP relay, only users who
    reside in your network should be able to send e-mail.

10. **C**   The purpose behind these hoax e-mails is to use social
    engineering to make users forward multiple copies of these e-mails to
    other people. The chain reaction of sending these e-mails can cause
    network and e-mail server performance problems.

P A R T

II

Network Infrastructure

Network Security

ETA	NEWBIE	SOME EXPERIENCE	EXPERT
	3 hours	2 hours	1 hour

Securing a network and its systems requires protection against a variety of attacks. These attacks might affect only certain areas of operations, such as a spam attack through your e-mail server, or they can disrupt your entire network, such as a denial-of-service (DoS) attack. Some attacks are attempts to gain unauthorized access to a system or to damage one particular user account or one server. Other attacks try to disrupt the entire network infrastructure itself or prevent customers from accessing a public company web site.

Attacks are launched for a variety of reasons. A casual hacker might be testing the security of the system and doing no damage at all. Malicious hackers could try to damage parts of your system or cause you to lose valuable data. Other unauthorized users might want access to confidential records in an act of corporate espionage.

Exam Tip

Some malicious hackers attack a network for "bragging rights" for being able to get past the security to perform the attack, and in other cases the intent is a malicious attempt at identity theft, fraud, disruption of network communications, or damage of data.

The purpose of the attack is not the main concern, however: The main concern is how the attacks occurred and how to prevent attacks from succeeding. By being aware of the various types of attacks, tools, and resources used by malicious users, you can protect yourself and your systems with knowledge. By knowing where and how to expect attacks, you can enact preventative measures to protect your systems.

Security must also include the devices, methods, and communications technologies that enable users to access the network's resources, and organizing your network into security zones to protect networks from external attacks and unauthorized access between them. Network devices such as routers, switches, and firewalls can be compromised, causing potentially much more damage than the simple theft of a laptop computer. Communications channels such as wireless LANs, remote access systems, and Internet access must be secured from unauthorized intrusion. The physical transmission media of the communications network, including physical cabling and communications infrastructure that allows information from one system on a network to transfer data to another system, are also vulnerable to threats and risks.

This chapter discusses the various types of networking threats and vulnerabilities and describes the procedures necessary to mitigate them.

Network Ports and Protocol Threats

Objective 3.01
CompTIA Security+
Objective 2.1

One of the most overlooked problems with securing network activity is that of unknown ports, services, and protocols running on a system. For example, a simple file server might be set up for file sharing, but the server might also be running software such as a web service, File Transfer Protocol (FTP) service, and Simple Mail Transfer Protocol (SMTP) service. Although these running services might not be used on your system, they could create security vulnerabilities because unauthorized users can still connect to the file server using their protocols and ports. By compromising the vulnerabilities inherent in those services, malicious hackers might be able to gain access to the files on that system, bypassing any authentication or access control.

Unfortunately, many operating systems install some of these services by default. For example, someone setting up a Microsoft Windows server might want to use it only for file sharing, but by installing the OS using the standard default configuration, the system could also install a web server or other Internet services by default. When installing server OS software, you must ensure that you install only the services and protocols you need for the purposes of that system. Deselect or disable any other services that would be installed by default during the installation process.

> ### Travel Advisory
> When installing OS and application software, use a custom installation method that enables you to pick and choose which services you want to run. Running the default installation could install a number of programs and services you do not need. The bottom line is, the more software running on your systems, the more vulnerabilities that exist.

Before pinpointing a system or network for attack, malicious users often perform *ping sweeps* in which the Internet Control Message Protocol (ICMP) ping utility is used to find a valid range of IP addresses to attack on the network. A ping sweep performs a quick ping of all the devices in a certain IP address range, and if those devices respond to the ping request, the utility logs the address so the user can then perform more detailed scanning on that address. After the valid IP addresses are found, an unauthorized user can try to find open security holes in a specific system or network using special types of software called *port scanners* that will analyze a system for every service and protocol it is currently using. This is accomplished by looking for open service ports listening for requests.

TCP/IP Network Ports

A Transmission Control Protocol/Internet Protocol (TCP/IP) port is a special numerical port used by a particular service. For example, HTTP web servers use port 80 by default for web surfing. Other services, such as Domain Name System (DNS) and Post Office Protocol 3 (POP3), use ports 53 and 110, respectively. These services are usually waiting for a request, such as a Dynamic Host Configuration Protocol (DHCP) server waiting for a client request for a new IP address. By scanning these ports, a malicious hacker can determine what types of software and services are running on the server. From there, he can use that information to employ other methods for compromising the security of those services because of software bugs or security vulnerabilities that have not been fixed.

Exam Tip

A port scanner can be used to analyze a system for open TCP/IP ports. For example, a web server that also runs SMTP might show port 80 and port 25 as open and waiting for connections. The port scanner can run through an entire port range looking for common open services.

To protect your systems, the administrator should examine each server carefully and ensure it is running only services and protocols required for its specific function. Any other services should be disabled or uninstalled. In addition, any current services that are required should be examined to ensure that all systems are using the latest versions of the software with the most recent security patches installed. On a Windows system, for example, the administrator can run the netstat command to view any ports on the system listening for requests.

Exam Tip

Know the port numbers of some of the most common protocols and services.

The administrator can run her own port scanner on her system to discover whether any open ports and services are listening for requests. Table 3.1 lists the most common, well-known protocols and services and their corresponding TCP/IP ports.

TABLE 3.1	Well-known TCP/IP Services and Port Numbers

Service	TCP/IP Port Number
DNS	53
DHCP	67
FTP (Data)	20
FTP (Control)	21
HTTP	80
IMAP (Internet Message Access Protocol)	143
LDAP (Lightweight Directory Access Protocol)	389
NNTP (Network News Transfer Protocol)	119
NTP (Network Time Protocol)	123
POP3	110
SMTP	25
SNMP (Simple Network Management Protocol)	161
SSH (Secure Shell)	22
Telnet	23

Travel Assistance

See www.iana.org/assignments/port-numbers for a full list of network ports assigned by the Internet Assigned Numbers Authority (IANA).

Travel Advisory

Many service ports also listen on User Datagram Protocol (UDP) as well as TCP. For example, DNS uses TCP port 53 for zone transfers and UDP port 53 for DNS queries.

Network-based Attacks

Many of the types of attacks that can assault a network and computer system are geared toward specific system accounts, system services, or applications. The most damaging and, obviously, the most popular attacks by hackers involve disrupting the network itself. Because the network is the infrastructure that allows all systems and devices to communicate, disrupting those communication lines can be the most damaging attack a network can suffer.

The following sections outline some popular types of network-based attacks that have been used to intercept or disrupt communications and describe how to prevent them.

> **Exam Tip**
>
> Know these different types of network-based attacks and how to prevent them.

Denial of Service

Denial-of-service (DoS) attacks are well known for their ability to deny access to a particular web or Internet site, but DoS attacks can be launched against any type of network or system. In a DoS attack, a hacker overloads a specific server with so much data that the server is too busy to service valid requests coming from real clients on the network. System performance slows to a crawl. This affects a web site's ability to service legitimate requests because the client will not receive responses to queries. This type of attack can also be performed on entire networks, as the DoS is targeted at the central router or firewall where all data passes through. The network traffic becomes so high that nothing can get in or out of the network. The DoS attack is more serious than a single-server attack because network bandwidth is being compromised, which effectively denies access to all systems on that network rather than just one.

In a more organized and devastating attack, a *distributed denial of service (DDoS)*, the flood of data originates from multiple hosts simultaneously. The combined effects quickly overload any server or network device. As opposed to a DoS attack with a single origin, with a DDoS, a network administrator cannot pinpoint and deny access by one host because the attacks come from multiple hosts distributed throughout the Internet. Usually, these originating hosts are not willfully engaged in the attack. Malicious hackers can secretly install software on an insecure server somewhere else on the Internet and use that remotely to flood another host with data. This effectively hides the true origin of the attack, especially when the IP addresses are spoofed to show different originating addresses than those actually used in the attack.

The most common form of attack uses simple TCP/IP utilities, such as Packet Internet Groper (ping), the command used to determine whether a certain host (classified as the *destination host*) is functioning and communicating with the network. A user sends a ping or query packet to the destination host. The destination host sends back a reply that it is indeed working and on the network. In a DoS attack, a malicious user can send a continuous stream of rapid ping attempts, called a "ping of death." The host is then overloaded by having to reply to every ping, rendering it unable to process legitimate requests.

Another type of DoS attack is the synchronous (SYN) flood. *SYN* is an aspect of TCP/IP that allows systems to synchronize with each other while communicating. One system sends a SYN packet that is acknowledged by another system. The target system then waits for another acknowledgement from the sender.

This process can be abused by a malicious hacker by sending forged SYN packets to a host that is unable to reply to the request because the return address is incorrect. This causes the host to halt communications while waiting for the other system to reply. If the host is flooded with a high number of forged SYN packets, it will be overloaded and unable to respond to legitimate requests.

DoS attacks can be difficult to stop and prevent, but some simple configuration changes on the local routers and firewalls can help prevent them. The simplest way of protecting against ping flood types of attacks is to disable ICMP at the firewall or router level, so the host will not acknowledge any ping attempts from outside the network.

Travel Advisory

Turning off ICMP can deprive you of important feedback from network troubleshooting tools, because commands such as ping and traceroute use ICMP to function and can provide important network diagnostics information.

Other types of attacks, including SYN floods, are caused by vulnerabilities in the network protocols themselves. The TCP/IP implementation of your OS should be upgraded to the latest version by installing recent service packs and security patches. Some firewalls and other security products can also detect network flood attacks, actively block them, and try to trace them back to a source.

Back Door

A *back door* is traditionally defined as a way for a software programmer to access a program while bypassing its authentication schemes. The back door is coded in by the programmer during development so at a later time she can break into her own program without having to authenticate to the system through normal access methods. This is helpful to programmers because they need not access the program as they normally would in a typical user mode (where they would be forced to enter authentication information, such as a user name and password).

In hacking terms, a back door is a program secretly installed on an unsuspecting user's computer so the hacker can later access the user's computer, bypassing any security authentication systems. This can also be an unauthorized account that is created on the system that the unauthorized user can access at a later time. The back-door program runs as a service on the user's computer and listens on specific network ports not typically used by traditional network services. The hacker runs the client portion of the program on his computer, which then connects to the service on the target computer. Once the connection is established, the hacker can gain full access, including remotely controlling the system. Hackers usually do not know what specific systems are running the back door, but their programs can scan a network's IP addresses to see which ones are listening to the specific port for that back door.

Back-door software is typically installed as a Trojan horse as part of some other software package. A user might download a program from the Internet that contains the hidden back-door software. Anti-virus programs can detect the presence of back-door programs. Personal firewalls can also detect suspicious incoming and outgoing network traffic from a computer. Port-scanning software can also be used to identify any open ports on the system, including those you do not recognize. These open ports can be cross-referenced with lists of ports used by known back-door programs.

NULL Sessions

NULL sessions are a type of attack on Windows-based servers in which weaknesses in the NetBIOS networking protocol are exploited to allow a user to create an unauthenticated connection with a Windows server. NetBIOS allows these unauthenticated connections to allow users and devices to browse the Windows network. To the Windows system, the user appears as an anonymous user; however, a malicious user can use a low-level remote procedure call (RPC) and other probing utilities in an attempt to glean information on services running on the system, attempt privilege escalation, or access user account and passwords information. Worms have also been known to spread via RPCs in NULL sessions.

Simple registry and access permissions settings allow administrators to prevent anonymous NULL session connections and enforce authenticated access for non-system service–related access. Newer versions of Windows are not generally vulnerable to the risk of NULL session exploitation via default configuration parameters, but older versions of Windows such as Windows 2000 and NT still have these vulnerabilities.

Spoofing

One of the more popular methods for hacking a system is *spoofing* network addresses, which involves modifying the header of a network packet to use the source address of an external or internal host that differs from the original address. By spoofing the IP address, the destination host could be fooled into thinking the message is from a trusted source. The cause of this problem is that the architecture of TCP/IP has no built-in mechanism to verify the source and destination IP addresses of its network packets. A hacker can spoof the IP address to make it look as though it is coming from a different location—in fact, it can even be made to look like the IP address of an internal system.

IP spoofing is mainly used by malicious hackers to hide their identity when attacking a network system, especially in a DoS-type attack. By spoofing the IP addresses of the incoming packets, network administrators could have a difficult time determining the real source of the attacks before they can set up a filter to block out that IP address.

Another use for spoofing is to emulate a trusted internal system on the network. For example, if a local server has an IP address of 192.168.17.5, and it accepts only connections from that network, a malicious hacker can modify the source address of the packet to mimic an internal address, such as 192.168.17.12. This way, the server thinks the packets are coming from an internal trusted host, not a system external to the network, as shown in Figure 3.1.

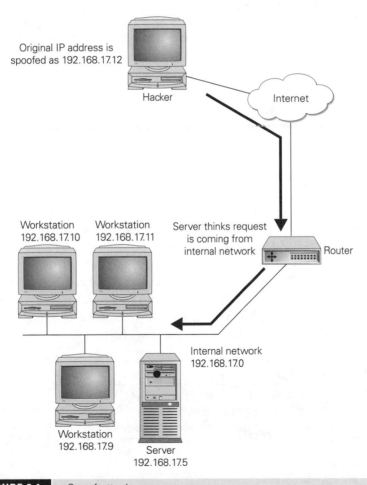

Original IP address is
spoofed as 192.168.17.12

Hacker

Internet

Workstation
192.168.17.10

Workstation
192.168.17.11

Server thinks request
is coming from
internal network

Router

Internal network
192.168.17.0

Workstation
192.168.17.9

Server
192.168.17.5

FIGURE 3.1 Spoof attack

To help prevent spoofing attacks, your router or firewall might be able to filter incoming traffic to restrict network traffic coming into the external interface. By configuring the filter to prevent external packets originating from internal addresses, spoofed addresses can't enter the network.

Smurf Attack

A *smurf* attack uses a spoof attack combined with a DDoS attack to exploit the use of IP broadcast addressing and ICMP. ICMP is used by networks and through administrative utilities to exchange information about the state of the network. It is used by the ping utility to contact other systems to determine whether they are operational. The destination system returns an echo message in response to a ping message.

A hacker uses a smurf utility to build a network packet with a spoofed IP address that contains an ICMP ping message addressed to an IP broadcast address. A *broadcast address* includes all nodes of a certain network, and messages to that address will be seen by all of them. The ping echo responses are sent back to the target address. The amount of pings and echo responses can flood the network with traffic, causing systems on the network to be unresponsive, as shown in Figure 3.2. To prevent smurf attacks, IP broadcast addressing should be disabled on the network router, because this broadcast addressing is used only rarely.

TCP/IP Hijacking

An unauthorized user can effectively *hijack* a network connection of another user. For example, by monitoring a network transmission, an attacker can analyze the source and destination IP addresses of the two computers. Once the attacker knows the IP address of one of the participants, she can knock them off their connections using a DoS or other type of attack, and then resume communications by spoofing the IP address of the disconnected user. The other user is tricked into thinking he is still communicating with the original sender. The only real way to prevent this sort of attack from occurring is installing some sort of encryption mechanism, such as Internet Protocol Security (IPSec).

Local Lingo

IPSec   Stands for Internet Protocol Security, a set of protocols to support secure exchange of packets at the IP layer. IPSec is typically used to secure and encrypt communications on a virtual private network (VPN).

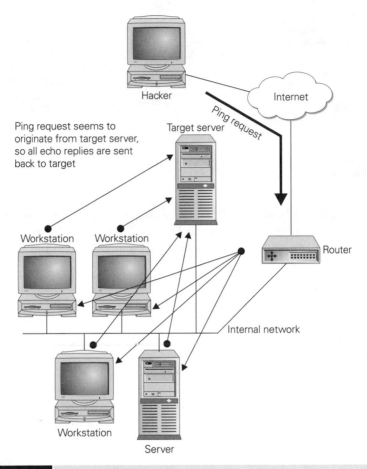

Ping request seems to
originate from target server,
so all echo replies are sent
back to target

FIGURE 3.2   Smurf attack

Man-in-the-middle

A *man-in-the-middle* attack occurs when a person uses a packet sniffer between
the sender and the receiver of a communication on the network and intercepts
or listens in on the information being transferred, modifying its contents before
resending the data to its destination. These types of attacks usually occur when a
network communications line is compromised through the installation of a
network packet sniffer, which can analyze network communications packet by
packet. Many types of communications use plain, clear text, and this can be easily read by someone using a packet sniffer. During an encrypted communication, a hacker can intercept the authentication phase of a transmission and
obtain the public encryption keys of the participants, as shown in Figure 3.3.

Hacker intercepts SSH
encryption host keys and
impersonates the client
and server, or just listens in

Fake server

Fake client

SSH

Hacker
man-in-the-middle

SSH

Client

Server

FIGURE 3.3   Man-in-the-middle attack

To prevent man-in-the-middle attacks, a unique server host key can be used to prove its identity to a client as a known host. This has been implemented in newer versions of the SSH protocol, which was vulnerable to man-in-the-middle attacks in the past.

Replay

A *replay* attack occurs when an unauthorized user captures network traffic and then sends the communication to its original destination, acting as the original sender, as shown in Figure 3.4.

To prevent replay attacks from succeeding, timestamps or sequence numbers can be implemented. This allows the authentication system to accept only network packets that contain the appropriate stamp or sequence number. If the timestamp is beyond a certain threshold, the packet is discarded.

DNS Poisoning

The *DNS poisoning* technique takes advantage of a DNS server's tables of IP addresses and host names by replacing the IP address of a host with another IP address that resolves to an attacker's system. For example, a malicious user can

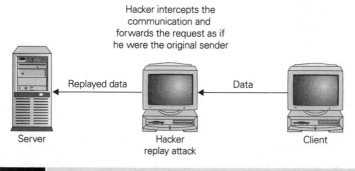

Hacker intercepts the
communication and
forwards the request as if
he were the original sender

Replayed data

Data

Server

Hacker
replay attack

Client

FIGURE 3.4   Replay attack

masquerade her own web server by poisoning the DNS server into thinking that the host name of the legitimate web server resolves to the IP address of the rogue web server. The attacker can then spread spyware, worms, and other types of malware to clients connecting to her web server. This type of attack has a great potential for damage, as several thousand clients can be using the DNS server or its cache of IP addresses and host names, and all of them will be redirected to the poisoned address in the DNS cache tables.

The malicious attacker can perform this attack by exploiting vulnerabilities in a DNS server that does not perform authentication or any type of checks to ensure the DNS information is coming from an authentic source. This information can be passed from one DNS server to another, almost like a worm, and the rogue address can be quickly spread.

DNS poisoning attacks can be mitigated by ensuring that your DNS sever updates its information only from authoritative sources by proper authentication or the use of secure communications. Most DNS software has been updated to prevent these types of attacks, and typically only out-of-date DNS software is vulnerable to DNS poisoning.

ARP Poisoning

ARP (Address Resolution Protocol) poisoning is a type of network attack technique in which the ARP cache of systems on the network is modified to point to an IP address with the Media Access Control (MAC) address of an unauthorized user. ARP is used by systems on a network to associate an IP address of a system with its hardware MAC address. The attacker sends spoofed ARP messages to the network and masquerades as another system so that returned network packets will go to the attacker's system and not its original destination. The malicious user can then modify the data in transit or modify the routing information to use the data as a DoS attack against a router.

ARP poisoning and spoofing can be mitigated by using DHCP or other network services that help network clients keep track of the MAC address of connecting systems to detect receipt of an ARP that does not resolve properly. Physical access to the network should also be controlled by disabling unused ports on network switches and hubs and using port security to limit who can connect to the enabled ports.

Domain Kiting

Domain kiting refers to the practice of registering a domain name, then deleting the registration after the five-day grace period, and then re-registering it to start another five-day grace period. This results in the domain being registered to the user without his having to pay for the registered domain.

The central authority for domain registrations, Internet Corporation for Assigned Names and Numbers (ICANN), allows a five-day grace period before the registrar has to pay for a new domain registration. This helps prevent mistaken domain registrations, typos, copyright infringements, and other issues related to domain name registration.

Some unscrupulous domain *registrars*, the organizations that register domains on a user's behalf, take advantage of the five-day grace period by deleting the registration before the end of the grace period. The domain is then immediately re-registered to allow the registrar to register a domain name indefinitely without actually having to pay for it.

Malicious users or registrars have also been known to do this with recently released domains that have not been renewed (either purposely or accidentally) and effectively own the domain with no chance for the previous owner or a new owner interested in the domain name to officially register it.

A similar practice, called *domain tasting*, utilizes this five-day grace period to test certain domains to track the amount of traffic they receive. These domains' names often use common misspellings or popular web site domain names. The domains that receive the most traffic are re-registered every five days to take advantage of the grace period and continue to generate advertising revenue for a domain that has never been paid for. These practices are often performed using fraudulent user names and addresses of domain registrars, and a single registrar can perform this with hundreds of thousands of domain names.

Legal domain registrars and other Internet advocacy groups have been working with ICANN to try to find a way to curb this activity by forcing fees for every registration and have obtained the support of Internet advertising companies who have started blocking kited domains.

Network administrators with several domains under their control must be wary of their domains and their expiry dates to ensure they are properly registered and renewed each time they are close to expiry to prevent the domains from being stolen by another individual or registrar. Many legitimate registrars offer several security features to prevent domain names from being transferred or renewed by a third party.

Objective 3.02
CompTIA Security+
Objective 2.2

Network Design Elements and Components

Depending on the size and complexity of the network, the administrator must examine the security implications of several different types of systems and communications—from the networking equipment, such as routers, firewalls, and switches, to the protection of the internal hosts that communicate through the Internet with the outside world. Compounding the issue are the several types of Internet services that most companies and organizations need to run their business: web services, e-mail, and file transfer servers. These types of applications require special attention to security. At the same time, you need to protect your internal network hosts and servers from unauthorized access from the public Internet.

To provide maximum security with the least amount of administrative overhead, the use of security zones is recommended. *Security zones* are created when parts of your network are divided into special areas in which similar systems and servers reside. By putting all your Internet servers in one zone and your internal network in another zone, you create a protective wall to regulate access between them. This type of topology is created through the use of a firewall that controls access to the various zones through a rules-based access system.

Other network protection schemes, including the use of network address translation (NAT), network access control (NAC), virtual local area networks (VLANs), and tunneling protocols, can help you divide the network into more manageable zones to secure access.

Security Zones

Dividing your network into separate security zones lets you create physical and logical barriers between the different areas of your network. You can allocate different types of security to different zones, depending on the sensitivity of the data and network equipment within that zone. Creating zones is the equivalent of setting up fences or walls between buildings at a facility that prevents users of one building from entering another building that they are not authorized to enter.

A firewall is used to set up zones on the network. The firewall device is used to regulate network traffic and prevent access to the private network from a public network such as the Internet. The firewall uses a special set of rules to permit or deny network access, as appropriate, such as allowing only FTP traffic to a specific server. By setting up the firewall to split the network into different zones, creating firewall rules to allow access to servers in those zones is much easier.

The three main zones into which networks are commonly divided are the *external public network*, the *internal private network*, and a *demilitarized zone (DMZ)*, as shown in Figure 3.5.

DMZ

The DMZ is an area of the network where a high number of publicly accessed Internet systems should be located. The firewall administrator controls what type of traffic is allowed to reach servers in the DMZ from the public Internet. In

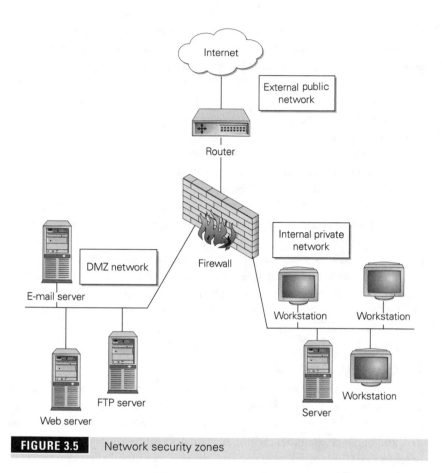

FIGURE 3.5   Network security zones

an overall network security topology, the DMZ is situated between the public (Internet) and protected zones (private network), as shown in Figure 3.6.

The DMZ provides a buffer zone between external network devices, such as routers, and the internal network that makes up your servers and user workstations. The DMZ usually contains popular Internet services—web servers, mail servers, and FTP servers. These services need to be accessed by users on the public network, the Internet. Your company might use a web site that hosts certain services and information for current clients and potential clients. A public FTP server in the DMZ might serve files to all users or only to certain clients. Your mail server needs to allow a connection from the Internet to let e-mail be

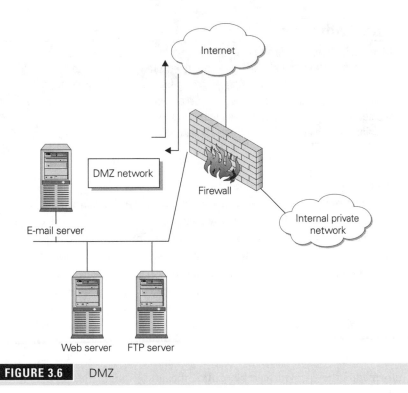

FIGURE 3.6 DMZ

sent to and from your site and to provide mail access for your own users who might be accessing the system remotely.

Exam Tip

Know the purpose of the DMZ and how a firewall can be configured to separate Internet services from the internal network.

Internet services, however, should be separated from the internal LAN. If you were to host a web server on your internal LAN that is accessible from the Internet, you would create vulnerabilities in your network, because an unauthorized user might be able to compromise the web server and gain full access to the LAN. If the web server is on your DMZ and it is somehow compromised, the malicious hacker could get only as far as the DMZ because the internal LAN is on another network, protected by the firewall.

| Travel Advisory |

Many web servers act as a front end for access to database servers, which need to be located on the internal LAN. Take care to ensure that only those ports needed for access to the database are opened by the firewall and that access can be granted only from that web server. If a hacker were to compromise the security of the web server, she might be able to use it as a jumping point to get to the database server on the internal LAN.

Intranet

An *intranet*, or internal network, is a locally available web network that is not accessible via the public Internet. Many companies provide web services that are relevant only to internal employees and not to the public or the company's customers. These web pages usually contain such services as a directory of contact information for everyone in the company, web pages dedicated to specific departments (such as human resources or engineering), or finance web pages dealing with the company's stock and financial plans. Web-enabled applications for internal use can also be created, giving employees access to internal services via a web browser.

The intranet lets only internal employees access these web pages because the information they provide can be confidential and shouldn't be accessed by the public, especially by rival companies. The web servers that host intranet services are located on the private internal LAN in the overall security zone model to prevent access from both the public zone and the DMZ.

Extranet

An *extranet* is an extension of your private network or intranet. An extranet extends outside the body of your local network to enable other companies or networks to share information. For example, an automobile manufacturing company could have an extranet that connects selected business partners, so they can access and share specific information on availability and inventories between the networks. These are often referred to as *business-to-business (B2B)* communications or networks because one company uses the internal resources and services of another.

Extranets can open security vulnerabilities in your network unless they are properly configured. Older types of extranets used dedicated communications links between the companies, which are much more difficult for an unauthorized user to penetrate. Nowadays, extranets use virtual private network (VPN) tunnels over the Internet to communicate, which makes them more susceptible to intrusion. To ensure extranet communications are secure, your VPN, encryption, and firewall configuration must be carefully planned to limit access by an intruder.

Networking Security

In addition to dividing the network physically into zones to secure network communications, you can use several software-based network configurations to aid in securing your network from unauthorized intruders. These enable you to reconfigure the network logically instead of physically, which reduces administrative overhead and removes the need to purchase additional expensive networking equipment.

Network Access Control

Any network is often vulnerable to internal attacks from hosts on its own network rather than malicious entities attacking from outside the network. *Network access control (NAC)* lets your network devices allow or deny access to clients based on predefined access policies. These policies set out rules for what clients can access the network and define a minimum set of parameters to which clients must adhere to ensure they are properly configured. NAC policies help prevent viruses and worms that have infected a client on your network from infecting other systems by denying the client access to the network based on its current status.

NAC policies can assess a connecting host and examine several factors, such as the computer's OS and application patch update level, the existence of anti-virus software and the date of their signature files, the existence of network vulnerabilities, and the access rights of the user that is logged in, and then decide whether to limit access to network resources based on these factors. Any clients that do not meet the minimum policy guidelines can be denied access or have severe restrictions on their access, such as the inability to see and use network resources such as file servers.

NAC-aware appliances are typically inserted into the network before major access switches and routers are connected. Ideally, NAC-aware routers and switches can be deployed on your network to remove the need for having separate devices on your network and allow your routers and switches to control access policies for your network. Because each vendor typically has its own version of NAC support, successful implementations of NAC on your network require that all network infrastructure devices such as routers and switches be from the same vendor; interoperability with other types of NAC systems may result in incompatibility and blocked access for major portions of your network.

Most NAC methods require that NAC *agent software* be running on the client. This agent can be permanently installed as a service on the client system or, in some cases, temporary agents can be installed over the network using ActiveX or Java web plug-ins. In the event someone brings an unauthorized client into your network, the temporary agent is helpful because it is doubtful that the system would be running the permanent NAC client service on their system, and it enforces policies on all systems on the network, not just those that have NAC client software installed. However, these methods require some administrative overhead, especially in regard to access for other devices (such as printers, personal digital assistants, and other network-aware devices) that do not have OSs or anti-virus software running. Most NAC systems allow you to whitelist (allow full access without scanning the device) based on the system IP address or hardware MAC address.

Network Address Translation

Network address translation (NAT) is a service that allows private IP addresses on your internal network to be translated into routable addresses for communication on the Internet. NAT was initially created to solve the problem of the lack of IP addresses available for private networks to use on the Internet. The numbers of remaining IP address ranges were scarce, so an alternative method of using already existing addresses was needed. Private networks can make use of special private IP address ranges internally, and, when they communicate with the Internet, the address is replaced by NAT with a public external address. Most companies have only a certain amount of external Internet IP addresses to use. To work around the problem, a NAT service can be installed, so when an internal client wants to communicate with the outside world, it is assigned an external IP address for that communication. From the outside world, any communications from that internal network seem to come from one external IP address. The NAT service takes care of handling what requests go back to which clients on the internal network by keeping tables of internal and external address mappings, as shown in Figure 3.7.

NAT is also important for security, because the internal address of the client cannot be accessed from anyone in the outside world on the Internet. If an unauthorized user tries to see what is in that network, he can only get as far as the external router or firewall. Most routers and firewalls have the NAT service built in to provide this functionality.

Spoofing has been used in attempts to compromise a network using a firewall to make it appear as though the request is coming from the internal network. The NAT service helps prevent spoofing attacks because the addresses of the internal private network are hidden.

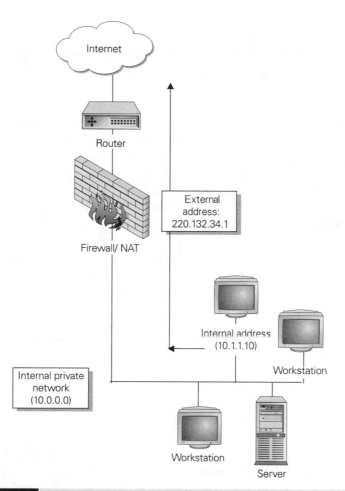

FIGURE 3.7   Network address translation

Internal Network Addressing

As part of the internal network security zone, the network is typically configured to use private IP address ranges. These standard private addresses can be
used by any internal network and cannot be routed externally on the Internet.
The following private address ranges can be used:

- **Class A network**   10.0.0.0 to 10.255.255.255
- **Class B network**   172.16.0.0 to 172.31.255.255
- **Class C network**   192.168.0.0 to 192.168.255.255

> ### Exam Tip
> Know the standard nonroutable private address ranges for different classes of networks.

Using these private internal network addresses ensures that any internal network communications cannot be communicated externally unless granted access by the organization's network firewall that uses NAT to convert the internal IP addresses to external addresses that can be routed on the Internet.

Three different types of NAT can be used:

- **Static NAT**   Provides a one-to-one address mapping in which one internal address is mapped to one public external address.
- **Dynamic NAT**   Provides a pool of various external IP addresses that can be used when an internal client wants to access something externally. Dynamic NAT helps in environments that have only a limited amount of external addresses to use and not all of the clients are going to be active at the same time.
- **Overloaded NAT**   Shares one single external address for all internal clients by assigning an individual port socket address that is mapped to the one external address. This technique is also called port address translation (PAT) and is widely used in home-based network devices.

Subnetting

Administrators can make use of network *subnetting* to break larger networks into more manageable subnetworks. Subnetting greatly reduces the amount of network "chatter" and broadcasts that are sent to all systems on a network by isolating this networking activity to specific segments.

Subnetting logically divides the network regardless of its actual physical layout. The router device creates and controls the borders between different subnetworks. The router facilitates communication between the subnets, while keeping inter-subnet traffic isolated on its originating network. These subnetworks can be physical Ethernet segments or VLANs in which the segmentation is not physical but logical.

Subnetting provides network security by ensuring that network details are hidden from external networks and that networking data for each subnet, especially potentially dangerous traffic such as excessive broadcasting, is isolated on its own segment.

Tunneling Protocols

To connect two networks together or to let users remotely access local network servers, VPNs are the communications technology of choice. Before VPNs, to connect the networks of two companies or to connect two offices of the same company in different locations, an expensive wide area network (WAN) communications link needed to be run. With the growth of extranets that connect the internal networks of different companies and organizations over the Internet, VPNs allow the existing Internet to be used to link them together. VPNs are much more secure, and less expensive to install and maintain, than running expensive WAN links between offices.

A VPN makes use of *tunneling protocols* to connect networks together. A tunneling protocol allows an existing internal protocol, such as Internetwork Packet Exchange (IPX) or a network with private IP addressing, to be encapsulated and relayed over the Internet to its destination. The VPN link should be protected with strong encryption and authentication mechanisms to provide secure access to a private network over the public Internet.

Virtual LAN

A VLAN is a type of logical network that exists as a subset of a larger physical network. Smaller networks can be fairly easily divided into segments, with little administrative overhead. Splitting a network into segments allows network data and broadcast traffic to stay on the local segment, without broadcasting data to the entire network. Segmentation of LANs also provides extra security, because a user on one LAN will not have access to another LAN without special permission.

Unfortunately, segmenting a larger network into smaller networks can be tedious and can involve the purchase of extra networking equipment, such as switches, routers, and extra cabling to separate them. Instead, VLANs can allow the network segmentation to be performed through software on a switch, rather than through hardware. VLANs can isolate network traffic on specific segments and even provide crossover functionality to enable certain VLANs to overlap and allow access between them.

Exam Tip

Know how VLANs can increase security and performance in a network, as well as the different ways they can be implemented.

The ability to create VLANs depends on the abilities of your network equipment. Most modern switches and routers support the use of VLANs, which can be enabled simply through changing the configurations of the network devices. Three basic types of VLANs exist:

- **Port-based VLAN**   Uses the specific port of a network switch to configure VLANs, where each port is configured as part of a particular VLAN. To assign a client workstation to that VLAN, it must be plugged into that port.

- **MAC address-based VLAN**   Tracks clients and their respective VLAN memberships through the MAC address of their network card. The switches maintain a list of MAC addresses and VLAN membership, and they route the network packets to their destinations, as appropriate. The advantage of MAC address-based VLANs is if their VLAN membership changes, they needn't be physically moved to another port. One drawback of this method is that being part of multiple VLANs can cause confusion with the switch's MAC address tables. This model is recommended for single VLAN memberships.

- **Protocol-based VLAN**   The most flexible and logical type of VLAN uses the addresses of the IP layer to assign VLAN settings, so an entire IP subnet can be assigned a certain VLAN membership.

Figure 3.8 shows an example of a typical VLAN network configuration that is divided by network subnets, configured as part of a certain VLAN. The switches are using a port-based VLAN configuration across two floors of a building. One VLAN cannot communicate with systems on the other VLAN.

<table>
<tr><td>Objective 3.03</td></tr>
<tr><td>CompTIA Security+
Objective 2.5</td></tr>
</table>

Network Device Vulnerabilities

Network device security protects the network's assets from theft, damage, and unauthorized access. Any device that is configured to connect to your network is a potential access point for unauthorized users to gain entry to the system. The following sections describe the major security risks and threats to network devices.

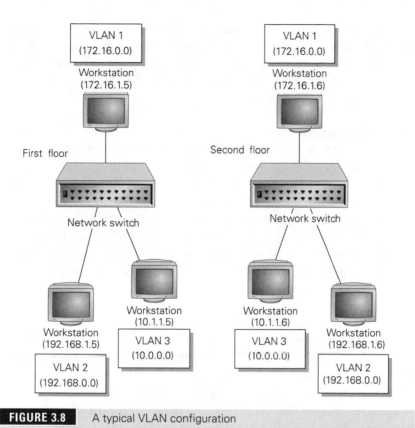

FIGURE 3.8 A typical VLAN configuration

Network Device Threats and Risks

Several weaknesses can be exploited and threats can compromise devices on your network, including weak passwords and account security, software and firmware vulnerabilities that lead to unauthorized access, and direct network attacks on the device itself.

Weak Passwords

Like servers and workstations, network devices control access via login credentials, and it is critical that the accounts and passwords used are secure. Passwords to critical network devices must be very strong to prevent unauthorized users from connecting to the device and attempting to log in and guess the password or use some other brute-force method. Select a password that is at minimum eight characters in length, that includes both uppercase and lowercase characters, numbers, and special characters such as the @ symbol. Passwords should never be written down. If necessary, password and account information can be written down, or stored on an encrypted USB key and stored in locked safe only accessible to authorized users.

Default Accounts

Most network devices have a preinstalled default administrative account, usually called *admin* or *administrator*. Because an unauthorized user can easily guess this account name and use it to try to log in to the device, you should disable this account and create another account with administrative rights and with an account name that does not represent its function. If your team consists of several administrators, you might use their names or other identifying information to help audit access and configuration changes to the device. Any guest accounts or other accounts with diminished access rights should also be disabled.

Back Doors

A *back door* is a program secretly installed on, or that takes an advantage of, an existing vulnerability on an unsuspecting system or device so that a malicious hacker can later access the device, bypassing security authentication systems. The back-door program can be run as a service on the device and listens on specific network ports not typically used by traditional network services. The malicious hacker runs the client portion of the program on her computer, which then connects to the service on the target system. Once the connection is established, the hacker can gain full access, including remotely controlling the network device. Alternatively, the hacker might be able to use a special login credential when logging in to the device that provides her with a back door to administrative access.

Administrators should be always running the latest firmware and software updates on their network devices to ensure that any known exploits or back doors are fixed by the latest updates. Port-scanning software can also be used to identify any open ports on a device that you might not recognize. The open ports can be cross-referenced with lists of ports used by known back-door programs.

Privilege Escalation

Privilege escalation refers to the practice of exploiting coding bugs that exist within software. In certain situations, it can be possible for an unauthorized user to gain more privileged access to a network device by taking advantage of the bug exploit to bypass the device security and perform commands with higher privileged access than expected.

Vulnerabilities that typically lead to privilege escalation scenarios are most often found as buffer overflow attacks, where conditions and boundaries are not properly checked on user-entered fields in a network device's firmware or operating system and allow highly privileged command execution.

In the event that a documented exploit is found in a network device firmware or OS, a patch must be installed (if available) to fix the bug to prevent proof-of-concept exploits from turning into real security threats. Systems administrators must be diligent in ensuring the network device software is running the latest patch level so that all known bug fixes are deployed.

Denial-of-Service (DoS)

When a malicious hacker overloads a specific network device with data, it cannot process data fast enough to keep up with legitimate demands. The DoS attack affects a device's ability to service legitimate requests because the clients will not receive responses to their queries. A DoS attack targeted at a central router or firewall where all data passes through can stop an entire network dead in its tracks so that nothing can get in or out.

Network Device Hardening

One of the most important steps in securing your network and systems is to make sure that the devices that form the infrastructure of your network are examined for security vulnerabilities. Several aspects of networking devices can create a number of security holes if not properly examined or configured, including firmware, configuration, and ACLs.

Firmware Updates

Firmware is software that controls the functions of the network device—like a device OS. Firmware is typically encoded in flash memory and can be updated just like any other software application by obtaining a newer version of the release and then installing it into the device's flash memory.

Like any other OS or application software, the system should be running the most recent versions with the latest security and bug-fix patches installed. Some firmware updates also include additional security functionality that was not in previous versions. For network devices such as firewalls and routers that form the first line of defense in network security, you should regularly update the firmware to maintain maximum security.

Configuration Settings

The administrator must examine the configuration settings of a network device after installation to make sure that the default configuration is suitable for the network's security needs. Typically, the default configurations of most devices provide the least amount of security. The administrator should enable secure settings and disable any options that are not required by the current setup.

Optional services can create security vulnerabilities. For example, in many network devices, SNMP is enabled by default to allow the device to be examined by network monitoring equipment. Unfortunately, SNMP's many security vulnerabilities can be compromised to gain administrative access to a router or a firewall. Another protocol used for network diagnostics, ICMP, is used by utilities such as ping and traceroute. Enabling ICMP leaves the network device open to DoS attacks that can quickly disable a router and cut off the communications flow for your network. ICMP can also be used for identification of systems that are live and accepting connections, which can lead to them being attacked.

Access Control Lists

ACLs are used by routers and other networking devices to control traffic in and out of your network. They can be general in nature or specific to certain types of communications. *Access lists* are typically used in firewalls to control communications between public and private networks, but they can also be used on internal routers to regulate traffic within the network. An access list entry that is contained inside the ACL usually includes the origin of the network packet, the destination, the protocol used (TCP or UDP), the TCP/IP port used, and whether access is allowed or denied.

The following types of parameters can be controlled using an access list:

- **Source address** Specifies the originating source IP address of a packet, whether an internal or external machine or an internal address that it proxies to an external address.
- **Destination address** Specifies the IP address where the packet is going, which can be internal or external to the network.
- **Port numbers** Specifies the TCP/IP port number the communication is using. Each type of TCP/IP service uses a standard port.
- **Protocol** Identifies the protocol being used in the transmission, such as FTP, HTTP, or DHCP, and is usually used in conjunction with a port number that's standard to that protocol or service. This parameter can also be used to define whether the protocol is using TCP or UDP.
- **Permit or deny** Permits or denies the communication specified in the access list entry.

The following is an example of code for an ACL entry for a router:

```
permit source 192.168.13.2 destination 10.1.5.25 tcp port 80
```

The syntax used by your router or network device will be similar to this entry but varies from vendor to vendor. In this example, the ACL entry permits TCP traffic on port 80 (the default port for HTTP) from a host 192.168.13.2 to a host on network 10.1.5.25. The destination might be some type of secured web server that needs to be accessed from a web browser client on the source host. This prevents any other system—internal or external—from connecting to that web server, as shown in Figure 3.9.

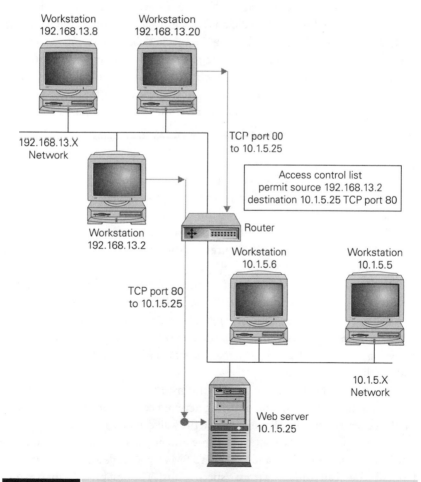

FIGURE 3.9 Access control lists prevent other systems from connecting to a web server

---

Travel Advisory

Denying all access by default is most efficient because it lets you add access to certain systems and service ports that you need. This way, you start off with full security and slowly add rules to allow access as needed.

Networking Device Security

Device security begins with the protection of the backbone of your network communications. If an unauthorized individual were able to tap into any part of your network, she would have access to virtually everything connected to that network. With the Internet, a malicious hacker need not be on site at a physical computer console. She can be far away in another country, trying to log in to your mail server from a home computer. Several key devices within your network can be configured to increase security against unauthorized intrusion. This is your first line of defense against incoming network attacks, and it is vital that these devices be secured and all security holes fixed. The main networking equipment includes the firewall, routers, switches, and wireless access points.

Firewalls

Although a firewall provides a barrier that protects the internal network from outside communications, a company might have some servers, such as web or FTP servers, that need to accept connections from the outside world. The firewall usually splits off these servers into a DMZ, where more generous access from Internet users can be configured. Figure 3.10 shows an example of how a firewall is positioned within a LAN.

The firewall can also act as a proxy for internal users trying to access Internet services. The internal networks usually have their own IP addressing scheme that will not work on the public Internet. The proxy forwards their requests and acts as a point of contact for the particular service being used, such as web browsing. The firewall uses NAT to masquerade the internal IP of a client with a real, public Internet address.

To configure the firewall, an administrator must set up a number of rules to use each time on incoming and outgoing network communications. These rules can be general or specific. For example, a firewall can be configured with a rule that states that any HTTP traffic can come and go on a specific network. It can also be much more detailed and state that a SMTP packet destined for a particular mail server can come only from a specific host. The best practice to use when configuring a firewall for the first time is to deny everything by default and then create rules to allow the access you need. This ensures you are starting off with

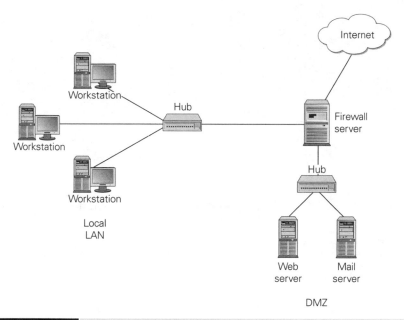

FIGURE 3.10   Network firewall deployment

the most secure model and working backward to configure the firewall to accept certain types of communications.

A firewall can be an independent hardware device or a software application running on a computer or server. In either case, the firewall software should always be kept current with the latest versions and patches. This will ensure you are using the most recent software that does not contain known software bugs and security vulnerabilities.

Travel Advisory

Documenting the rules applied to the firewall and why you are implementing them is important. When auditing these at a later date, you might find you are allowing access to services that do not exist anymore and the rules can be removed.

Routers

A router is a network device that connects several networks together and relays data between them, as shown in Figure 3.11. A router usually contains a number of network interfaces, each representing a different network. Smaller companies generally have only one main router, while larger companies could have several routers to relay information from all their networks.

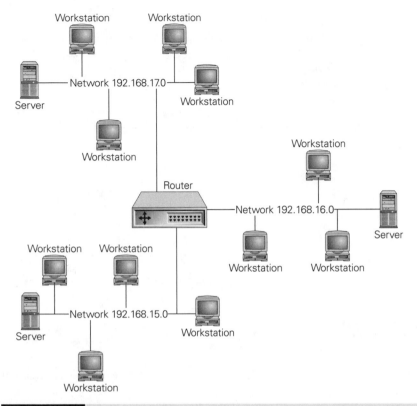

FIGURE 3.11 Router deployment

Router software contains a lot of the same protection found in firewalls, including packet filtering and ACLs that let you carefully control the protocols, services, ports, and source and destination of the information that flows through the router. For example, you can configure the router to accept only FTP communications to a certain network. Other security features of routers include the capability to protect against spoofing and DoS attacks.

Router software can be complex and practically an OS in itself. Just like any other piece of software, router software can contain a number of bugs and security vulnerabilities. Always ensure you have the latest software and patches for your system that can fix any bugs or security issues.

Switches

A switch is a network device used to segment networks into smaller, more manageable sections and to relay packets between the segments. Switches are used for performance and security reasons, and you can configure the switch to accept only data from certain MAC address ranges. These ranges can be spoofed by a hacker, though, so they can access the switch and usually mount some form of DoS attack by flooding the switch with packets.

Most attacks are usually directed at the administrative console of the switch that is used for configuration. Many administrators do not change the default account password, and this provides easy access to an unauthorized user who knows the default passwords used by the switch vendor. If possible, remote access methods, such as the use of Telnet to connect to the switch, should be disabled. This will prevent users from accessing the device, unless they are physically attached to it with a cable.

The use of the SNMP on switches lets you use network monitoring programs to analyze information on the switch. But SNMP has been known to contain a number of security vulnerabilities and sends its data in clear text, so disabling its use is best. SNMP also makes use of a type of password system called *community strings*, which are used as simple pass phrases for SNMP to access each device. Most administrators leave the default community string *public* as is, but this opens up a vulnerability because anyone knowing the community string can connect to the SNMP-enabled device. SNMP passwords should be immediately changed from the default if set up on the switch.

Exam Tip

Remember that SNMP has been known to contain many security vulnerabilities and should be disabled if it is not required, as it is often enabled by default on network devices. The default *public* community name string should be changed when SNMP is installed.

Wireless Devices

Wireless communications have created many security vulnerabilities of which administrators can be unaware. Unlike LANs, for which an unauthorized individual must gain access to a physical connection or connect remotely to a system on the network, a *wireless LAN* creates a network with a varied boundary that can provide access for anyone with a wireless device, even if the person is not inside the facility. Wireless security creates a number of issues that must be added to current security procedures.

Wireless clients access a regular LAN through the use of wireless access points, which accept connections from wireless clients and connect those wireless clients to the LAN. The access point usually has its own wired network connection to the network. Without proper protection, unauthorized clients can use these access points to gain entry to the network. Following are some of the more important security configurations that should be enabled on a wireless LAN.

Travel Assistance

See Chapter 4, "Network Security Tools and Wireless Security," for more detailed information on wireless security.

MAC Address Filtering The access point can be configured to accept connections only from certain hardware MAC addresses. This lets you create a list of all devices that use the wireless LAN and add them to the filter on the access point. Any other device trying to connect that is not on the list of known addresses is denied access. This is an excellent, but impractical, procedure for larger wireless networks because the amount of administration required in keeping the list of addresses and uploading them to each access point would be daunting. MAC addresses can also be spoofed, making MAC address filtering unreliable.

Service Set Identifier A special network name, or *service set identifier (SSID)*, can be configured on the wireless LAN so that only clients that have configured their system to use that identifier are granted access. This is a simple scheme, much like using a public password, and it can be easily compromised if someone learns the SSID. Access points broadcast the SSID in clear text that can be intercepted by a network packet sniffer; however, this broadcast can be disabled to prevent rogue wireless clients from discovering the network.

Exam Tip

Remember that SSIDs should be set to a unique value and should not be broadcast. However, SSID security alone can be easily bypassed and should be used in conjunction with other wireless security techniques.

Encryption The best protection for a wireless LAN is the use of encryption to secure network communications. Encryption is used to convert clear, plain text communications into secure encrypted text. If the communication is captured, the data cannot be read unless it is decrypted with the corresponding encryption key. The client must be configured with the same type of encryption and also the correct public encryption key. This prevents unauthorized users from capturing network transmissions that contain confidential data. Some earlier forms of encryption, such as 40-bit, are weak and can be cracked by a hacker. Using larger bit key systems—such as 128-bit and higher—is best because they are much less likely to be compromised.

Remote Access Devices

In today's corporate environments, many employees need to access the resources of the computer and phone networks when they are not physically in the building. This requires the use of modems to connect to a network using a phone line and more advanced methods, such as encrypted VPN access over the Internet. A VPN is a special, encrypted communications tunnel between one system and another and is used to secure remote access in most modern networks.

These remote access methods offer opportunities for hackers to compromise systems that do not install proper security mechanisms. Through a modem or the Internet, an unauthorized user need not physically be at a console inside the location. He can be halfway across the world in another country, merely using a simple dial-up Internet connection. To protect these communications from unauthorized access, a security policy must be in place to provide authentication measures and data encryption.

To ensure communications security, the use of network monitoring and intrusion detection tools can aid in proactively monitoring the network for suspicious and unauthorized activity.

The modem was, and still is, an important tool for remote communications. A modem allows two computer systems to communicate over an analog phone line. While this is a much slower method than modern VPN and remote access solutions that use broadband Internet access, modems are still in use today as secondary methods of contact, especially for mobile laptop users who must be able to call in from a hotel or an airport where this is no other network access such as wireless.

At minimum, any type of modem access to a network should require authentication before the session can begin. Adding other types of security is ideal, especially because the laptop can be stolen. An important feature to implement is *call-back security,* which requires that after the user connects to the system, the system dials him back and lets his modem answer to continue the connection.

In corporate networks, some users install modems to their work systems so that they can dial in and access it from home, bypassing any security that was set up by the administrator, such as a firewall or VPN system. Unfortunately, most users do not properly configure their modem to authenticate when someone calls, meaning that any unauthorized user can gain access to the corporate network if she knows the right phone number. The administrator must be vigilant in not allowing any type of modem access that bypasses normal security measures.

Remote Access Services

Remote Access Services (RAS) typically refers to the service provided with Microsoft Windows servers to allow remote access to a network through a specific system equipped with a modem. When a user dials in to the server, the RAS handles the procedure of authenticating the client, allowing them access to the rest of the network through that server.

A number of authentication protocols can be used with the RAS server, including Password Authentication Protocol (PAP) and Challenge Handshake Authentication Protocol (CHAP). CHAP is considered to be more secure than PAP and its variants because it does not need the transfer of a password, encrypted or not, between the client and the server.

The system should also be configured with the ability to allow only certain protocols that are used on the network. For example, in a TCP/IP network, communication using other protocols such as IPX/SPX or AppleTalk should be restricted. RAS servers also support *client callback*, which requires the server to call the client computer back to ensure authentication and the origin of the communication.

One of the problems with RAS is that users need a modem to call a RAS across a great distance, which creates an expensive long-distance call. One of the benefits of VPN is that users can make a local call to an Internet service provider (ISP) to get an Internet connection, and then call the VPN server across the Internet at no additional cost. After connecting to the VPN server, the user has a secure channel between her and the network to which the VPN server is attached, enabling her access to network resources.

Users can now access their corporate networks from any Internet connection, whether over a modem or broadband connection. To protect these communications and to reduce the possibility of any Internet user gaining access to a corporate network, most companies use a VPN. The VPN creates an encrypted communications tunnel between the user's computer and the corporate system through the Internet. Users are authenticated with a login and password. The use of special encryption keys provides added security.

Another feature of VPN is the use of *protocol encapsulation*, which enables a client to communicate using an internal network protocol, such as IPX. IPX is then encapsulated into a TCP/IP packet for travel over the Internet. Another way to protect VPN communications is to allow the VPN to assign IP addresses as the user connects and to allow only these blocks of IP addresses to access the network. A VPN is shown in Figure 3.12.

Telephony Services

In most organizations, telephony services also come under the information technology (IT) banner because they are just as much a part of the everyday communications of the company as the computer network. Instead of assigning a direct line for each user, which can be expensive, most large companies prefer to use a phone switch system, such as a Private Branch Exchange (PBX). The

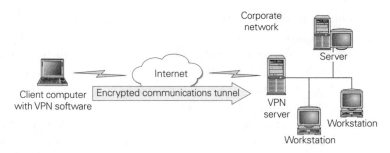

Corporate
network

Server

Internet

Client computer
with VPN software

Encrypted communications tunnel

VPN
server

Workstation

Workstation

FIGURE 3.12   VPN (Virtual Private Network)

PBX allows the company to maintain a certain number of internal and external lines. For example, a company of 200 people could have only 50 incoming lines and 20 outgoing lines. Internal users also have the ability to call other internal users using only three- or four-digit extensions. A centralized voice mail system is also usually a part of the entire phone network, which can generally be accessed from an outside line, in case someone wants to check voice mail while working at home or traveling.

Security for phone systems, however, has traditionally been lax compared to that for computer networks. If an unauthorized user were to gain access to the PBX, he might be able to make expensive long-distance phone calls, all charged to the company. Unauthorized voice mail access can invade the privacy of individual users and can also be used to glean information for corporate espionage. Important to note is that most phone PBX systems are equipped with a modem to allow remote access for the service technicians from the system vendor. If this modem is not secured with proper authentication systems, anyone might be able to call that number and access the phone system. A good practice is to unplug this modem when it is not in use and plug it in when a technician needs access to the system.

The voice mail system should be configured to allow only secure passwords for user voice mail boxes, with a minimum of six to eight characters of uppercase and lowercase letters, numbers, and symbols. The same rules should also be applied to the PBX administrator account.

Voice over IP

The last few years have seen an exponential growth in *Voice over IP (VoIP)* communications, in which clients use TCP/IP to communicate over traditional computer networks. VoIP clients include basic phone services but also include video conferencing and other types of multimedia applications that are used to communicate over a network.

The advantage of VoIP services is that the long-distance costs associated with traditional phone networks practically disappear as phone services can be deployed globally to enable communication over existing Internet lines. A user in an office in New York, therefore, can call an office associate in Tokyo using a VoIP phone that communicates over Internet and VPN connections between their offices, completely bypassing the traditional phone system network.

Security concerns regarding VoIP have grown because it uses computer networks and is open to the same types of computer vulnerabilities that can attack a computer, such as DoS attacks, spoofing, eavesdropping, call interception, man-in-the-middle attacks, and even voice mail spam. VoIP also offers less availability in the event that an Internet connection fails, as none of the VoIP phones will work with no IP communications available. Most organizations use VoIP for specific applications such as video conferencing and continue to use traditional phone networks for the majority of their users because of their inherent security and high-availability risks.

Telephony communications over a computer network require the same types of security safeguards that are used on traditional networks and must be part of your overall network security infrastructure plan.

Objective 3.04
CompTIA Security+
Objective 2.6

Transmission Media Vulnerabilities

Although the physical transmission media of your communications network is rarely considered a security risk, real threats and risks exist for the physical cabling and communications infrastructure that allows information from one system on a network to transfer data to another system that is physically connected to another part of the network. Beyond the computer network, phone and other telecommunications equipment are all vulnerable to the same risks and threats.

The following sections describe the vulnerabilities associated with transmission media and identify the steps required to mitigate these vulnerabilities and protect your communication networks from attack.

Exam Tip
Be aware of which cabling types are more secure and which are more suited for particular types of environments.

Network Cabling

The physical cabling of the computer and telecommunications networks is a critical part of the infrastructure, because the entire network operation would not work without the miles of wires that connect one device to another. Although many companies do not consider cabling a security priority, the physical network cabling offers an opportunity for an unauthorized individual to tap directly into the network to perform malicious functions.

Several types of network cabling are in use today, each with its own advantages and disadvantages, especially in the area of security. Cabling security includes not only intrusion protection but protection against the physical environment as well.

Coaxial Cabling

Coaxial cable has a copper core surrounded by layers of insulation and protective shielding, all rolled into an outer jacket. This cabling is used most often with Ethernet networks, in both thin and thick versions. Each end of the coaxial network must be terminated with a resistor, and each cable segment is connected to the other using several types of connectors, such as a T barrel, or Bayonet Neill-Concelman (BNC), connector. ThinNet, or 10Base2, is much easier to work with than ThickNet, or 10Base5, and is used for smaller distance runs. ThickNet is used for distances of up to 500 meters. Connecting workstations to ThickNet is more complicated because it requires the use of transceivers and "vampire" tap connectors, which pierce the cable.

Local Lingo

vampire tap   A special connector used in coaxial cabling that uses a number of sharp metal teeth to clamp down on a cable and pierce into it to connect to the core copper wire. Vampire taps have been used to hack into a network by tapping directly into the communications cable.

Although not as popular as twisted-pair cable, coaxial cable is most often used in manufacturing environments, where the inherent industrial dangers require a cable that can withstand the physical and electromagnetic environment.

The disadvantage of coaxial cabling is if one segment is disconnected without being properly terminated or broken, that segment will disconnect the entire network. In fact, all you need to do to disable a coaxial network is unplug one of the end terminators. Overall, coaxial networks are less reliable than other cabling options, such as twisted-pair or fiber-optic cables.

Of concern security-wise is that an unauthorized user can access the cable and tap into the connection with his own vampire tap or, in the case of ThinNet, add on another segment to the network and then add a new unauthorized computer or device.

UTP/STP Cabling

Twisted-pair cabling is the most popular type of network cabling today and is also used for virtually all phone-system cabling. Twisted-pair cabling typically consists of four to eight copper wires, surrounded by an outer, protective jacket. The wires are twisted together, which prevents signal crossover interference among the wires.

Two basic types of twisted-pair cabling exist: unshielded twisted pair (UTP) and shielded twisted pair (STP). These are essentially the same, except STP provides an additional foil-shielded layer to provide extra protection against electromagnetic interference (EMI).

Disadvantages of twisted-pair wiring include its susceptibility to EMI, especially in the case of UTP, and attenuation, which means the signal becomes weaker over greater distances.

UTP comes in several different categories representing different applications and transmission speeds:

- **Category 1 (Cat1)**   Used primarily for phone networks
- **Category 2 (Cat2)**   Up to 4 Mbps, used primarily for Token Ring networks
- **Category 3 (Cat3)**   Up to 10 Mbps, used primarily for Ethernet 10BaseT wiring
- **Category 4 (Cat4)**   Up to 16 Mbps, used primarily for Token Ring networks
- **Category 5 (Cat5)**   100 Mbps (usually called 100BaseT) and supports distances of up to about 100 meters
- **Category 5e (Cat5e)**   Gigabit Ethernet support (1000 Mbps), similar to Cat5, but can support speeds up to 1000 Mbps
- **Category 6 (Cat6)**   Gigabit Ethernet support (1000 Mbps), similar to Cat5e, but contains a protective separator between the four pairs to help reduce EMI

Twisted-pair cabling is considered the least secure of network cabling because someone can easily connect it by connecting a computer or network device to an existing cable from a wall jack or to a central hub. Twisted-pair cabling is also easy to damage physically and can be opened up and the cables spliced and reattached to an unauthorized device.

> ## Exam Tip
> Remember that twisted-pair cabling is the least secure of network cabling types.

Fiber-optic Cabling

Fiber-optic cabling, as opposed to other cabling that uses electrical signals over copper wire, uses light as the medium to transfer information. Fiber cabling consists of a central glass core surrounded by protective layers of cladding. Fiber can transfer information quickly and over greater distances than conventional copper wire cabling. Fiber cabling is also immune to EMI, and it does not emit or radiate signals that can interfere with other cables.

Fiber-optic cabling, however, is expensive compared to other forms of wiring and is typically used as a main network backbone. Copper wiring is then used to break off into smaller networks, right down to the desktop computer.

With the added performance advantage of fiber-optics comes the security of knowing unauthorized users cannot tap into a fiber cable to snoop network traffic as they can with a copper-based cable. The main disadvantages of a fiber-optic cable are the expense, its susceptibility to being damaged, and difficulty of repair. Very long fiber-optic cable runs are heavily protected by additional cladding and typically run with redundant cabling via hard-shell conduits. If a cable is damaged, the redundant cable is activated and plugged in, while a new fiber-optic cable must be run to replace the damaged one.

> ## Exam Tip
> Know that fiber-optic cabling is the most secure type of network cabling.

CHECKPOINT

✔ **Objective 3.01: Network Ports and Protocol Threats**   Network administrators must ensure that any unused or antiquated protocols on network devices are disabled or blocked. Be aware of the potential attacks against the network, such as denial-of-service and man-in-the-middle attacks, and DNS and ARP poisoning.

✔ **Objective 3.02: Network Design Elements and Components**   To provide maximum security with the least amount of administrative overhead, the use of security zones is recommended. This type of topology is created with a firewall, which controls access to the various zones through a rules-based access system. Other network protection schemes, including the use of network address translation (NAT), network access control (NAC), virtual local area networks (VLANs), and tunneling protocols, can help you divide the network into more manageable zones to secure access.

✔ **Objective 3.03: Network Device Vulnerabilities**   Several weaknesses and threats can compromise the devices on your network, such as firewalls, routers, switches, and remote access equipment. These threats include weak password and account security, software and firmware vulnerabilities that lead to unauthorized access, and direct network attacks on the device itself.

✔ **Objective 3.04: Transmission Media Vulnerabilities**   Your physical network cabling offers an easy opportunity for an unauthorized individual to tap directly into your network to perform malicious functions. Fiber-optic cabling is the most secure type of cabling as it is not susceptible to electromagnetic interface and cannot be tapped into physically. Twisted-pair and coaxial copper types of wiring are the least secure as they can be easily tapped into via vampire taps and are susceptible to damage and electromagnetic interference.

REVIEW QUESTIONS

1. Which of the following protocols should be disabled on a critical network device such as a router?

   A. TCP/IP

   B. ICMP

   C. IPX/SPX

   D. RIP

2. What feature of a network device, such as a router or switch, can control access permissions for network data?

   A. DNS protocol

   B. Firmware update

   C. Firewall

   D. Access control lists

3. Which zone of a network security topology should contain your Internet servers, such as web, FTP, and e-mail servers?

   A. DMZ

   B. VLAN

C. VPN

D. Intranet

4. Which network service allows internal addresses to be hidden from outside networks and allows several internal hosts to use the same external address?

A. NAT

B. VPN

C. VLAN

D. IP spoofing

5. What networking technology would be used to divide an internal network into smaller, more manageable, logical segments?

A. NAT

B. Tunneling

C. VPN

D. VLAN

6. You have been tasked to cable the network backbone of a new section of a manufacturing plant. Which of the following is the most secure type of cable to use for this environment?

A. 10BaseT

B. Cat3

C. Cat5

D. Fiber-optic

7. During a DoS attack, a network administrator blocks the source IP with the firewall, but the attack continues. What is the most likely cause of the problem?

A. The DoS worm has already infected locally.

B. The attack is coming from multiple, distributed hosts.

C. A firewall can't block DoS attacks.

D. Anti-virus software needs to be installed on the target server.

8. A port scan has been performed on your e-mail server. Which of the following services and ports should be disabled?

A. TCP port 21

B. TCP port 25

C. TCP port 110

D. TCP port 143

9. Which type of network attack results in an unauthorized user being able to capture and manipulate network data as it passes through the network?

    A. SYN flood

    B. Spoofing

    C. DDoS

    D. Man-in-the-middle

10. If not required, which of the following services or protocols should be disabled on a router?

    A. UDP

    B. TCP/IP

    C. SNMP

    D. ACL

REVIEW ANSWERS

1. **B**   Internet Control Message Protocol is a reporting protocol used by utilities such as ping and traceroute to acknowledge network activity from a device. Unfortunately, this protocol can also be used as a basis for DoS attacks, such as a ping flood, to prevent the device from acknowledging legitimate requests. Such utilities are also used by an intruder to discover which hosts exist on the network.

2. **D**   An access control list (ACL) of rules can be entered on a network device to control access between networks. For example, all HTTP access can be denied from one network to another, except for a specific subnet of clients.

3. **A**   The demilitarized zone (DMZ) is a network that contains Internet servers and services that are accessible from the outside world. The DMZ ensures that incoming connections for these services don't reach the internal LAN.

4. **A**   Network address translation (NAT) allows an internal host with nonroutable Internet addresses to access the Internet using an external address. NAT also hides the IP information of the internal network from the outside world.

5. **D**   A virtual LAN (VLAN) is used to segment a network into smaller logical units to aid in security and performance.

6. **D**   Fiber-optic cable uses pulses of light to communicate network data and cannot be comprised via a vampire tap or be disrupted by electromagnetic interference from a manufacturing environment.

7. **B**   A distributed denial of service (DDoS) attack comes from multiple, geographically distributed hosts, making it difficult for the network administrator to block it.

8. **A**   TCP port 21 (FTP) is not required on your e-mail server, and it should be disabled to prevent hackers from connecting to the e-mail server on this port.

9. **D**   A person using a packet sniffer between the sender and the receiver of a communication on the network (man-in-the-middle attack) can intercept or listen in to the information being transferred and modify its contents before resending the data to its destination.

10. **C**   Simple Network Management Protocol (SNMP) allows administrators to monitor network devices remotely. This protocol, however, can create a number of security risks and vulnerabilities by allowing remote access to the device. If not in use for monitoring, SNMP should be disabled.

Network Security
Tools and Wireless
Security

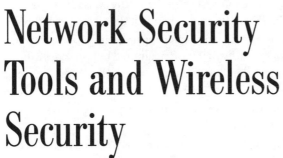

	NEWBIE	SOME EXPERIENCE	EXPERT
ETA	2 hours	1 hour	0.5 hour

Network devices and security tools offer a first line of defense for detection and prevention of attacks at the network border. Several network security tools are available, such as intrusion detection systems (IDSs), firewalls, proxy servers, honey pots, and content filters that do more than just detect network threats: they take proactive steps to stop attacks from entering or leaving your network.

Another aspect of network security that is often ignored but provides a direct threat to your internal systems is the use of wireless networks. Without proper security procedures, any person armed with wireless devices can connect to your network and eavesdrop or access private data by bypassing the traditional security defenses used in wired networks.

This chapter discusses network security tools and their ability to detect and prevent network security threats, and it includes information on the security risks posed by wireless networks and the procedures used to protect them.

Determine and Apply Appropriate Network Security Tools

Objective 4.01
CompTIA Security+
Objectives 2.3 & 2.4

Although several protection mechanisms can be implemented to prevent malicious attacks and unauthorized access to your network, they usually aren't proactive in nature, and after an incident, security must be reviewed and stronger new techniques must be created to prevent future attacks. The following sections describe several network security tools that can aid the administrator in protecting networks and systems from a variety of security threats and in taking proactive steps to mitigate attacks.

Intrusion Detection and Prevention

As a first line of defense, the implementation of an *intrusion detection system (IDS)* greatly enhances the security of your network. An IDS can monitor your network and host systems for suspicious behaviors that can indicate someone is trying to break in or damage your system. By proactively monitoring the system, the IDS can notify an administrator of the intrusion immediately through an e-mail, instant message, or pager. Some systems, called *intrusion prevention systems (IPSs)*, can self-repair the problem and either disconnect suspicious network connections or turn off network services that are being attacked.

Two primary types of IDS can be used:

- **Network-based system**   Analyzes network traffic going in and out of the network and between devices on the network. It can detect suspicious behavior that can indicate unauthorized access or network attacks against network hosts.

- **Host-based system**   Protects one specific host or device. By analyzing incoming and outgoing network activity, suspicious system behavior, and logging user logins and access, it can detect any possible attempts to compromise security.

IDSs can also be either active or passive. In an *active* detection system, intrusion attempts are dealt with immediately by shutting down network connections or services that are being attacked. A *passive* detection system relies on notifications to alert administrators of an intrusion.

Exam Tip

Know the difference between network and host-based intrusion detection systems, as well as the difference between active and passive versions of these systems and how they mitigate threats.

Network-based IDS

To prevent intrusions into your network systems, a network-based IDS (NIDS) can be installed to monitor incoming and outgoing traffic in your network. A NIDS analyzes network activity and the data packets themselves for suspicious activity against hosts on the network.

A NIDS can examine network patterns, such as an unusual amount of requests destined for a particular server or service, such as an FTP server. The headers of network packets can be analyzed to determine whether they were changed in transit or contain suspicious code that indicates malformed packets. Corrupted packets and malformed data can bring down a web server that's vulnerable to such attacks.

A NIDS typically consists of the following components, as shown in Figure 4.1.

- **Detection agent**   These agents are usually physically installed in a network and attached to core network devices such as routers, firewalls, and switches. Detection agents can also be software agents that use network management protocols, such as Simple Network Management Protocol (SNMP). They simply collect the data passing through the network and send it to the network monitor for analyzing.
- **Network monitor**   The network monitor is fed information from the detection units and analyzes the network activity for suspicious

behavior. This is the heart of the IDS; it collects information from the network, analyzes it, and then uses the notification system to warn of any problems.

● **Notification system** This is used for notification and alarms, which are sent to the administrator. Once the network monitor recognizes a threat, it writes the incident to a log file and uses the notification system to send an alert, such as an e-mail or a page, to an administrator. The notification system is usually configurable to allow for a variety of methods of communication.

To protect the entire network, the NIDS is usually located at a central point, such as a main router, switch, or firewall. An IDS can monitor only what it sees, so placing it further down in the system lessens the chance of finding intrusions, especially because your firewall and routers are the entry points to the network. This characteristic makes a NIDS much more important than a host-based system (described a little later) because of its ability to detect intrusions at the entrance to the network. The disadvantage of a NIDS is that it is specifically designed to detect intrusions originating from outside the internal network. This is why also using host-based IDSs in your overall security model is important.

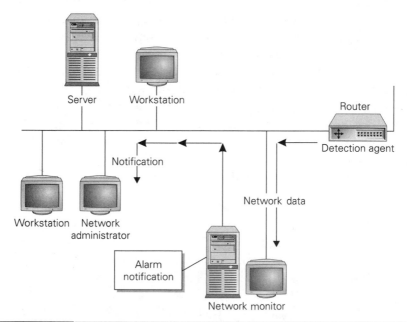

FIGURE 4.1 Network intrusion detection system

Network-based IDSs also are ineffective at monitoring encrypted communications, because the IDS would need to see the contents of the packet in order to analyze it.

When an intrusion is detected, the system works in either an active or a passive way to alert an administrator of the problem. A passive system will send warnings and alarms through log files, e-mail or instant message notification, and paging. An active system tries to fix the problem by shutting off certain services or preventing connections from a suspicious host.

Active Detection   A network-based IDS that uses active detection methods can take immediate steps to halt an intrusion. These types of systems are also called *network intrusion prevention systems (NIPSs)* because they actively attempt to prevent intrusions rather than just detect them. An active NIPS can attempt to prevent an intrusion from continuing and prevent the suspicious activity from ballooning into actual damage or data loss. This is a great advantage over passive based detection systems, which merely log the incident or send an e-mail to the administrator who might not see the message for many hours before he can perform any preventative actions. By then, it could be too late.

Exam Tip

A Network Intrusion Prevention System (NIPS) tries to prevent an intrusion from continuing or spreading throughout the system after detecting the intrusion.

Network-based active detection systems can automatically reconfigure logical network topologies to reroute network traffic in case of network attack, such as a denial of service (DoS) attack. They can also detect suspicious activities on a network connection and terminate them, logging the originating IP address to prevent any further connections from that origin. The detection system can also sense attacks on certain ports or services, such as an SNMP port on a router, and shut it down to prevent more attacks on that service port.

The disadvantage of active detection systems is the occurrence of false alarms that can cause the system to shut down services or network connections for legitimate requests.

Passive Detection   Passive detection by NIDSs involves alerting an administrator of the intrusion, so he can take the necessary actions to stop it. The system will not take any active steps to prevent the detected intrusion from continuing. With a passive system, the administrator might not get the alert immediately, especially if he is offsite and not carrying a pager, cell phone, or other mobile device. By the time he reaches the system, the intrusion damage can have already been done.

Passive detection methods usually consist of some form of utility that logs events as they happen and stores them for later examination or notifies the administrator of high-level warnings and errors. If no type of messaging alert function is configured, the administrator must scan the log files regularly for suspicious behavior.

Host-based IDS

A *host-based intrusion detection system (HIDS)* differs from a network-based system because it monitors a specific host or device for suspicious behavior that could indicate someone is trying to break into the system. An HIDS monitors inbound and outbound network activity, networking service ports, system log files, and timestamps and content of data and configuration files to ensure they have not been modified by unauthorized users.

An HIDS needs to be installed on a specific system or network device. This differs from NIDS, which needs to install monitors only at certain points on the network. The host-based system can monitor only the system on which it's installed and should be used only for critical server systems rather than user workstations.

The advantage of an HIDS is that it can detect attacks that occur from someone physically working at the system console, rather than over the network. The unauthorized user might be trying to access an administrator account or trying to copy files to or from the system. The IDS is able to alert the administrator if someone has tried to log in to an account unsuccessfully too many times.

Like NIDSs, a host-based system can provide both active and passive protection.

Active Detection   An HIDS using active methods of detection can take immediate steps to halt an intrusion. This is the preferable method because it prevents the suspicious activity from continuing. An active detection system can terminate network connections from clients who seem to be performing some type of suspicious activity and prevent any further connection from that particular network address. Another method of preventing an intrusion is shutting down the network service that is under attack. For example, a web server can immediately stop accepting HTTP requests to prevent the attack from continuing.

If the intrusion appears to originate at the system console, the system can shut down and disable that user account. This type of detection is used by most network OSs that disable accounts if a predefined number of unsuccessful logins occurs.

The disadvantage of active detection is the potential of a false detection: the system might automatically shut down services when no attack is occurring, which can cause unnecessary and often costly downtime.

Passive Detection   Passive detection methods do not take active steps to prevent an intrusion from continuing if it is detected. These methods typically include logging events to a system log, which can be viewed by an administrator at a later time or, if configured to do so, forwarding the log entries through a pager or e-mail system. The latter method is preferable because it enables the administrator to be notified as the intrusion is happening, giving the administrator a chance to catch the unauthorized user in the act and to prevent any damage or data theft. If the administrator isn't immediately notified, she must be sure to audit system log files regularly for critical warnings and errors that indicate suspicious activity.

On the down side, passive methods merely log the incident or send an e-mail to the administrator who might not see the message for many hours before she can do something about it.

Network Firewalls

A firewall protects an internal network from unauthorized access by unauthorized users on an external network, as shown in Figure 4.2. The external network can be the Internet, or it can be another network within the same organization.

A network firewall is critical in an organization's overall security architecture. The firewall controls and monitors access between different networks by filtering inbound and outbound traffic, manages access controls to requested locations, and typically blocks all services except those explicitly permitted by the administrator. Most firewalls log network traffic and activity and activate alarms if it detects anomalous situations.

The firewall implements security, authentication, and access controls at multiple levels while remaining completely transparent to internal users. Firewalls generally provide the following services and security features:

- **Packet filtering**   The firewall server analyzes each network packet destined for inside or outside the network and can filter out dangerous malformed packets, attacks, and spoofed IP addresses to prevent unauthorized access. Packets are also analyzed and acted upon depending on the rules enabled by the administrator that are based on information in the headers that specify the source and destination IP addresses and ports used by the packet.

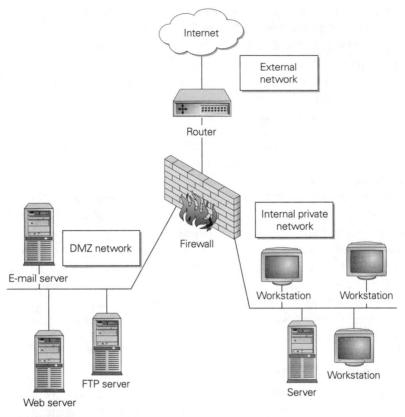

| FIGURE 4.2 | Network firewall deployment |

- **Stateful inspection** Stateful inspection of packets ensures that the firewall maintains a record of the connections that pass through and monitors their state from when they are connected to when they close. This ensures the firewall is not only tracing packets but also analyzing the state of the entire connection. Depending on the access rules configuration, certain actions can be taken when an anomalous change of state occurs (such as a connection hijack). Stateful inspection allows the firewall to track a network conversation and know what type of packet is expected next in the sequence. This is more advanced than a typical packet-inspecting firewall that only filters traffic based on the header information. Packet filtering doesn't know about the context of a conversation, and if the filter conditions are met, the packet filtering firewall allows the traffic in.

- **Access and authentication control** The firewall can restrict access to networking services by source and destination IP address, type of service, time/day of the week, and also via authenticated access. Most firewalls have flexible access control policies that can be fine tuned by the administrator to secure access for specific users and networks.

* **Application layer filtering**   Firewalls can be aware of specific applications and services such as Domain Name System (DNS) and Simple Mail Transfer Protocol (SMTP) e-mail. This allows the firewall to analyze network traffic and apply access rules that are specific to that application. For example, a firewall can act as an application gateway for e-mail servers to help secure the connections between external e-mail servers and local e-mail servers and clients that send and receive messages. The firewall can detect whether these services are trying to be accessed on unauthorized ports for that specific application. Generally, application layer firewalls inspect the application data, not just the header information, as the packet filtering firewall does.

* **Network address translation** (NAT)   Most firewalls use NAT to map source IP addresses of outbound connections so that the connection appears to have originated from the firewall's address. This allows internal networks to be hidden behind a single Internet IP address without any additional registered addresses required.

Proxy Servers

A *proxy server* is a network server or device that accepts and forwards requests from clients to other servers. The proxy server performs this function on behalf of the client. The proxy is typically situated between the clients and the Internet and can be used to forward requests for many types of traffic and data transfers such as web and FTP. This protects the specific addresses of internal clients from being revealed to external servers and allows the proxy server to filter incoming and outgoing requests to prevent attacks and malicious software from reaching the client systems.

The most commonly used type of proxy server is for web browsing. A web client will request a specific URL from the web browser, which is sent to the proxy server. The web proxy server will then forward the request to the destination web site using its own IP addresses as the source of the request. When the data is sent from the web site to the proxy server, the proxy server may cache or content filter the data before sending the data to the requesting client. Web proxy servers are used primarily for their caching ability that boosts web browsing performance by storing content retrieved from an external web server. The next time a client retrieves the same web data, the web proxy can serve the information to the client without sending another request to the external web server. This greatly reduces the amount of bandwidth required to retrieve numerous web requests for an organization and provides significant cost savings.

Internet Content Filtering

Most proxy servers provide some type of content filtering abilities that help protect an organization's clients from accessing host phishing and fraud sites or other web sites and downloads that are infected with worms, spyware, or malware. Organizations can also filter specific URLs or file types from being accessed, such as adult sites and other types of content that should not be viewed or used on a corporate or public network, such as at a library. The web proxy will have a predefined list of sites that are allowed or blocked as required via policies. If a client tries to access a blocked web site or file, the user will receive a warning message and will not be allowed access to that particular site. Public block lists that contain lists of web sites that are most commonly blocked because of their content can be consulted for help with setting up access restrictions.

Some proxy servers allow only clients with authenticated access to traverse the proxy server and access content outside the network. In addition, users' web surfing habits can be tracked to monitor content and/or bandwidth usage.

Outbound Filtering

As privacy concerns increase and certain types of organizations (such as financial or medical companies) must adhere to specific government regulations regarding the release of private data, the control of outbound content has become a priority for proxy server deployments.

Several rules must be followed by financial organizations to protect the security and privacy of data. For example, Payment Card Industry (PCI) is a compliance policy that defines the minimum amount of security required for credit card, debit card, ATM system, and other financial transactions. Most major credit card and banking companies are PCI-compliant. These compliance rules are primarily based on the storage and transmission of sensitive financial information. For example, a bank must ensure that a private customer's credit card or banking details are not transmitted outside of their networks, or if they must be transmitted, they must be encrypted.

Medical and health providers must adhere to strict rules, such as those required by the Health Insurance Portability and Accountability Act (HIPAA). These rules ensure that organizations are accountable for the privacy and security of their patients' medical records. Outbound content filtering can ensure that messages with specific identifying information can be blocked from being sent outside of the organization.

An outbound content filter on a proxy server can monitor outgoing e-mails (including deep content scanning of e-mail attachments) and web connections to scan the content for patterns of credit card or account numbers. If they are encountered in a message, the message can be blocked or quarantined; policies can also require that messages be automatically encrypted before leaving the organization's network.

Protocol Analyzers

Beyond basic filtering services, *protocol analyzers* have become another defense in organizations' security arsenal to prevent attacks and exploits from reaching their server and client systems. Protocol analyzers can be stand-alone applications or used in conjunction with other network monitoring and intrusion detection applications to monitor and capture network data right down to the packet and frame level.

The network administrator can analyze each frame of network data to look for abnormalities and inconsistencies in network requests and responses that can indicate an intrusion or other malicious application running on the network. Due to the enormous amount of data that floods through a network, it would be impossible for a network administrator to examine each and every frame passing through the primary network router. Stand-alone analyzers are most useful for detecting isolated problems with specific systems or on a small subnet of clients.

Protocol analyzers can also be used in conjunction with intrusion detection and prevention systems to analyze large blocks of the network and network protocols such as web HTTP and FTP data. This deep-level scanning of network data can detect specific behaviors of known exploits or network attacks, such as anomalous data in an HTTP request. This information can be communicated to the IDS, which can block those network packets from reaching the client. This technique is similar to how anti-virus and anti-spyware applications detect malicious programs, by comparing them to known behaviors based on a signature file. To ensure efficiency, this signature file must be kept up to date with the latest known network and application exploits.

Honey Pots

A *honey pot* is a device or server used to attract and lure attackers into trying to access it, thereby removing attention from actual critical systems. The name refers to using a pot of honey to attract bees, which in this case are malicious hackers. The honey pot server is usually situated in the network DMZ and runs popular Internet services that are vulnerable to attack, such as web or FTP services. The server does not have many basic security features enabled, and it freely advertises open Internet ports that can be picked up by malicious hackers' port scanners, as shown in Figure 4.3.

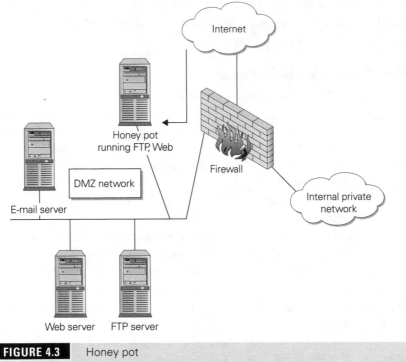

FIGURE 4.3   Honey pot

A slight security danger exists if the honey pot isn't configured correctly. If an unauthorized user hacks into the server, she might be able to attack other systems on the DMZ. To prevent this scenario, some honey pot systems can emulate services, instead of actually running them.

Travel Advisory

To ensure your honey pot system does not allow an intruder to attack other machines, use service emulation rather than running the full services, or isolate the honey pot on its own network segment.

Honey pots can be used as decoy devices that attract attention away from real production servers, or they can be used by network administrators to learn the identity of malicious hackers through logging and auditing. By keeping accurate logs of the IP addresses being used by an attacker, the administrator might be able either to track down the source of the attack or to pass information to legal authorities. From a legal standpoint, however, doing this can be tricky, especially if the server advertises files for downloading or viewing, because this is considered entrapment and is illegal.

Honey pot systems are best suited for understanding the different types of attacks that can happen to your network. You can log when and what types of attacks are occurring in the system logs, and then use that information to secure your network even further by including protection against attacks that were overlooked in the original security plan.

Exam Tip

You should know that a honey pot is the name given to a device or server used to attract and lure attackers into trying to access it, diverting their attention from actual critical systems.

Objective 4.02
CompTIA Security+
Objective 2.7

Explain Wireless Networking Vulnerabilities and Implement Mitigations

One of the greatest changes in networking technology is the phenomenal growth of wireless communications. Wireless networks use radio frequency technology to transmit data through the air, effectively bridging the gap between data connectivity and user mobility. Wireless networks allow the mobile world to reach the Internet, not only with laptop computers, but also with other telecommunication devices, such as wireless-enabled cell phones, personal digital assistants (PDAs), and many other devices.

Wireless connectivity lets a user perform daily computing functions, such as checking e-mail, voice mail, and calendar scheduling, without physically plugging into a network. Wireless applications also extend into the business world, where inventories are taken by handheld devices and entire floors of a building are set up with wireless networks to enable mobile users to move their laptops from room to room without the encumbrance of wires.

The popularity and explosive growth of wireless networks, however, have also introduced increased concerns for the security of wireless data. More so than traditional wired networks, wireless security heavily involves the use of encryption technologies, coupled with traditional security mechanisms such as access control and authentication.

Wireless security depends on the different types of wireless network configurations available and the types of devices that will connect to them. The following sections discuss the various wireless network configurations, wireless threats and risks, and the protocols, hardware, and software that make them work.

Wireless LAN Technologies

Wireless LANs (WLANs) use electromagnetic airwaves to transfer information from one point to another without the need for a physical connection. To communicate these signals, the sender and receiver need to be tuned to the same radio frequency. The receiver tunes in one radio frequency, rejecting all others. WLANs can comprise a range of technologies, each with its own set of strengths and limitations.

Narrowband Technology

A *narrowband* system transmits and receives data only on a specific radio frequency. The signal frequency is kept as narrow as possible—large enough to communicate only the required information. Crossover between communications streams is prevented through the use of separate channel frequencies. The radio receiver filters out other radio signals, accepting only those on its designated frequency. The disadvantage of narrowband technology is that a Federal Communications Commission (FCC) license must be issued for each site where it is employed.

Spread Spectrum Technology

Most WLAN systems use spread-spectrum technology to transmit their information. *Spread-spectrum* technology is a wideband radio-frequency technique used to ensure reliable and basic security for communications systems. More bandwidth is consumed than in a narrowband transmission, but spread-spectrum technology produces a stronger signal. Two types of spread-spectrum radio exist—frequency hopping (FHSS) and direct sequence (DSSS):

- **FHSS**   *Frequency-hopping spread-spectrum* uses a narrowband carrier that changes frequency in a pattern known to both the transmitter and the receiver. When synchronized, a single logical channel is maintained. FHSS uses a lower data rate (3 Mbps) than DSSS systems but can be installed into virtually any location without fear of interference interrupting its operation. FHSS is used by the Bluetooth standard.
- **DSSS**   *Direct-sequence spread-spectrum* generates a redundant bit pattern for each bit to be transmitted. Through the use of these bit patterns, transmissions can be easily recovered if interfered with or damaged, without the need for retransmission. DSSS delivers higher speeds than FHSS and is used by the 802.11 wireless standards.

Infrared Technology

Infrared (IR) systems use high frequencies, just below visible light in the electromagnetic spectrum, to carry data. Like light, IR transmissions can't go through solid objects, and its application is mostly for short, line-of-sight communications between devices. Infrared technology is rarely used in wireless network applications. Instead, it is geared more toward implementing fixed networks for allowing devices such as PDAs to communicate with each other when in line of sight of their IR ports.

Wireless Access

In a typical WLAN setup, a device called an *access point* is connected to a wired network from a fixed location using standard LAN cabling. The access point acts as a gateway, connecting the wireless and the wired LAN together. A single access point can support a small group of users and can function within a range up to several hundred feet. The access point is usually mounted at the top of a wall or ceiling to provide maximum coverage for the wireless area. The access point and any wireless device usually contain an antenna that can be extended to aid in signal reception.

To access the WLAN, the user can use a regular PC with a special WLAN adapter, a notebook computer with a wireless PC card, or even a hand-held device, such as a PDA or other device. The wireless adapter appears to the OS of the computer or device as a typical network adapter.

Site Surveys

An initial site survey should be performed before installation of a wireless network to ensure the environment will be conducive to wireless communications. The survey can also help determine the best placement and coverage for your wireless access points. The following are some important issues to remember for the site survey:

- **Antenna type and placement**   Proper antenna placement is a large factor in maximizing radio range. As a general rule, range increases in proportion to antenna or access point height.
- **Physical environment**   Clear or open areas provide better radio range than closed or filled areas.
- **Obstructions**   Metal physical obstruction can hinder the performance of wireless devices. Avoid placing these devices in a location where a metal barrier is situated between the sending and receiving antennas.
- **Building materials**   Radio penetration is affected by the building materials used in construction. Drywall construction allows greater range than concrete blocks, while metal construction can hinder and block radio signals.

WLAN Topologies

WLANs can be as small and simple as two PCs or laptops networked together through their wireless interfaces. This type of peer-to-peer (P2P) network requires little configuration and administration, and the wireless devices would only have to be within range of each other to communicate. No intermediary access points or servers are on this *ad-hoc* network. Each client would have access only to the resources of the other client.

More complex networks can encompass a large number of access points, connected with many different wireless PCs, notebooks, or hand-held devices. Installing an access point can extend the range of a small wireless network, effectively doubling the area in which the devices can communicate. The access point is directly connected to a wired network, so any wireless clients accessing that access point can communicate with the resources of the wired LAN through the access point. Resources on the wired network that wireless clients might access include file servers, mail servers, and the Internet. Figure 4.4 shows an example of a typical WLAN access-point configuration.

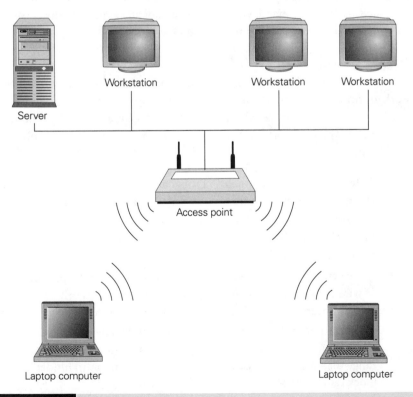

FIGURE 4.4   Typical WLAN configuration

An access point can accommodate many clients, depending on the number and the type of bandwidth transmission required. Typical access points can handle up to approximately 50 client devices. The disadvantage is that the more users connected to the access point, the less bandwidth available to each client.

Access points are limited by range—ranging from 100 meters indoors to 500 meters outdoors—depending on the physical environment. In large wireless environments, multiple access points are needed to provide a wide coverage area for the clients. The access point ranges must overlap, so network connectivity will not be lost roaming from one access point to another.

Wireless Protocols

Just like regular networked LANs, WLANs run on specific networking protocols optimized for use with wireless communications. As wireless networks began to proliferate, a number of competing wireless protocols were released that weren't always compatible with each other. A wireless device using one type of protocol might be unable to access a WLAN using an entirely different protocol. The industry has settled down somewhat, and the most popular protocol for wireless devices currently in use is the Institute of Electrical and Electronics Engineers (IEEE) standard, 802.11g, with the next standard 802.11n quickly gaining popularity, even though it has not been fully standardized. The following sections outline some of the most common wireless protocols.

Wireless Access Protocol

Wireless Access Protocol (WAP) is a specification that provides the delivery mechanisms for transmitting information to wireless devices. WAP supports the use of Wireless Markup Language (WML) instead of HTML to send web data to wireless devices, such as handhelds and cell phones. Through the use of WML, web site content can be tailored so that it can be handled by WAP browsers embedded into wireless devices. Wireless devices typically have small memory and processors, so the web content must be stripped down to work on these types of devices.

Security for WAP is handled through the use of Wireless Transaction Layer Security (WTLS), which provides authentication and encryption functionality similar to the Secure Sockets Layer (SSL) in typical web networking. The wireless client and the server must be authenticated for wireless transactions to remain secure and to provide encryption. WTLS resembles SSL in that both rely on certificates on the client and server to verify the identities of the participants involved.

Exam Tip

Know that WAP security for wireless networks is performed via Wireless Transaction Layer Security (WTLS).

Unfortunately, WAP hasn't caught on as strongly as other wireless protocols and architectures because it's limited to smaller hand-held devices and restricts its usefulness with higher bandwidth wireless solutions.

Bluetooth

Bluetooth wireless technology is designed to enable and simplify wireless communication between small, mobile devices. In an effort to implement wireless methods that eliminate the need for proprietary cables, Bluetooth attempts to allow connectivity between any device, including peripherals such as cameras and scanners. For example, no cables are needed to transfer digital photographs between a camera and a PC, or to transfer data between an address book program on your PC and your cell phone, because the communications can be performed using Bluetooth wireless. Bluetooth has low power consumption and transmits via common radio frequencies (2.4 GHz). Configuration is usually performed dynamically in the background, allowing seamless communications between Bluetooth wireless devices.

Bluetooth also enables devices to form small, wireless networks called *piconets*, which are established using a radio transceiver embedded within each Bluetooth device. This is designed to operate in a noisy radio environment and to provide a fast, robust, and secure connection between devices. The range for Bluetooth, however, is much smaller than typical wireless networks, allowing for a link range between 10 cm (about 4 in.) and 10 meters (about 33 ft.), because typical Bluetooth connectivity is used between one device and another. Figure 4.5 illustrates how a Bluetooth network works.

Several vulnerabilities in vendor implementations of Bluetooth have allowed unauthorized access to personal data on cell phones and computer devices. Bluetooth can also be susceptible to unauthorized messages, a practice called *bluejacking*. An unauthorized user can send unwanted messages to another Bluetooth device in range of the originating device. This has most often been used for Bluetooth spam advertising, in which a Bluetooth device such as a cell phone suddenly receives a text message containing the spam message. Bluejacking is relatively harmless and a nuisance much like spam e-mails, but there is the potential for harmful media to be transferred from one device to another.

A more serious Bluetooth vulnerability is called *bluesnarfing*. Many Bluetooth phones and devices use a discovery mode that allows a hacker to detect and connect automatically to other Bluetooth devices, much like a WLAN. Without proper authentication, an unauthorized user can connect to unprotected Bluetooth devices and access any data stored on the device. If an unsuspecting user leaves his device in discovery mode, it is not protected from access by other Bluetooth devices in the vicinity.

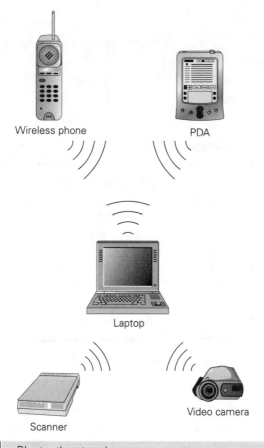

Wireless phone

PDA

Laptop

Scanner

Video camera

FIGURE 4.5   Bluetooth network

Bluetooth defines three security modes:

- **Nonsecure mode**   No security features are enabled.
- **Service-level security mode**   Application security policies are used, in which the actual applications on the wireless device are responsible for security.
- **Link-level security mode**   The most secure of the three modes authenticates the actual communications link before data transmission can begin. Data encryption can also be performed in this mode, once the link is authenticated. Authentication allows the devices to decide whether a connection will be formed based on available identification at the hardware level. Once the link is established, additional security might be applied to the data transmission using encryption. Stronger encryption can also be enabled at the software level, if needed.

Exam Tip

Remember that bluesnarfing is a serious Bluetooth security threat, and link-level security is recommended to secure the communications link and transfer of data. Bluetooth should be disabled if you are not using it.

802.11

802.11 refers to a family of specifications developed by the IEEE for WLAN technology. 802.11 specifies an over-the-air interface between a wireless client and a base station, or between two wireless clients. The IEEE accepted the specification in 1997.

Several specifications are included in the 802.11 family:

- **802.11**   Applies to WLANs and provides 1 or 2 Mbps transmission in the 2.4 GHz band using either frequency hopping spread spectrum (FHSS) or direct sequence spread spectrum (DSSS).

- **802.11a**   An extension to 802.11 that applies to WLANs and provides up to 54 Mbps in the 5 GHz band. 802.11a uses an orthogonal frequency division multiplexing encoding scheme, rather than FHSS or DSSS.

- **802.11b**   Also referred to as 802.11 High Rate or Wi-Fi, this extension to 802.11 applies to WLANS and provides 11 Mbps transmission (with a fallback to 5.5, 2, and 1 Mbps) in the 2.4 GHz band. 802.11b uses only DSSS. 802.11b was a 1999 ratification to the original 802.11 standard, allowing wireless functionality to provide performance comparable to the Ethernet 10BaseT standard, which runs at 10 Mbps.

- **802.11g**   Applies to WLANs and provides 54+ Mbps in the 2.4 GHz band.

- **802.11n**   Applies to WLANs and provides 150 to 300 Mbps in the 5.8 GHz band.

Travel Assistance

For detailed information on the IEEE wireless standards, see http://standards.ieee.org/wireless/.

Currently, the 802.11g standard is popular for home and business wireless users, with 802.11n devices already on the market, even though the standard has not been finalized (due in March 2009). The popularity of wireless networks, however, has created the need for even better security for WLANs at home and in the workplace. Without any type of security mechanisms, WLANs can be easily compromised; with no mechanisms for authentication or encryption configured, an unauthorized user can simply bring her own wireless laptop or wireless device into the range of the WLAN for instant access.

Travel Advisory

With the proliferation of home networks with high-speed Internet connections, many users have also added wireless systems to their home networks. Due to the lack of security on these home wireless networks, unauthorized users nearby can access a neighbor's network without subscribing to the service and perform illegal activities, using someone else's home network so it cannot be traced back to the hacker.

Wireless Threats

The following sections describe some common security issues with wireless networks.

Data Emanation

Data emanation is a serious issue, as unprotected and unsecured wireless communications can be easily intercepted and an unauthorized user can steal user names and passwords and sensitive private data. All information on an unsecured WLAN is transmitted in clear text, and any wireless user can use a protocol analyzer or sniffer application to view the data traversing the WLAN. All WLANs should communicate using secure encrypted channels to prevent eavesdropping from unauthorized users.

War Driving

Many corporate WLANs and home-based wireless networks are set up and configured with no encryption or access control. Hackers have been known to roam neighborhoods with a large corporate presence, using simple laptops with wireless connectivity to connect to unprotected WLANs and access their resources. This is called *war driving*. Several programs are available (such as Kismet) that allow unauthorized users to scan an area for open and unprotected wireless networks. After accessing the network, the user can attempt several types of attacks, such as eavesdropping and sniffing the wireless data, or accessing and capturing the data on other wireless devices on the network. Administrators can lower the susceptibility of their wireless networks to war driving attacks by encrypting their networks and disabling the broadcast of their service set identifiers (SSIDs). These and other techniques are discussed in the section "Securing Wireless Networks."

Rogue Access Points and Devices

With wireless networks, much of the typical physical security that prevents someone from plugging into a network is unavailable. Anyone within the vicinity of a WLAN can connect to it easily with the use of a laptop or other wireless-equipped device. Unauthorized users can also set up their own wireless access points to which unsuspecting users connect and transmit sensitive and private data, including user name and password credentials, directly on the hacker's network.

By setting a unique SSID name and encrypting the network, any rogue access points and devices will require the SSID name and encryption passphrase to connect to the network. In certain cases, Media Access Control (MAC) address filtering can also be used to allow only certain hardware addresses access to the network; however, this is not practical for networks with hundreds of wireless clients. Your networks should be routinely scanned for evidence of rogue access points or devices.

Local Lingo

MAC Address   Stands for Media Access Control Address, a unique hardware address assigned to network interface cards. This address is expressed in hexadecimal format.

Securing Wireless Networks

Securing a WLAN with as many layers of security as possible is extremely important. The following methods can collectively be used to secure access to 802.11 networks:

- Access point security
- An SSID
- MAC address filtering
- Encryption—Wired Equivalent Privacy (WEP) and Wi-Fi Protected Access (WPA and WPA2)
- A secure virtual private network (VPN)
- Personal firewall

Access Point Security

Security for a WLAN begins at its primary points of access, and the wireless access point security configuration is of critical importance to the network administrator. Most access points allow administrative configuration to be performed wirelessly; however, this creates a security risk because any user with wireless access can attempt to access the configuration via brute-force or other account cracking methods. If possible, configuration should be limited to a wired connection, and the administrator's machine must be physically cabled to the access point to perform these tasks. Remote configuration should be disabled if wired access can be performed on the access points. If wireless configuration must be used, network administrators should be sure that these occur over encrypted channels such as Hypertext Transfer Protocol over Secure Socket Layer (HTTPS) and SSL.

The administrator user name and password must be secure, like any user name and password used on an important server or router on the network. This includes modifying the *admin* account name (if possible) to something less recognizable and using a secure password of at least eight alpha-numeric characters, including uppercase, lowercase, and special characters.

From this point, several security features can be enabled for the entire WLAN that are discussed in the following sections. Ensure that all access points have the same configuration, or you may leave one of your access points with security weaknesses and vulnerabilities that can be exploited. For example, you may forget to disable SSID broadcast on one of your access points, which allows unauthorized users to attempt to access the network using the SSID name.

Service Set Identifier

The most simple wireless network access control is the use of a network password or name. This SSID can be set up on one or a group of wireless access points. It provides a way to segment a wireless network into multiple networks serviced by one or more access points. This is helpful in companies that are separated by departments or physical floor locations.

To access a particular network, client computers must be configured with the correct identifier. For roaming users, multiple identifiers can be enabled on their wireless devices, enabling them access to different networks as required. This type of security is minimal, however, because it simply employs a network password, which could easily be compromised by word of mouth or through access points that broadcast the network name.

> **Travel Advisory**
>
> Many access points advertise their SSID by default. For security reasons, check the settings of all your access points to disable this feature. The disadvantage of disabling broadcasts, however, is that clients cannot see the network if they do not know the SSID name. It is a best practice to disable SSID broadcasting, but at the same time, anyone who wants to crack a wireless network knows that even with SSID broadcasting disabled, the network is detectable with advanced hacking tools.

MAC Address Filtering

Access points can be identified with network names and passwords, but a client computer can be identified by the unique MAC address of its wireless network card. Access points can be configured with a list of MAC addresses associated with the client computers allowed to access the wireless network. If a wireless client's MAC address isn't included in this list, the wireless client isn't allowed to connect with the access point and the network. This is a much better solution than using network identifiers alone, but maintaining the list of client MAC addresses can quickly become a daunting task with larger networks. In addition, each access point must be configured individually, so each node contains the same list of addresses. This type of security is best suited to small networks because the administrative overhead quickly limits its scalability.

Exam Tip	
Enable MAC Address filtering on access points to control which clients can access the network.	

WEP Security

The WEP security protocol provides encrypted communication between wireless clients and access points. WEP uses a key encryption algorithm to encrypt communications between devices. Each client and access point on the WLAN must use the same encryption key. The key is manually configured on each access point and each client before they can access the network. Basic WEP specifies the use of up to 64-bit keys, but 40-bit WEP encryption has been proven to be vulnerable to attack because of a weak algorithm. Most devices now support up to 128-bit encryption, but even this has been cracked. If your devices do not support WPA, they should use 128-bit WEP encryption in conjunction with the MAC address filtering and network identifier methods described previously.

Exam Tip	
Know that the highest level of encryption available, such as WPA or WPA2, is best to use. Older levels of encryption, such as WEP, have been proven to be vulnerable.	

WPA and WPA2 Security

WPA is the most recent and secure form of encryption for wireless networks and was created to fix several weaknesses in the WEP standard. WPA can be used in two ways: using a preshared key or using an authentication server that distributes the keys. The preshared key method (also called Personal WPA) means that all devices on the WLAN must use the same passphrase key to access the network. The authentication server method (also called Enterprise WPA) is more suited for environments with hundreds of clients, where using a single passphrase key for each device is not scalable, and the authentication server takes care of key management between the wireless devices on the network.

Using WPA, data is encrypted using a 128-bit key that is actually routinely changed during sessions using Temporal Key Integrity Protocol (TKIP). This ensures that a single session key cannot be hacked by the time the protocol changes keys. WPA also provides for improved integrity checking of data traversing the wireless network to ensure it cannot be intercepted and changed on the way to its destination. This provides much more protection than the original WEP protocol.

The strength of a WPA network, however, is only as strong as the passphrase used. A WPA passphrase can be from 8 to 63 characters, and it is recommended that this passphrase be as strong as possible and not based on known dictionary words. It should include numbers, uppercase and lowercase characters, and special characters such as the @ symbol. All devices on the WPA network must share the same passphrase, including all access points.

WPA2 is the most recent version of WPA and adds Robust Security Network (RSN) support that includes added protection for ad-hoc networks, key caching, preroaming authentication, and the Counter Mode with Cipher Block Chaining Message Authentication Code Protocol (CCMP) that utilizes the Advanced Encryption Standard (AES) cipher to replace TKIP. All currently manufactured devices support WPA2 in addition to WPA.

If your network devices support WPA2, they should use this type of encryption. However, many older devices do not support WPA2, and you will have to use WPA or some other common encryption method that can be supported by all your clients.

VPN

For larger networks with high security requirements, a VPN wireless access solution is a preferable alternative or addition to the other solutions discussed. VPN solutions are already widely deployed to provide remote workers with secure access to the network via the Internet. The VPN provides a secure, dedicated path or tunnel through a public network such as the Internet. Various tunneling protocols are used in conjunction with standard, centralized authentication solutions using a login and password.

The same VPN technology can also be used for secure wireless access. In this application, the public network is the wireless network itself. Wireless access is isolated from the rest of the network by a VPN server and, for extra security, an intermediary firewall. Authentication and full encryption over the wireless net-work are provided through the VPN server. The VPN-based solution is scalable to a large number of users. Figure 4.6 illustrates the architecture of a VPN-based wireless network.

Personal Firewall

In addition to the overall wireless network security, all wireless systems should be equipped with personal firewall software protection. Similar to home com-

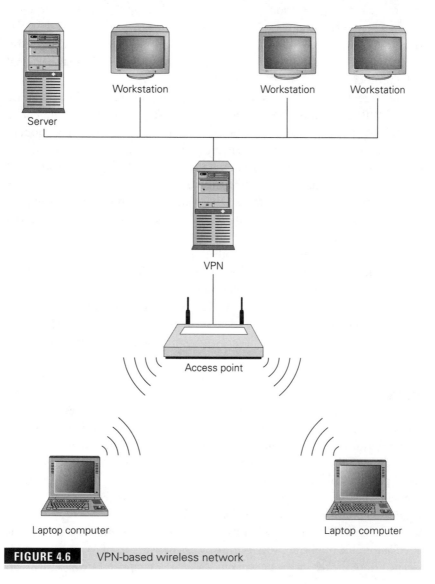

FIGURE 4.6   VPN-based wireless network

puters with permanent cable modem and DSL Internet access connections, wireless clients can be vulnerable to attacks by unauthorized users accessing the same network. The personal firewall software can be used to protect the roaming user's confidential local data against many types of possible attacks for both incoming and outgoing connections.

Exam Tip
Be aware of the advantages and disadvantages of all the wireless access security solutions. Depending on the type of network and the scope of security required, some of the detailed security solutions won't be acceptable, or they'll need to be augmented by other methods.

CHECKPOINT

✔ **Objective 4.01: Determine and Apply Appropriate Network Security Tools**   Use intrusion detection and prevention systems to detect and mitigate threats at your network borders. Host-based intrusion detection systems must be set up on specific servers to prevent console-based intrusions. Use network firewall and proxy servers to hide the internal details of your network from external networks. Use content filtering services to examine and filter incoming content for malicious and inappropriate files and prevent private and sensitive data from leaving your network. Use honey pots to attract network attacks away from legitimate servers and services. Use protocol analyzers to provide deep-level scanning of network data between systems on the network.

✔ **Objective 4.02: Explain Wireless Networking Vulnerabilities and Implement Mitigations**   More so than security for traditional wired networks, wireless security heavily involves the use of encryption technologies, coupled with traditional security mechanisms such as access control and authentication. Wireless networks should use WPA or WPA2 encryption with a strong passphrase, should disable SSID broadcasts and use a unique SSID name, should use MAC address filtering if possible, and should have access points that are properly secured with a strong password for administrative configuration, with remote configuration disabled.

REVIEW QUESTIONS

1. What is the primary difference between a network intrusion detection system (NIDS) and a network intrusion prevention system (NIPS)?

   A. A NIDS system only detects TCP/IP attacks.

   B. The NIPS system actively tries to mitigate an incoming intrusion rather than just detect it.

   C. The NIDS system can raise alarms when it detects an intrusion.

   D. A NIPS system is only host-based, not network-based.

2. Which of the following is the strongest encryption that you should use for your wireless network if all devices support it?

   A. WAP

   B. WPA

   C. WEP-128

   D. WPA2

3. Many of your users are downloading MP3 song files from the Internet and using up valuable bandwidth. Which technology would best be suited to help block the transfer of these files from the Internet?

   A. Content filtering

   B. Honey pot

   C. Protocol analyzer

   D. NIDS

4. The ability to access data on a Bluetooth device remotely without proper authorization is referred to as what?

   A. Bluesnarfing

   B. Bluespoofing

   C. Bluejacking

   D. IP spoofing

5. What should be done to ensure that unauthorized wireless users cannot access or learn the SSID of your wireless network?

   A. Enable SSID broadcast

   B. Enable SSID tunneling

   C. Disable SSID snarfing

   D. Disable SSID broadcast

6. After a number of network-based attacks against a web server, what technology would be best suited for diverting network attacks away from your primary web server?

    A. DMZ

    B. Proxy server

    C. VLAN

    D. Honey pot web server

7. Wireless MAC address filtering is defined as which of the following?

    A. Allows access only to specified MAC addresses

    B. Prevents access only from specified MAC addresses

    C. Encrypts wireless device MAC addresses

    D. Personal firewall

8. The most secure and efficient method of authorization and access control for wireless security is

    A. WEP 40-bit encryption

    B. VPN

    C. WPA2

    D. Network security identifier

9. Which of the following types of technologies is best suited for caching and filtering web content?

    A. Web proxy server

    B. Firewall

    C. Authentication proxy

    D. Intrusion detection system

10. Which of the following network security tools would be best used for examining network traffic between your primary router and your e-mail server?

    A. Host-based intrusion detection system

    B. Proxy server

    C. Protocol analyzer

    D. Firewall server

REVIEW ANSWERS

1. **B** The NIPS system actively tries to mitigate an incoming intrusion. A NIDS actively monitors for intrusions and will alert the administrator when one is detected, but the NIPS system goes a step further and tries to prevent the intrusion just as it is occurring.

2. **D** WPA2 is currently the strongest level of encryption security available for a wireless network. WPA2 is the most recent version of WPA and adds Robust

Security Network (RSN) support that includes added protection for ad-hoc networks, key caching, preroaming authentication, and the CCMP that utilizes the AES cipher to replace TKIP.

3. **A** A content filtering server can analyze network traffic and block specific file types, such as MP3 music files, from being downloaded. The end user will receive an error when he tries to access the file.

4. **A** Bluesnarfing is a hacking method in which an unauthorized user can connect to unprotected Bluetooth devices and access any data stored on the device. An unauthorized user can leave her device in discovery mode and automatically connect to unprotected Bluetooth devices in her vicinity.

5. **D** By disabling SSID broadcast, your access points will not advertise the SSID they are using to wireless clients. A user would have to know the SSID of the network before he could access it.

6. **D** By setting up a honey pot web server that contains a number of open ports and vulnerabilities, you can divert attacks away from your secure servers so that the honey pot server is the prime target. Using the log files on the honey pot server can help you identify the types of attacks and their sources and help you understand how best to protect your real servers.

7. **A** A list of authorized client MAC addresses must be configured on each access point for the network. If any client tries to communicate with the access point and its MAC address isn't in the list, it will be denied access.

8. **B** Through the use of an existing VPN, wireless communications can be authorized and encrypted just like any other type of remote device.

9. **A** Web proxy servers are used primarily for their caching abilities that boost web browsing performance by storing content retrieved from an external web server. Most proxy servers provide some type of content-filtering abilities that help protect an organization's clients from accessing dangerous host phishing and fraud sites or web sites and downloads that are infected with worms, spyware, or malware.

10. **C** A protocol analyzer is best suited for examining and capturing network packets and frames between two devices. The amount of data captured scanning the entire network would be much more difficult to examine and sort through.

PART

III

Access Control

Access Control

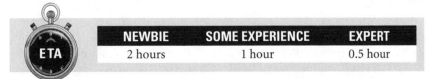

	NEWBIE	SOME EXPERIENCE	EXPERT
ETA	2 hours	1 hour	0.5 hour

155

Two simple and often overlooked aspects of security are access control and authentication. In many business environments, access involves a single login to a computer or a network of computer systems that provides the user access to all resources on the network. This access includes rights to personal and shared folders on a network server, company intranets, printers, and other network resources and devices. These same resources can be quickly exploited by unauthorized users if the access control and associated authentication procedures aren't set up properly.

Access control refers to permissions applied to resources that determine which users can access those resources. *Authentication* goes hand-in-hand with access control by identifying users to be sure they are exactly who they claim to be. After a user has been authenticated, the resources for which the user has appropriate permissions become accessible.

As an administrator, you must carefully consider system and network security when creating access and authentication policies. Basic security practices such as login IDs and passwords must be augmented with advanced logical access control techniques, such as the use of long, non-dictionary, alphanumeric passwords; regular password rotation and expiration; and password aging. Finally, the protection of personal and shared data resources on network file servers must be maintained through the use of directory and file access control permissions on a per-user or group basis.

Without carefully considering your authentication methods and policies, any weaknesses in your network and system security can be quickly penetrated by unauthorized users, both within and outside of the network.

Objective 5.01
CompTIA Security+
Objective 3.1

Identify and Apply Access Control Methods

Access control methods determine how users interact with resources and computer systems. Resources must be protected from unauthorized modification or tampering. Access controls must be enforced on a network to ensure that unauthorized users can access neither its resources nor the network and computer system infrastructure itself.

Users and Resources

Your first task is to define who are the *users* and to what *resources* they need access. A *user* in this sense doesn't always mean a specific person. A computer might act as a user when it tries to connect to the resource of another computer system. A *resource* can be anything from a simple text file on a file server, to a network laser printer, to an Internet proxy server. A user of a resource might also be a computer account used by a system to back up other computer systems' resources and data to a tape drive. This *backup* user account must also have its access control defined properly so it can securely perform its job function.

Just as your users must be carefully defined, the resources offered by your computer network need to be categorized and access controls defined for the resources' security. Your resources must be categorized with the following attributes in mind:

- **Sensitivity** How confidential is the data from this resource? Should it be seen only by certain users or should access be open to anyone? An example of sensitive data would be payroll or human resources data. The ability to access this resource should be available only to users from those departments. Sensitivity issues can be secured via access controls.

- **Integrity** Should users only be able to read from this directory or can they modify the files within? If the integrity of the data is vital, this resource should have its access permissions set to read-only. For example, a datasheet of released company financials to shareholders should never be modified after distribution. Integrity issues can be addressed via access controls, primarily file and directory security.

- **Availability** How available should the data be as a resource? Does this data need to be available at all times or only during certain time periods? Is this information so critical that it must be available whenever a user requests it? Typically, availability decreases with increased security, so the needs of protecting the data must be balanced with the necessary level of availability. Availability issues can be addressed via backups, clustering, and redundancy solutions.

Travel Advisory

In real-world situations, friction can exist between management and the information technology (IT) department over the need for availability against the need for security. IT departments must emphasize the need for security over ease of availability and balance the requirements accordingly.

Levels of Security

Before a user can access a resource, three levels of security must be passed:

1. **Identify** The user must initially identify himself as a valid user for that network. This is usually provided through the form of a network login ID.

2. **Authenticate**   The user is then authenticated to the network, using his logon ID and a password. If these two criteria are matched with the database of user logon IDs and passwords stored on the network, the user is granted access to the network.

3. **Authorize**   When the user tries to access a resource, the system must check to see whether that user ID is authorized for that resource and what permissions the user has when accessing it. Just because a user has been identified and authenticated to a network doesn't mean he should be able to access all resources.

Once a user has been authorized for that resource, he can use it according to the access permissions he was granted.

Exam Tip

Be aware of the differences between identifying a user, authenticating, and authorizing. In a secure access-controlled environment, these terms correspond specifically to different steps in the access control process.

Access Security Grouping

Administrators need to visualize the relationships among users and groups and the resources they need to perform their jobs. A network administrator assigning access permissions individually to resources on a per-user basis would likely be inefficient and extremely time-consuming. For small networks, this might be a viable option, but for mid-sized to large corporate networks, it would be an unwieldy strategy. Grouping users, depending on similarities in their attributes, is far more efficient. Typically, you can identify groups of users in three main ways: by job function, department, and physical location.

Job Function   Users who perform the same job will most likely need access to the same resources. For example, a number of financial analysts might need access to the same data directory on a specific file server. By grouping these users into one entity, you can assign the resulting group access to the data without needing to perform this configuration for each user. This model can also be defined hierarchically, as shown in Figure 5.1, where management might have more access to resources than nonmanagement personnel.

Department   Users who belong to the same department in an organization will probably need access to the same data and resources. All employees within a department aren't always working in the same physical location. Because of the virtual nature of many large corporate networks, a sales employee in the United

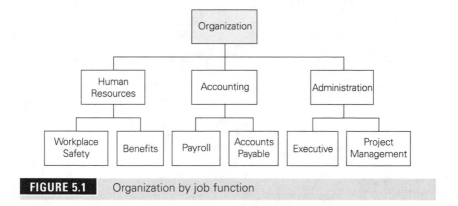

Organization by job function

States might need access to the same sales database used by a sales employee in Japan. All users from the sales department can be assigned to the same group: Sales. The network administrator has to configure access only to the sales database once for the Sales group, without having to assign access for each individual salesperson. This model is shown in Figure 5.2.

Physical Location   A company could be located in a single building, in several buildings, or in different cities and countries. Many companies divide their resources among physical locations, so, for example, an office in New York might not need access to resources to a file server in Los Angeles. In this way, the security model can be set up by physical location, where users are grouped depending on the office to which they belong, as shown in Figure 5.3.

In the most efficient security model, data resources are organized based on need-to-know criteria. Resources should be available only to users who need access to that information. In most cases, the users in a sales department wouldn't need access to the data resources of accounting or human resources, for exam-

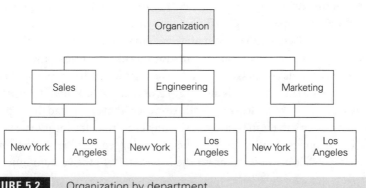

Organization by department

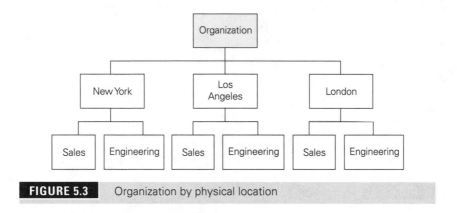

FIGURE 5.3   Organization by physical location

ple. Each resource must have its access controls specifically set to allow access only to users authorized for that resource. This also flows down into more granular levels of security, in which a user might have access to read a file, but not modify or execute it. For example, an employee assigned to print a directory of documents should need only read and print access to the file; she does not need access to modify or delete. The best practice is to grant only the lowest level of access permissions a user needs to perform her job.

Travel Advisory

When setting up a new network, you should create a user hierarchy based on one of the previous security models. Trying to change the model down the road can be difficult after it is already in place.

Centralized and Decentralized Management

In early computer systems, when networking wasn't as easily available as it is today, each individual computer contained a set of resources a user could access. The user needed a specific login ID and password to gain access to a computer and its resources. Setting up each separate system within a company was tedious business for computer users and administrators alike because of the frequency with which accounts and passwords had to be reset for each computer when users forgot them. This scenario is an example of *decentralized management*.

Nowadays, modern networks provide resources that are spread throughout a computer network that can be accessed by any user from any location. The user can be onsite on his own computer, or he can be logged in from home or on the road by using dial-up methods or via the Internet. With the vast amount of resources that can be contained on a large computer network, the concept of different logins and passwords for each resource has been eliminated in favor of a single logon to the network. Using this *centralized management* system, the user has to be authenticated only once on the network to access the resources on that network.

Centralized administration is a much more efficient way for a network administrator to control access to a network. User account policy templates can be created and used network-wide, forgoing the need to configure each user's account settings individually, except for a unique login ID and password. Access control methods, such as directory and file permissions, are used to provide more granular security on the resource level. Examples of centralized management systems are Microsoft Active Directory and Novell eDirectory.

Access Control Best Practices

Several best practices for access control to data include methods for increasing security through proper organizational structures and data security principles. They are outlined here.

Separation of Duties

To make sure that all employees and management personnel know their roles in the company, the organization's structure should be clear, with positions properly defined with formal job titles and descriptions, definitions of responsibilities, and reporting structures that define the lines of authority.

To increase security and reduce risk from security compromises, part of the effort should be directed toward both a clear organizational structure and a specific separation of duties. A *separation of duties* can ensure that one individual isn't overtasked with high-security and high-risk responsibilities and that users aren't accessing restricted resources because of jobs that haven't been properly defined.

To separate duties that involve high-security situations, a certain amount of collusion must take place. *Collusion* means that to proceed with a certain task, more than one person is required to allow the procedure to take place. In a banking situation, for example, opening the main safe could require the authorization of at least two people, because each authorized person possesses a key, and both keys are needed to open the safe. This prevents a single individual from opening the safe without supervision. Like a safe, computer system access needs to be protected. The more people involved, the less chance of a single person making a poor security decision that could compromise the entire network.

> **Exam Tip**
>
> Separation of duties ensures that one individual isn't tasked with high-security and high-risk responsibilities, and that users aren't accessing restricted resources because of jobs that haven't been defined properly. Collusion requires that more than one person allow a specific procedure to take place to ensure that important security decisions are not relegated to a single person.

Rotation of Job Duties

Job rotation provides employees with workforce skills improvement and increased job satisfaction, but it also enhances the security of an organization. Job rotation exposes employees to new skills and opportunities by allowing them to perform different jobs within an organization. Job rotation also ensures better security, as no single employee retains the same amount of access control for a particular area for an extended period of time. This can prevent internal corruption that can occur, for example, when a long-term employee, because of her deep knowledge of a particular area of duty, might take advantage of the position and security access. Job rotation also boosts accountability when another person takes over a specific job duty and examines potential inefficiencies or evidence of security lapses.

Suppose, for example, that a server administrator and network administrator switch roles. Each administrator has an opportunity to increase her knowledge by applying her security skills and knowledge of security procedures to a different part of the organization. The switch also allows each administrator to scrutinize the security aspects of the other role with a fresh perspective.

Implicit Deny

Implicit deny refers to the security principle of starting a user out with no access rights and granting permissions to resources as required. This principle states that a security policy must implicitly deny all access to provide a full secure baseline. Only then can the administrator grant a user access to resources.

The implicit deny principle is more secure than starting out with a policy that grants a user default access to all resources, and then denies access permissions to certain resources. It is too easy for administrators to overlook several aspects of resources that require access to be controlled and denied as appropriate.

> **Travel Advisory**
>
> Network firewalls should be implemented with an implicit deny policy so that all traffic is denied access unless access is specifically granted.

The implicit deny policy should be applied to all aspects of an organization's security, from physical security and access control, to file and resources permissions on a file server, and to network firewall and router rules. By starting out with the strongest security policy and then working backward from that to allow access permissions, administrators know that all access is denied by default, and each access control permission granted is an exception to that policy.

Exam Tip

Implicit deny means that all access is denied by default, and access permissions are granted only to specific resources as required.

Need-to-Know Principle

The *need-to-know* principle grants users only access rights they need to perform their job functions. This requires giving users the least amount of privileges possible to prevent them from abusing more powerful access rights. For example, a user might need access to certain files to print them for a manager. The network administrator should give the user only enough access rights to read the file and print it, without including privileges to delete, modify, or add information to the file.

The function of management is to decide exactly what a person needs to know or for what areas the person requires access for a particular position. The network administrator must enact the decision. When in doubt, the network administrator should be cautious and allow only minimal access until someone can authorize more privileges on behalf of the user. Increased privileges should never be handed out at the request of the user who needs them.

Exam Tip

Data access should be based on the need-to-know principle, which ensures that users have access only to the data they need to perform a job function and nothing more.

Objective 5.02
CompTIA Security+
Objective 3.2

Explain Common Access Control Models

To control how users access data, each company employee should be structured logically to define access privileges depending on the type of user, the groups to which she belongs, and her specific role in the company. The following sections outline key topics concerning privilege management.

Access control models are policies that define how users access data. These policies form a framework based on the security and business goals of the organization. The rules of the framework are enforced through access control technologies. The following sections cover the main access control types.

Mandatory Access Control

In a mandatory access control (MAC) model, the network operating system (OS) is in control of access to data. Most data owners can assign permissions to their own files and share them however they see fit, but OS access controls override any data owner settings. Users have little freedom to adjust access controls, except for specific data under their control. When defined on the system, users are given certain access rights representing a certain level of trust. The data resources themselves also have security classifications that define the level of trust a user must have to access the data. If a user doesn't have the appropriate access rights to use the data, he is denied access. This type of model is centralized and is often used in high-security environments, such as the military or government offices, where access control is tightly guarded through strict OS security policies. Military classifications such as Classified, Secret, and Top Secret are examples of MAC in which specific security access is restricted depending on the classification of the data.

Discretionary Access Control

Discretionary access control (DAC) enables data owners to specify which users can access certain data. Access to resources is allowed only to authorized users through permissions on the resource. This is the most common model used in Windows- and Unix-based environments in which administrators create a hierarchy of files, directories, and other resources that are accessed based on user privileges and access rights. Resource owners are typically allowed to control who accesses their resources. For example, an individual user can share specific files or directories to users they authorize. This model is a less-centralized version of the mandatory access control.

Role-Based Access Control

Role-based access control (RBAC) is also referred to as non-discretionary access control. This centrally controlled model allows access to be based on the role the user holds within an organization. Instead of giving access to individual users, access control is granted to groups of users who perform a common function. For example, many organizations have special "contractor" roles comprising employees who work on a contract basis and are not full-salaried employees;

these workers are given less access to certain resources or parts of the network. In an IT department, for example, a user given the role of "backup administrator" might have access to controlling backup and restore operations, but he would not have privileges to add users or assign access permissions, which are reserved for a system administrator. No matter who is assigned the backup administrator role, access permissions will be the same. Database servers such as SQL servers often use role-based permissions to restrict access to certain portions of the database.

Rule-Based Access Control

Rule-based access control provides enhanced granularity when specifying access control policies and indicates specifically what can and cannot happen between a user and the resource. This type of access control policy is typically defined by an access control list (ACL), which specifies a set of rules that must be followed before access is granted. Unlike the DAC method, rule-based access control does not necessarily have to be tied to an authorized identity and could involve access permissions based on network location, content of messages (such as e-mail text or attachments), and other types of content filtering. These rules are typically implemented in network access devices such as routers, firewalls, and content-filtering systems, and they apply to all users regardless of their identity.

Objective 5.03
CompTIA Security+
Objective 3.3

Organize Appropriate Security Groups, Roles, Rights, and Privileges

P*rivilege management* involves the creation and use of policies defining the users and groups that access company resources, such as data files or printers. To control how users access data, employees need to be logically structured to define access privileges depending on the type of user, the groups to which the user belongs, or the user's specific role in the company.

When designing a company's security infrastructure, you must visualize the relationships among users and groups and the resources they need to perform their jobs. Although assigning access permissions individually to resources on a per-user basis might be viable for small networks, it would be an inefficient and extremely time-consuming strategy for mid-sized to large corporate networks. Grouping users according to similarities in job functions is much more efficient. Beyond this, user security can be designed according to user roles within the company.

User

A single user's access rights and privileges revolve around the data that person creates, modifies, and deletes. In addition to the user's own user access control privileges, she can also be part of a group, be assigned a specific role, and be assigned that role's privileges as well. For example, a user can have individual access rights to files in her home directory, but she can also have access to the Sales and Marketing group directory, as she also belongs to that group. In addition, the user might have an additional role such as auditor, so she has access to additional resources beyond her user and group access rights.

Group

In this model, several users who need access to the same data are organized in a group. Privileges can be distributed to the entire group of users, rather than to each individual user. This is much more efficient when applying permissions and provides greater overall control of access to resources. For example, users who are part of the same Sales and Marketing group would typically have access to and share the same data on a file server and, depending on their location, would share rights to the same printers. Group privileges typically provide additional access rights to users beyond their own individual access permissions to access shared data.

Role

A user might have different security privileges according to his role in the company. For example, a user who is also a database administrator might have extra privileges accorded to that role, on top of or replacing those privileges acquired as a user or part of a group. Predetermined permissions for a role can be created and then applied to users or groups that fit that role.

Travel Assistance

See the "Microsoft Windows Server 2008 Security Guide" for detailed information on securing Windows servers, including organizing security groups, roles, rights, and permissions. The guide is available at: http://technet.microsoft.com/en-us/library/cc514539.aspx.

Objective 5.04
CompTIA Security+
Objective 3.4

Apply File and Print Security Controls

Use of file and print servers can be involved in much of a user's daily work routine. *File servers* are used to store the user's data, including personal work files and departmental or company-wide information. *Print servers* are used to administer print services and print queues, in which a user's print jobs are organized and sent to the appropriate printer.

Security concerns with file and print servers center around authentication and access permissions. File servers should be configured so that no user can access the server through the network without first being authenticated via a user name and a password. Beyond that, various directories and files, depending on their ownership and confidentiality, need to be secured with access permissions.

Configuration Methodologies

Most files servers have directories arranged in hierarchies, typically according to user and departmental or group directories. For example, each user would have her own personal data directory, in which only she has access to create, delete, and modify the files and directories within. This prevents other users from accessing her files. Or the CEO of the company can store personal and important company files in a personal directory that only he can access; he wouldn't want other people in the company to have access to these files.

Typically, some directories are set up as departmental or group directories that provide a separate area for each department to store files to which everyone in that department needs access. For example, a directory could be set up for the finance department that allows each person in the finance group to access the confidential accounting files in that directory. The access permissions would be set so that no user or department could access that directory except those in the finance group. Other directories could allow only read-only permissions, such as a directory of company policy and benefit files that all employees need to access for reference, but shouldn't be allowed to modify or delete.

This same methodology should be used for printing services. Most printers are configured to allow any user to send print jobs to them. For more confidential printers, such as a printer used in the human resources department, where employment or termination notices might be created, the printer's access permissions would allow only HR department employees to print. The printer itself should also be physically located in a secure area with controlled access. More granular security-access permissions can be set, so users can't modify or delete jobs after they've been sent to the printer. Most of these controls are handled by the administrator, who controls the flow and access of print queues.

File and Print ACLs

Several different permissions can be assigned to files and directories on a computer system. This is typically defined in the ACL, which contains a list of permissions granted to users for each resource. Following are the most common permissions that can be assigned:

- **Read**   View the contents of a file or directory.
- **View**   View the contents of a directory; users can see that a file exists, but they won't necessarily have permission to read the contents of the file.
- **Write**   Create and save a new file or write to an existing file.
- **Print**   Print a file.
- **Copy**   Copy a file from one location to another. The Write permission would also be required in the destination directory.
- **Delete**   Delete a file or directory.
- **Execute**   Execute a program file or script.
- **Modify**   Modify the attributes of a file or directory.
- **Move**   Move a file from one location to another. The Write permission would be required in the destination directory. The Delete permission would be required to remove the file after the move is completed.

Exam Tip

Be aware of the differences between the various access permissions, especially those pertaining to files, directories, and file attributes.

The most basic types of security that can be set at the resource level are *full access* or *no access* at all. Using these settings is a bad practice, however, and must be avoided through the use of more granular security. An ACL should be created for every resource and applied for all users. When you first create an ACL for a resource, start with *no access* as a default. This lets you begin with a clean slate, where no access is the default permission. Then add access permissions based on the needs of the particular user or group, granting only the access permissions necessary to perform their job functions. Never grant Write or Modify permissions unless users need to make changes to a file.

Consider the following situation, for example. A sales database is used to keep track of clients and their pertinent information. Employees in the sales group must be able to read and modify this information and delete and add new users to the database. The administrative staff will initiate or take calls from clients, and they need access to the database to look up client information and print the results. The administrative staff doesn't need access to modify the contents of the client records in the database, however. To perform system maintenance and administration on the database, the database administration group needs access to perform all functions, including changing the file attributes of the database file. The sales group, however, doesn't want the database administration group to have Delete access. In this scenario, the following access rights should be defined for each group:

User	Access Rights Assigned
Sales	Read, Write, Delete, Copy, Move
Admin	Read, Print
Database Admin	Read, Write, Copy, Move, Modify

Travel Advisory

If a user asks to be given access rights to a file or directory, never grant it without first verifying the user's need for the access with his or her manager.

Objective 5.05
CompTIA Security+
Objective 3.5

Compare and Implement Logical Access Control Methods

Logical access controls are software-based components that authenticate users and allow them to access resources. These access controls are typically an integral part of an operating system or software application that provides user account, password, and access privileges management.

Enforcing the use of strong passwords can greatly diminish an unauthorized user's ability to guess a password (see Chapter 1). To ensure the usefulness and efficiency of login IDs and password, account and password policies must be created and strictly followed.

User Account Policies

Several policies can be created for account use to strengthen the security of the logon process. By setting restrictions on user accounts, you can narrow the risk of having your network compromised by an unauthorized user. Some of the most effective restrictions include the following:

- Using appropriate naming conventions
- Limiting logon attempts
- Setting count expiry dates
- Disabling unused accounts
- Setting time restrictions
- Setting machine restrictions
- Using tokens

Using Naming Conventions

When you configure and set up a company network, a best practice is to enact some form of account naming conventions. A common naming convention is employing a user's first initial and last name, or variations of it, as his account ID. Never use account names that represent job functions: A user account named *admin* is much more likely to attract the attention of an unauthorized user who is trying to hack into a system, because he knows the user ID could be the main administrative account for the network. If he's able to compromise that account, he will have full control over the network. Other names such as *human_resources* or *accounting* will also be more likely targets for an unauthorized user.

Limiting Logon Attempts

This parameter sets the maximum amount of incorrect logon attempts before disabling an account. This is an important feature because many hackers simply repeat attempts at accessing an account using different passwords each time. If no logon attempt restrictions exist, hackers can continue this brute-force attack until the account is eventually compromised. A best practice is to set a limit of three to five failed attempts, after which the account is locked and the user must contact the administrator to enable the account again.

Setting Account Expiry Dates

Setting an expiry date on a user account will disable it when the target date is reached. This is useful for contract workers who are employed for a limited period of time. When the contract date is reached, the user's login is immediately disabled. By setting an expiry on the account when a contractor is first hired, disabling the account won't be forgotten, and the account will be automatically disabled when the expiration date is reached. If the contract is renewed, the account can simply be re-enabled and the expiration date changed.

Disabling Unused Accounts

When an employee leaves the company, his account should be immediately disabled. This is especially important for any employee who is suddenly terminated for any reason. By immediately disabling the account, you deny access to further attempts by that user to access his account. Another best practice is to disable accounts you don't recognize as valid. Unauthorized users could have broken into the system and created their own "dummy" accounts to perform malicious activities unnoticed. If the account is valid, the user will contact you, because he can't log in. You can then verify whether the user should have access to the system.

Setting Time Restrictions

If your company operates only during certain hours each day, you can set time restrictions on access to the network. After hours, only a select few users might need access. You can set time restrictions on other users' accounts so they are able to log in only during operating hours. This will reduce the risk of unauthorized users trying to use an employee's account off-hours to break into the system.

Setting Machine Restrictions

You can allow logins only from certain machines on the network. Any computer on your current internal network can be set up to prevent anyone trying to access the system using an outside computer or laptop. Machine restrictions are usually set using a computer's network card MAC address, computer name, or the network IP address.

Using Tokens

To provide additional access control and authentication protection, many organizations use a two-tier form of authentication: in addition to an account name and password, the user also requires a physical or logical *token*, such as a special Universal Serial Bus (USB) key, that needs to be connected to her computer before she is allowed access. Certain types of physical tokens, such as RSA SecurID and CRYPTOCard, provide a logical token number that is generated in conjunction with the access control server that must be entered, along with a user name and password, to grant access.

Tokens provide an extra layer of security, because even if an unauthorized user has access to the physical token (if it was stolen from the user, for example), he still requires a user name and password to access the system. Similarly, if the unauthorized user knows a user name and password he can use, he still needs the physical or logical token to complete the authentication and access control process.

Exam Tip

Be aware of the different types of account restrictions and access control methods that can be used to increase the security of user accounts.

Password Management

Password management, although typically created and enforced by the network administrator, is becoming a special area of network security that should be covered in specific company policies. All users must be aware of the company's rules and procedures for managing user accounts and passwords that allow access to company resources.

Password Policies

Following are some basic, but important, password policies that can be set by the administrator to enforce strong passwords:

- **Minimum length** The minimum length for a password can be enforced by the network administrator. This prevents users from using small, easy-to-guess passwords of only a few characters in length. The password should be six to eight characters and should contain a mix of uppercase and lowercase characters, numbers, and special characters.

- **Password rotation** Most login and password authentication systems can remember a user's last several passwords and can prevent the user from using the same one over and over again. This is often referred to as *password history*. If this option is available, it should be enabled, so a user's password will always be different.

- **Password aging** The longer a password has existed, the easier it is for a malicious hacker to discover eventually, simply by narrowing the options over time. Forcing users to change their passwords regularly can prevent a malicious hacker from discovering a password through brute-force attacks and ensures that if the account password has been compromised, the hacker will lose access the next time the password is changed. Most organizations force their users to change their passwords every one to three months.

Domain Passwords

In environments that use the *single sign-on* type of account and password, such as a Microsoft Active Directory domain account, account and password security mechanisms must be strictly enforced, as each user will use one account and password to access all file and print resources for her domain. This strengthens security as both administrators and users only need to define, enforce, and utilize a single account and password policy for the entire domain. In the past, users had different accounts and passwords for each resource they needed to access, which usually meant that one or more of these resources was inadequately protected with a weak password. Having an overall domain account and password policy allows administrators to manage the security of these accounts using a single policy and allows end users to have to remember only one user name and password to access any resource.

CHECKPOINT

✔ **Objective 5.01: Identify and Apply Access Control Methods**   Use separation of duties, job rotation, implicit deny, and need-to-know principles when organizing your security infrastructure and grouping users and resources into appropriate security groups and zones.

✔ **Objective 5.02: Explain Common Access Control Models**   In a mandatory access control model (MAC), the OS of the network is in control of access to data. Discretionary access control (DAC) allows the data owners to specify what users can access certain data. Role-based access control (RBAC) allows access to be based on the role the user holds within an organization. Privileges can be assigned by user, group, or role in the company. Rule-based access control is based on ACLs and is not necessarily tied to the identity of a user; it provides access rules that are applied to all users in the organization.

✔ **Objective 5.03: Organize Appropriate Security Groups, Roles, Rights and Privileges**   Access rights can be typically assigned using user, group, or roles. User permissions are granted based on what resources users are specifically allowed to access. In a group model, several users who need access to the same data are organized in a group, and access privileges can be distributed to the entire group of users, rather than to each individual user. Users might have different security privileges according to their role in the company.

✔ **Objective 5.04: Apply File and Print Security Controls**   Each user should have her own personal data directory, where only she has access to create, delete, and modify the files and directories within. When you first create an ACL for a resource, use no access as a default. This enables you to start with a clean slate, and you can add access permissions based on the needs of the particular user or group, giving them only enough access permissions to perform their job function.

✔**Objective 5.05: Compare and Implement Logical Access Control Methods** Some of the most effective account restrictions include limiting logon attempts, using expiry dates, disabling unused accounts, setting time restrictions, restricting machine access, and using tokens. Use password policies such as regular password rotation, enforce strong passwords, and employ password aging to prevent password weaknesses.

REVIEW QUESTIONS

1. Which of the following access control principles concerns giving a user minimum access rights to be able to perform his job function?

   A. SLA

   B. Separation of duties

   C. Need-to-know

   D. RBAC

2. Which of the following privilege management access control models concerns the use of ACLs that do not necessarily have to be tied to the authorized identity of a user?

   A. Role-based access control

   B. Discretionary access control

   C. Rule-based access control

   D. Mandatory access control

3. Which of the following should be implemented to facilitate access control and user account management across several systems?

   A. Role-based access control

   B. Mandatory access control

   C. Remote access

   D. Single network logon

4. What should the default access level rights be?

   A. Full access

   B. No access

   C. Read access

   D. Write access

5. Which of the following is most likely to be assigned group access control permissions and privileges?

   A. A network subnet

   B. Two branch offices in New York and Tokyo of 1000 users each

    C. The admin user

    D. Users in the sales and marketing department

6. Which of the following best practices ensures that users do not have the same amount of access and privileges for too long a time, to discourage corruption?

    A. Need-to-know

    B. Separation of duties

    C. Job rotation

    D. Implicit deny

7. Implicit deny refers to which security principle?

    A. Users are by default denied access and have access permissions granted if required.

    B. Users have only the access rights they need to perform their job function.

    C. Users are by default allowed access and have specific access permissions denied.

    D. One single individual isn't tasked with high-security and high risk responsibilities.

8. Which of the following would prevent users from accessing resources beyond regular working hours?

    A. MAC address restrictions

    B. Time restrictions

    C. Account login timeout restrictions

    D. Account expiry dates

9. Which of the following prevents a user from reusing the same password when it needs to be changed?

    A. Password rotation

    B. Password expiry

    C. Tokens

    D. Password aging

10. Which of the following practices would help prevent against brute-force attacks against user accounts and passwords?

    A. Using account expiry dates

    B. Restricting the machine MAC address

    C. Limiting login attempts

    D. Setting time restrictions

REVIEW ANSWERS

1. **C** The need-to-know principle is used to ensure that a user has only the access rights he needs to perform his job functions. This requires giving users the least amount of privileges possible, to prevent them from abusing more powerful access rights.

2. **C** Rule-based access control is typically defined by an access control list (ACL), which specifies a set of rules that must be followed before access is granted. Rule-based access control does not necessarily have to be tied to an authorized identity and could involve access permissions based on network location, content of messages (such as e-mail text or attachments), and other types of content filtering.

3. **D** With a single network logon, a user has to be authenticated only once on the network to access the resources for that network. This type of centralized administration is a much more efficient way for a network administrator to control access to the network.

4. **B** The default access permission should be no access. The administrator can start adding permissions for users on the basis of what they need to accomplish their jobs.

5. **D** A specific group of users such as the sales and marketing department is more likely to be assigned group rights than entire large offices, single users, or network segments. The department would grant similar access permissions to every user, as each would access the same file server shares and the same group of printers for the department.

6. **C** Job rotation ensures greater security, as no single employee retains the same amount of access control for a particular area for an extended period of time. This can prevent internal corruption, whereby long-term employees, because of their deep knowledge of their area of duty, might be more inclined to take advantage of their position and enhanced access.

7. **A** Implicit deny refers to the security principle of starting out with no access rights and granting permissions to resources only as required. This principle states that a security policy must implicitly deny all access to provide a full secure baseline. Only then can administrators grant access to resources for a user.

8. **B** With time restrictions in place, only a select few users are granted system access after hours. Everyone else will be able to log in only during operating hours. This reduces the risk of unauthorized users trying to use an employee's account off-hours to break into the system.

9. **A** With a password rotation policy, login and password authentication systems remember the last five to ten passwords a user has used and can prevent her from using the same one over and over again. If this option is available, it should be enabled, so a user's password will always be different when it comes time to rotate the password.

10. **C** By limiting the amount of login attempts to three to five times, the account will automatically be locked when the threshold is reached, and a user must contact the administrator to enable the account again.

Authentication

	NEWBIE	SOME EXPERIENCE	EXPERT
ETA	2 hours	1 hour	0.5 hour

To use the resources of a computer system or network or enter a secure facility, a user must first be *authenticated*. Identification and authentication verifies that the user is who he says he is and has the credentials to access these resources. The most common form of authentication requires a user name and password, but more secure schemes can use multiple factors to strengthen the authentication process and confidence in the identity and credentials of a user.

Methods such as security cards, tokens, personal identification numbers (PINs), and more advanced techniques, such as *biometric* voice or fingerprint recognition, offer additional forms of authentication. When a user logs in to a system, he supplies a set of credentials or login identifiers that must be matched against credentials stored in an authentication database. If any of the information doesn't match, the user is refused entry or access to the system. Authentication and access control methods are only as efficient as the amount of time and planning spent setting up and configuring the system. The more complex the login process, the more difficult it will be for an unauthorized user to gain access to a system.

This chapter describes the types of authentication models, deployment methods, and other physical access control methods that offer more security during the identification and authentication process before a user can access a facility or resource.

| Objective 6.01 |
| CompTIA Security+ |
| Objective 3.8 |

Explain Identification and Authentication

Before a user is allowed access to a facility or resource, three main levels of security must be passed:

* **Identification**   The user must initially identify herself as a valid user for that network, usually with a login user name or account name. *Identification*, also referred to as *identify proofing*, ensures that a user (which could also be an application program or process) is who she claims to be. For example, before performing any type of online banking or telebanking, a customer must identify who she is and have sufficient physical identification (such as bank cards, passwords, PINs, and so on) to be able to prove her identity before the process goes any further.

- **Authentication** The user must then pass the *authentication* phase using her logon user name or account number and a password. If these two criteria are matched with the global database of login user names and passwords stored on the network, the user is authenticated and is granted access to the network. To be authenticated properly, the user must provide proof that she should be using the login name by supplying a password, PIN, or token. If the identity and password or PIN match the central database, the user is authenticated.

- **Authorization** Finally, when a user tries to access a resource, the system must check to see if that user ID is authorized for that resource and what permissions or privileges the user has when using it. Just because a user has been identified and authenticated to a network doesn't mean she should be able to access all resources. If the system determines that the user may access the resource, the user is authorized and allowed access with the privileges she has been granted.

Exam Tip

Be aware of the differences between identifying a user, authenticating, and authorizing. In a secure access-controlled environment, these terms specifically correspond to different steps in the process.

Objective 6.02
CompTIA Security+
Objective 3.6

Identify Authentication Models

A user authentication system must be able to confirm a user's identity and level of authorization. Three basic authentication components can be combined to provide the highest level of assurance in authenticating a user's identity:

- Something the user has in his possession (ID badge, smart card)
- Something the user knows (user name, password, PIN)
- A unique physical component of the user (biometrics, fingerprint)

The following sections describe how these factors or multiple sets of factors can be used to identify a user.

Single-Factor Authentication

Single-factor authentication refers to requiring only one factor (such as a password) to authenticate a user. The system compares the password for the account with the database of known user names and passwords and then authenticates the user if they match. This is the simplest but weakest form of authentication, because users' passwords tend to be weak.

Single-factor authentication can also involve a magnetic swipe card or token used to open a locked door. This is also a weak form of authentication, as the card or token can be easily lost and an unauthorized user can simply use the card or token to access the door without needing to provide any other credentials.

Two-Factor Authentication

Two-factor authentication typically combines two single-factor authentication types, such as something the user knows and something the user possesses. For example, most ATM banking transactions require two-factor authentication: the user inserts a physical banking card into the machine and then types a PIN, which is matched with the electronic information contained on the card's magnetic strip. One authentication factor should be physical, such as a smart card or access token (something the user possesses) or a biometric factor (something physically unique about the user), and the second factor should be a password or PIN (something the user knows). Without these two items, no access can be granted.

Three-Factor Authentication

Three-factor authentication is the strongest form of user authentication and involves a combination of physical items such as a smart card, token, or biometric factor, and non-physical items such as passwords, passphrases, and PINs. Typically, the biometric factor is the third and deciding factor used in combination with an access card and password. For example, before he can enter a high-security facility, a user might have to insert a smart card into a door, enter a PIN on a keypad, and then insert his finger into a scanner.

Single Sign-on

In early computer systems, when networking wasn't as available as it is today, each computer contained a set of resources the user could access. To access the resources of a computer system, she used a specific login and password. Each specific computer needed a separate login and password. This was tedious for computer users and administrators alike, because of the frequency with which login accounts and passwords needed to be reset for each computer if a user forgot them.

Nowadays, modern networks provide resources that are spread throughout the computer network and that can be accessed by any user from any location. The user can be onsite on her own computer, or she can be logged in from home or on the road by using dial-up methods or via the Internet. With the vast amount of resources that can be contained on a large computer network, the concept of different logins and passwords for each resource has been eliminated in favor of a *single sign-on* to the network; the user has to be authenticated only once on the network to access the resources for that network. This type of centralized administration is a much more efficient way for a network administrator to control access to the network. User account policy templates can be created and used networkwide to remove the need to configure each user's account settings individually, except for a unique login and password.

An example of single sign-on is a Microsoft Active Directory user name and password required for accessing directories, files, and printers on a network, along with MS Exchange mail servers and SQL database servers.

Objective 6.03
CompTIA Security+
Objective 3.7

Deploy Authentication Models

The methods used for authentication depend on the resources that these security mechanisms are trying to protect. Most computer networks rely on a login and password type system. The use of dial-up or virtual private network (VPN) accounts might require the use of encrypted communications on top of the typical user login and password process. Each authentication system must be geared specifically to the circumstances that define a user and resources and how those resources need to be protected. The following sections describe several authentication models and components, including remote access authentication.

Remote Access and Authentication

Remote access is an important network feature for companies and organizations that require users to access network resources from anywhere offsite. With the evolution of telecommunications, a variety of methods can allow a user to access a network remotely. Early methods included attaching a serial cable between two computers via their serial interfaces. The use of modems enabled users to dial into a system or network over a common phone line. Modern access methods include complex VPNs that let users access their corporate network from a public network, such as the Internet. Broadband networking technologies have enabled home users to break free of the bandwidth limitations of modems and phone lines; they create fast and secure communications channels to remote networks.

The most important factor in securing remote communications is the ability both to authenticate a client to a remote network and to encrypt the communications so they can't be captured. With the explosive growth of high-bandwidth home networks that communicate over the Internet with remote systems, the need for secure communications is critical.

Each type of communication system depends on the medium used by the client user to connect to the remote machine. A user in a hotel in another country could be trying to access his corporate LAN by using a modem to dial into his remote access server or via a public wireless connection. Another user might be connected to the Internet via a digital subscriber line (DSL) connection, using a virtual private network to communicate with a remote network. A network administrator might use Telnet or Secure Shell (SSH) to log in to a server remotely from home.

Each remote access method must be carefully examined for security vulnerabilities to make sure that users are properly authenticated to access the network's resources and that communications are encrypted to prevent someone from tapping into the transmitted information.

Dial-up

For many years, the most common way of accessing remote services to a corporate local area network (LAN) or the Internet was through the use of a dial-up connection using a modem over a common phone line. A modem, short for modulator-demodulator, is used to convert the digital signals of a computer to analog for transmission over an analog phone line. A modem at the receiving end converts the signal back into digital for the remote computer. Many companies don't properly protect their remote access services because they think their regular company firewall will protect them. Unfortunately, the firewall protects the network only from traffic that comes from the Internet—not traffic that dials into the network.

Travel Advisory

One of the oldest modem-hacking methods is the use of war dialing, in which a malicious hacker uses a program to call phone numbers in quick succession to look for those attached to a modem. Once a number is found, the hacker can dial in to the modem and try to break the authentication to gain access.

For remote access to a network, a client machine initiates a call to a remote access server. The remote access server is connected to a modem, or several banks of modems, to provide enough connections for multiple remote users, as shown in Figure 6.1.

When the client and remote modems are connected, the server typically provides some form of authentication, often user name and password, before granting the client access to the network's resources. The authentication system could be built into the remote access server itself or it could be a separate service running an authentication protocol, such as Terminal Access Controller Access-Control System (TACACS) or Remote Authentication Dial-in User Service (RADIUS). Additional forms of authentication that can secure communications even more include the use of security tokens, a type of card or token that displays a key code that cycles every few minutes. When synchronized with the server, the token creates another form of authentication that's tied to a user account. Because the sequenced number is cycled with a defined algorithm, the same number can't be used twice within a certain period of time.

Travel Advisory

Security tokens are combined with traditional usernames, passwords, and PINs; if the token card is stolen, the unauthorized user still needs the other credentials to gain access.

Another type of dial-in security check is the use of a *call-back feature*: When the client first connects, the remote access server will hang up and try to dial back the client with a preconfigured phone number. Once the client answers, a

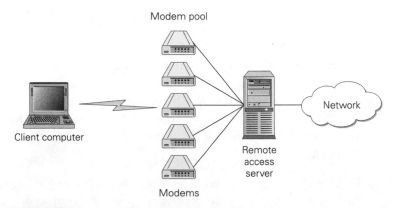

Modem pool

Client computer

Network

Remote access server

Modems

FIGURE 6.1   Remote access via modem

user name and password can authenticate the client for access. This call-back feature ensures the caller is who he says he is and allows the company to absorb any long-distance charges incurred because of the call.

ISDN

Integrated Services Digital Network (ISDN) technology was created to replace the use of common phone lines for network communications. A special ISDN line must be run to your location, and both your client computer and the re- mote computer must use a special ISDN adapter. Unlike a modem, an ISDN adapter doesn't convert signals from digital to analog and back again; instead, ISDN connects digitally between the two adapters over the ISDN line.

Each ISDN connection is divided into channels:

- **B-Channels**   These channels transmit data, such as voice or computer data communications. The channels can be used individually or combined to create higher bandwidth.
- **D-Channels**   These channels transmit control and signal information for managing the transmission of data.

Three main types of ISDN implementations exist, depending on the level of bandwidth a customer requires:

- **Basic Rate Interface (BRI)**   This interface is targeted for lower bandwidth home installations and can run over conventional phone lines. It uses one 16-Kbps D-Channel, and two 64-Kbps B-Channels. The data channels can be combined to provide 128-Kbps communications.
- **Primary Rate Interface (PRI)**   This interface is for business customers who have higher bandwidth needs. It contains one 64-Kbps D-Channel and twenty-three 64-Kbps B-Channels for data, providing bandwidth up to 1.544 Mbps.
- **Broadband ISDN**   This interface can handle many different services at the same time and is usually used within a telecommunications carrier backbone. Broadband ISDN is most often used in fiber-optic and radio-type networks, such as fiber distributed data interface (FDDI), Asynchronous Transfer Mode (ATM), and synchronous optical networking (SONET).

ISDN has generally been passed over in favor of cable modem and DSL com- munications. These methods are much less expensive and easier to set up and configure because they use the existing cabling infrastructure in the home.

Cable Modem

Cable modems are one of the most popular ways of connecting home computers to the Internet. Cable modems are misnamed, though, because they don't operate like a typical modem, which translate signals between analog and digital. A cable modem enables you to connect to your home's coaxial cable lines, which are then connected by common Ethernet cable to your computer's network interface card (NIC).

The speed of cable modem communications decreases when more homes are connected to the same cable line. For example, in most neighborhoods, several homes are connected to the same segment of a coaxial cable run. If many people are using the Internet at the same time, the bandwidth is shared among them, so the individual connections are slower.

The security risk involved with cable modems is that, unlike dial-up connections, the connection to the Internet is permanent and always on, until the system is turned off or unplugged from the cable network. As long as a system is connected to the Internet, it's open to attacks from hackers, who continually scan networks for security vulnerabilities in online systems. To secure these connections, the use of a firewall is recommended to protect your computer against these intrusions.

> **Travel Advisory**
>
> Malicious hackers make use of port scanner programs to analyze a bank of IP addresses on a network, looking for open service ports and applications that can be compromised. To prevent a port scanner from viewing your system while you're connected to a cable modem or DSL network, a firewall can be installed, which prevents your system from replying to such scans.

DSL

A DSL is another popular method of connecting a home computer or small business to the Internet. DSL runs over common copper telephone lines but requires the connection to be in close proximity to a phone company's access point. The closer your system is to the access point, the faster your connection.

DSL can be used for communicating voice and data transmissions over the same phone line. Home users can talk on the phone while still connected to the Internet. This type of communication was impossible over normal dial-up modem methods. DSL also differs from a typical modem in that it doesn't require modulating the signal from digital to analog and vice versa. DSL uses the entire bandwidth of the phone line for digital transmission.

Like cable modems, a DSL network connection is always on until the system is switched off or unplugged from the DSL network. To protect your system, use a firewall.

Remote Access Applications

Remote access applications are used to provide remote access to a machine from a client system. The communication that connects the two systems can be anything from a dial-up modem connection, to a direct cable connection, to a TCP/IP network. Typically, these applications consist of server and client components. The server software is installed on the system made available for remote access. The server is then connected to a modem or a network. Sometimes the client and server computer are connected with a simple network or serial cable. The server software is then configured to accept communications as a host server. If a modem is attached, the program sets it up to answer incoming calls. Once the client connects to the server by dial-up or some other communications medium, it should be authenticated before being granted access. The authentication credentials are usually a user name and a password.

Once connected, the client can remotely control the machine as if she were sitting in front of it on the console. This type of application can create severe security vulnerabilities if it isn't properly secured. This security should include strong authentication and encryption methods and, if possible, a call-back function that will call the client back at a specific number to authenticate the client's identity.

Travel Advisory

Be wary of users on your network who hook up modems to their work computers so they can dial in from home using a remote access application. They might not set up any authentication or security at all, leaving a large security hole in your network. Remote access standards must be enforced so users are always communicating using known secure methods.

Telnet

Telnet is a text-based terminal emulation utility that's part of the TCP/IP suite of protocols. It allows a system to connect to a remote host to perform commands as if the user were on the console of the remote machine. For Telnet to work properly, the remote machine must be running a Telnet server service, which listens for Telnet requests from other hosts. When the client connects, it must authenticate to the remote system using a user name and password specific to that system. Once authenticated, the user can run commands on the remote system as if she were directly on the command console.

Unfortunately, Telnet provides little security other than basic authentication. This means transmissions, including the user name and password, are sent in clear text and can be easily discovered by someone monitoring and capturing the communication using a protocol analyzer. The Telnet service should be disabled to block from being used in connecting to a certain host. Although Telnet is a basic utility of TCP/IP communications, its use has been discouraged in favor of more secure methods of remote access, such as SSH, which encrypts its communications.

SSH

SSH is a secure form of terminal access to other systems. Like other terminal communications utilities such as Telnet, SSH enables a user to log in to a remote machine and execute commands as if he were on the console of that system. Unlike Telnet, however, SSH provides a secure, encrypted tunnel to access another system remotely. SSH is sometimes used as a low-cost alternative to normal VPN communications because of its simple installation and delivery of well-encrypted, secure communications.

When a client connects to a system using SSH, an initial handshaking process begins and a special session key is exchanged. This begins the session and an encrypted secure channel is created to allow the access.

Vulnerabilities have been discovered in some versions of SSH, so you should make sure that you are using the latest version. Early versions of SSH were susceptible to man-in-the-middle attacks because a malicious hacker could capture the headers of the handshaking phase to intercept the session key.

Exam Tip

Other utilities that send their information in clear text include remote login (rlogin), File Transfer Protocol (FTP), and remote shell (rsh). Whenever possible, a secure method, such as SSH, should be used for remote console access and file transfer. SSH utilizes TCP port 22.

VPN

A *VPN* is a secure and private connection over a public network. The connection between the client and the remote network is provided by an encrypted tunnel between the two points, as shown in Figure 6.2.

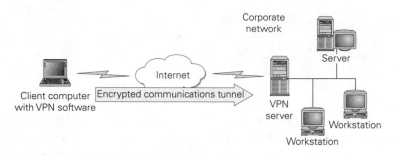

FIGURE 6.2   VPN deployment

In addition to remote access, VPNs are also used for connecting two remote routers to form a secure wide area network (WAN). For a VPN to work properly, the sender and receiver must be running the same type of VPN, with the same protocols and encryptions settings.

VPNs grew out of the need for users to access their corporate network remotely from home or on the road, without the need for dialing up over a slow modem connection, especially one that incurs long-distance charges. VPNs can be used *over* dial-up connections, but the use of high-speed broadband networks has allowed VPN technology to take advantage of the increased performance. The VPN enables the remote user to be connected locally to a public network such as the Internet, while also being directly connected to the corporate network through the use of the encrypted VPN tunnel. This connection can be a dial-up through a modem or a direct Internet connection, such as a cable modem or DSL.

The user must first complete his connection to the Internet, using either Point-to-Point Protocol (PPP) over dial-up or connecting with a cable modem or DSL connection. The user then starts his VPN software, which creates a virtual connection to the VPN access server on the corporate network. After the connection is negotiated, the client must authenticate itself using a user name and password before the VPN will grant access to the corporate network. A VPN is only as secure as the tunneling and encryption protocols used on the connection. Early types of VPNs used older encryption methods, which can be cracked by today's savvy attackers.

Remote Access Protocols

For remote access communications to work, the data must be transmitted using one or several network protocols. These protocols must be able to travel through different networks and different physical infrastructures. A home user who wants to connect her computer to the Internet must use a modem to dial up to and connect with an ISP over a phone line. Different protocols, such as Serial Line Internet Protocol (SLIP) or PPP are needed both to facilitate the transmission of digital data over analog phone lines and encapsulate TCP/IP over the serial-line modem communications.

Exam Tip
Know the advantages and disadvantages of the protocols discussed here, as well as with what types of communications they can be used.

SLIP

SLIP is one of the earliest Internet protocols used for encapsulating IP packets for transmission over serial communications, such as a phone line or serial cable. SLIP is able to work with most types of protocols, such as IP, Internetwork Packet Exchange/Sequenced Packet Exchange (IPX/SPX), and NetBIOS Extended User Interface (NetBEUI), and does not require a static network address; however, SLIP is considered difficult to configure, inefficient, and unreliable. SLIP isn't used much these days and has been replaced by PPP.

PPP

PPP is used to enable a connection between two computers using a serial interface, usually over a phone line. PPP is the most popular protocol used by an ISP to enable users to dial into the Internet network from home using a modem attached to a home computer. The main function of PPP is to encapsulate IP packets and send them over the Internet. PPP is considered much more reliable and easier to use than SLIP, because it contains error checking and the ability to run different types of protocols over a variety of media methods. Common authentication protocols used with PPP are Password Authentication Protocol (PAP), Challenge Handshake Authentication Protocol (CHAP), Microsoft Challenge Handshake Authentication Protocol (MSCHAP), and Extensible Authentication Protocol (EAP), which are discussed later in the "Authentication Protocols" section.

VPN Protocols

The following types of protocols are used by VPNs to tunnel over a public network and to provide encryption for protecting transmitted data.

PPTP   *Point-to-Point Tunneling Protocol (PPTP)* is a Microsoft implementation of secure communications over a VPN. Because PPTP is an extension of PPP, it has become one of the most widely used tunneling protocols and allows network packets to be encapsulated within PPP communications for transfer over another network, such as the Internet through a dial-up connection.

Previous remote access technologies allowed remote access only through a dial-up modem to the corporate network. Depending on where this user is located, the long-distance charges could be enormous, and, sometimes, a company would need to create its own expensive toll-free phone service for long-distance dial-in access. Tunneling protocols allow users connected to a public network, such as the Internet (through dial-up or faster cable modem or DSL service), to create their own private connections to their corporate LANs.

PPTP decrypts and encapsulates PPP packets to create the VPN connection. The security mechanisms within PPTP include authentication and data encryption. One major security problem with PPTP is that when a connection is negotiated, the communication is transmitted in clear text. This data can be captured by an unauthorized user who can use the information to try to hack the connection. PPTP connections for VPNs are typically authenticated using Microsoft Point-to-Point Encryption (MPPE), which uses the RSA RC4 encryption algorithm with support for 40-bit, 56-bit, and 128-bit session keys. These keys are changed on a regular basis, which greatly improves security and lessens the chance of the keys being broken.

Exam Tip	
Remember that PPTP uses TCP port 1723 for communications.	

L2TP   *Layer 2 Tunneling Protocol (L2TP)* combines the best features of PPTP with the Layer 2 Forward (L2F) protocol created by Cisco Systems. L2TP is most often used with other media technologies, such as Frame Relay.

L2TP consists of two main components:

- **L2TP Access Concentrator (LAC)**   The LAC is responsible for terminating the local network connection and tunneling PPP packets to the LNS.
- **L2TP Network Server (LNS)**   The LNS is situated on the remote end of the connection and terminates the PPP connection originating from the LAC.

Through the use of the LAC and LNS, the connection can be localized, because the L2TP components terminate the endpoints of the PPP connection, as shown in Figure 6.3.

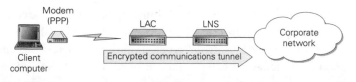

Modem
(PPP)

LAC   LNS

Client
computer

Corporate
network

Encrypted communications tunnel

FIGURE 6.3   L2TP deployment

The main difference between L2TP and PPTP is that L2TP can run on top of and tunnel through other network protocols, such as IPX and Systems Network Architecture (SNA), while PPTP can run only on top of IP networks. L2TP, however, doesn't provide any type of native encryption, so it must be combined with another encrypted protocol, such as Internet Protocol Security (IPSec). Unlike PPTP, L2TP supports TACACS+ and RADIUS for authentication.

Exam Tip	
Know that L2TP uses UDP port 1701 for communications.	

IPSec   *IPSec* is a standards-based method of providing privacy, integrity, and authenticity to information transferred across IP networks. IPSec works on the IP layer to encrypt communications between the sender and receiver. It is most often used to secure VPN communications over an open network, such as the Internet.

IPSec uses two types of encryption modes: transport and tunnel. In *transport* mode, IPSec encrypts only the data portion of each packet, but not the header. This can be used only in host-to-host communications. *Tunnel* mode encrypts both the header and the data of the network packet. This is used to host VPN gateway communications, which is the most common form of VPN. The receiver of the packet uses IPSec to decrypt the message. For IPSec to work, each communicating device needs to be running IPSec and share some form of public key, such as a preshared key, Kerberos, or a public key.

IPSec consists of component protocols, including *authentication header (AH)* and *encapsulating security payload (ESP)* headers. The AH is an IP header that is added to a network packet and provides its cryptographic checksum. This checksum is used to achieve authentication and integrity to ensure that the packet has been sent by a specified source and has not been captured and changed in transit. ESP is a header applied to an IP packet after it has been encrypted. It provides data confidentiality so that the packet cannot be viewed in transit. In newer IPSec implementations, the AH functionality is always performed within the ESP header, resulting in a single combined ESP/AH header.

Security associations (SAs) are the basic building blocks of IPSec communications. Before any two devices can communicate using IPSec, they must first establish a set of SAs that specify the cryptographic parameters that must be agreed upon by both devices before data can be transferred securely between them, including the encryption and authentication algorithms and keys.

The primary way of establishing SAs and managing VPN keys is via Internet Security Association and Key Management Protocol (ISAKMP) and Internet Key Exchange (IKE). ISAKMP/IKE is the protocol for performing automated key management for IPSec. The ISAKMP/IKE process automatically negotiates with the remote VPN device to establish the parameters for individual SAs. An SA is established so that all key exchanges can be encrypted and no keys need to be passed over the Internet in clear text. Once the SA is established, a session SA is negotiated for securing normal VPN traffic, referred to as IKE Phase-1 and Phase-2 negotiations. The session SAs are short-lived and are renegotiated at regular intervals, ensuring that the keys are discarded regularly. The same keys are used only for a small amount of time and for limited amounts of data.

Authentication Protocols

Just as a user on a wired LAN connection needs to authenticate to the network before accessing its resources, specific authentication mechanisms must be set up for remote access users who connect to the network through other methods, such as dial-up or VPN, over the Internet.

Authenticating remote users requires additional security measures, because they're usually communicating over an open line such as a dial-up modem connection or using remote access applications over the Internet. This enables an unauthorized user to snoop or perform other network attacks, such as a replay or a man-in-the-middle attack. A good remote access method needs to secure the password database tables with which the user's credentials are compared and the communication lines with which the client sends a user name and password information.

Exam Tip

Be aware of the authentication protocols discussed here, including their uses and strengths and weaknesses.

PAP

Password Authentication Protocol (PAP) is the most basic type of authentication that consists of comparing a set of credentials, such as a user name and a password, to a central table of authentication data. If the credentials match, the user is granted access. PAP is most often used with dial-up remote access methods using PPP, such as connecting to an ISP or Remote Access Services (RAS) that supports PPP.

Although the password tables used by PAP are encrypted, the actual communications between the client and authentication server are not, allowing the user name and password to be sent over the network in clear text. This can easily be captured by an unauthorized user monitoring the network. Typically used for dial-up authentication, PAP is also the default authentication protocol within HTTP. Because of its weaknesses, CHAP is usually used in place of PAP.

CHAP

Challenge-handshake authentication protocol (CHAP) is much more secure than PAP. Once the communications link is completed, the authenticating server sends a random value to the client. The client sends back the value combined with the user name and password credentials, plus a predefined secret, calculated using a one-way hash function. The server compares the response against its own calculation of the expected hash value. If the values match, the client is granted access.

CHAP provides protection against *replay attacks*, which are used by hackers to capture data and then resend it again. To prevent this type of attack, CHAP uses an incrementally changing identifier and a variable challenge value, and the authentication can be repeated any time while the connection is open using the new identifiers.

> **Travel Advisory**
>
> Microsoft has its own version of CHAP called MSCHAP, which extends the functionality of CHAP for Microsoft networks.

Extensible Authentication Protocol (EAP)

Extensible Authentication Protocol (EAP) is used primarily in wireless networks, but it can also be used in traditional LANs and remote access methods to extend PPP authentication. The EAP framework provides an extension of the types of authentication protocols that are typically used in PAP and CHAP methods. For example, instead of a simple user name and password, additional methods can be used such as tokens, Kerberos, biometrics, and Transport Layer Security (TLS).

RADIUS

Remote Authentication Dial-in User Service (RADIUS) is the most common Internet standard used for authenticating clients in a client/server environment, especially for dial-in users. A typical remote access solution for a company includes a pool of modems a user can dial into from a remote location. When communicating through the modem with the remote access server, the user is authenticated to the network by the RADIUS server, which compares the user's login and password credentials against those of the server's authentication database. If the credentials match, the user is granted access to the rest of the network. The client's credentials that are sent to the RADIUS server are encrypted to prevent someone from capturing the transmission. RADIUS servers also include accounting and reporting functions that can monitor and log data on each connection, such as packet and protocol types, as well as length of time connected. Figure 6.4 shows an example of how a RADIUS server authenticates a remote access client.

LDAP

Lightweight Directory Access Protocol (LDAP) can be used to look up information in a database for other users and network resources. A *directory* is a database that's often compared to the telephone white pages or the yellow pages because the information can be searched and quickly found within the indexed database. The directory database itself can consist of a wide variety of information, including not only basic user contact information, such as e-mail addresses or phone numbers, but also objects, such as printers and computers. Some directory services are used to configure and control access to every single network resource object on the entire network or to contain a centralized database of logins and passwords. With such a critical collection of network data, security is of prime importance when using directory access protocols such as LDAP.

All LDAP servers have some security controls in place for allowing read and update access to the directory database. Typically, all users can read a majority of the information held in the database, but only a few users have update privileges. Large directories usually have multiple information administrators who have access to update only information pertaining to their departments or regions.

For a client to access an LDAP server, it must first be authenticated, unless the server allows anonymous connections. This type of access control allows the LDAP server to decide exactly what that client can access and what information it can update.

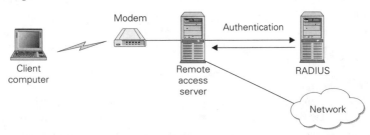

FIGURE 6.4   RADIUS server authentication

Many LDAP servers support the use of encrypted secure channels to communicate with clients, especially when transferring information such as user names, passwords, and other sensitive data. LDAP servers use the Secure Sockets Layer (SSL) protocol for this purpose.

> ### Exam Tip
> Remember that LDAP (unencrypted) uses TCP port 389, LDAP over SSL uses TCP port 689, and LDAP over TLS uses TCP port 636.

TACACS

Terminal Access Controller Access Control System (TACACS) is an older type of authentication protocol that's similar to RADIUS. A remote access user dials into a network with a modem and is authenticated by the TACACS server before being allowed access to the network's resources. Three versions of TACACS have been used:

- **TACACS**   The original protocol, which performs both authentication and authorization.
- **XTACACS**   Extended TACACS, which builds on TACACS by separating the functions of authentication, authorization, and accounting.
- **TACACS+**   This added the use of both a user name and password for authentication or other authentication methods, such as Kerberos or dynamic passwords through security tokens. All communications are encrypted.

Unfortunately, the TACACS protocols have several security vulnerabilities, including a weak encryption algorithm. This has decreased its use in favor of the standards-based RADIUS authentication protocol.

Kerberos

Kerberos is an authentication system that uses a special key ticket assigned to the client that is embedded in all its network data to identify the client to other clients on a nonsecure network. Kerberos uses symmetric key cryptography, where the same key used to encrypt a message is used to decrypt the message. The Kerberos client needs to authenticate only once to the Kerberos server, which provides the client with a ticket that proves to other clients on the network that it has been authenticated. This type of authentication requires a Kerberos server to authenticate clients and manage the tickets assigned to them. This is also its weakness, as all the keys are stored on the Kerberos server; if it is compromised or crashes, the security of the entire Kerberos authentication system is compromised or unavailable to authenticate clients.

802.1X

The *IEEE 802.1X* standard is an authentication mechanism for wireless networks. Its goal is to provide a centralized authentication framework for wireless LANs (WLANs), which include both wireless clients and the access points that connect them to the network. In most current WLANs, a client automatically connects to the closest access point and then authenticates to the network by directly communicating with the network's native authentication. Unfortunately, unless the LAN is protected with a strong encryption method, the client can perform certain network functions without authentication, such as performing networking functions such as ping.

Using 802.1X, when a client connects to an access point, the wireless port is set to an unauthorized state, so it can't perform any network functions, which includes receiving an IP address from a DHCP server. The access point then asks the client for authentication credentials, such as a user name and password. Once received, this data is forwarded to an authentication server running a service such as RADIUS. If the client is accepted as an authorized user, then the client port on the access point is switched to an authorized state, and normal communications can commence.

802.1X can be helpful in allowing WLANs to scale upward in size easily, while maintaining a centralized authentication system. This authentication, however, should be coupled with a strong communications encryption mechanism to provide full security.

Travel Assistance
See Chapter 4, "Network Security Tools and Wireless Security," for more detailed information on wireless security.

Certificates (Mutual Authentication)

Certificates are a form of *mutual authentication*, which uses a third party to establish the identity of a user for access control purposes. A certificate is like a digital piece of paper that contains a user's credentials. Digital certificates are used mostly in dealing with secure web communications and encryption. Each user needs another user's certificate to authenticate the other user before exchanging secure confidential information.

A user obtains a certificate by registering with a third-party service. To receive the certificate, the user must supply credentials such as a driver's license, Social Security number, address, and phone number. The certificate authority then issues a certificate to the user, along with any encryption keys they'll be using. This certificate proves the user's legitimacy.

Biometrics

Although typically available only to extremely high-security installations because of the great costs, biometric access controls offer the most complete and technologically advanced method for securing access to a facility. *Biometrics* uses a unique physical attribute, such as a fingerprint, voice scan, or retinal scan, to identify a user.

Initially, the user requesting access must have the respective attribute scanned, so a perfect copy is on file for comparison when the user tries to gain access in the future. These types of biometric systems are complex and sensitive, and they can often result in false permissions and denials for access. They must be constantly calibrated, and repeated measurements of users' biometric data are required.

The following are the most common types of biometric access systems:

- **Palm/fingerprint scan**   No two fingerprints are alike. A user must place his hand on a biometric scanner, which will compare it to the palm scan and fingerprints on file for that user. This is the most effective of all biometric methods.

- **Hand geometry scan**   The size and shape of a person's hand varies significantly among different people. Similar to a fingerprint scan, the user places his hand on a biometric scanner, which measures the length and width of the hand, including the sizes of the fingers.

- **Retinal/iris scan**   A person's retina contains a varied pattern of blood vessels and is a unique attribute, similar to a fingerprint. The user must place her eye up to a device that projects a light beam into the eye to capture the retinal pattern. The *iris,* the colored part of the eye that surrounds the pupil, can also be used for scanning because it contains many unique characteristics.

- **Voice scan**   The voice is also a unique characteristic. By recording the user speaking a set of access words, the captured voice print can be compared to the same spoken words the next time the user tries to gain access.

- **Face scan**   A facial scan records the unique characteristics of each user's face, such as bone structure and the shape of the eyes and nose. These characteristics can be captured in the scan and compared to the facial scan on file.

- **Signature scan**   Considered one of the weakest types of biometric security, a signature scan records the written signature of a user and then compares it to subsequent signatures when the user attempts to gain access. Two types of signature scans exist: static and dynamic. A static scan merely compares the two signatures for accuracy and can't be considered accurate. A dynamic scan can record the motions of the signature using electrical signals. These unique characters make a dynamic signature scan much more reliable.

Exam Tip	
Be aware of the characteristics of a biometric access control system that differentiates it from other traditional access control methods.	

Objective 6.04
CompTIA Security+
Objective 3.9

Apply Physical Access Security

Physical security differs from computer security: When securing a computer system or network, you're attempting to prevent unauthorized users from accessing the resources of your system. Physical security, however, is implemented to prevent unauthorized users from accessing an environment—anything from the entire facility to a small network closet that contains networking equipment and wiring.

Much time and expense is spent on securing a computer network from unauthorized external access, but typically not enough resources are used on physical security to prevent unauthorized internal access. The possible result of lax physical security includes equipment theft, physical damage and vandalism, service interruptions, and the unauthorized release of confidential data. Physical security is required to protect employees, company data, equipment, and the facility itself. Physical security concepts include planning, facilities security, access control, and physical and environmental protections.

To secure access to the facility, access systems should be installed to identify employees and control what areas of the facility they can enter. Access control security also includes surveillance and monitoring of company property and the installation of physical barriers to prevent unauthorized intruders from trespassing on a company's property.

Your first line of defense is the security of the perimeter of the facility or the boundaries of its property. It's critical that unauthorized people are prevented from accessing the property or its buildings. This could involve unique security mechanisms for use during daily working hours and for use when the facility is closed. Building security includes the use of physical barriers, surveillance, and access control.

Physical Barriers

To deter unauthorized people from accessing a facility, physical barriers can be the most effective form of security. *Fencing* can close off the perimeter from people who are simply passing by and could be inclined to trespass on company property. Depending on the level of protection required, fencing can be as simple as a 4-foot fence that protects against casual trespassers or animals. Higher fences of at least 8 feet should be constructed to make it difficult for the average person to climb over them. For the most protection, barbed wire can be installed at the top of the fence.

Lighting

In the interest of security and safety, all areas of the property—including all the company's buildings and the parking lot—should have proper lighting installed to discourage intruders and provide a safe environment for employees. Flood-lights are an effective way to illuminate a large area. The entire lighting system should also be set on a timer, or photoelectric technology can be used to detect outside light levels.

Video Surveillance and Monitoring

To maintain the physical security of the property, surveillance and monitoring devices should be employed. The simplest form of surveillance is the use of common security procedures, such as using security guards. Cameras can be set up throughout the facility, which can be constantly monitored by security guards. Although effective, these options can be costly because of the high price of surveillance equipment and the ongoing wages that must be paid to security guards. Camera surveillance can be coupled with recording equipment that can monitor and record all activity 24 hours a day. If a burglary or vandalism occurs, the culprits could be captured on video, which can then be analyzed to identify the unauthorized intruders.

Camera placement is key, both in terms of efficiency of surveillance and equipment costs, and at minimum all entrances, doors, and access ways should be included in the coverage. All people who enter and exit the facility will be recorded on the cameras. In high-security environments, additional cameras are typically placed inside server rooms and other networking equipment areas that form the hub of the communications network.

The use of intruder detection equipment can ensure that a surveillance and monitoring system is proactive by alerting you to suspicious behavior without the need and expense of constant monitoring by security guards. Several intrusion detection technologies options are available:

- **Proximity detector** Senses changes in an electromagnetic field that surrounds a small area or object; when a change is detected, an alarm will sound.

- **Motion detector** Detects motion in a certain area; most often used in conjunction with floodlights that turn on when motion is detected. The light serves as a warning that an intruder has been detected.

- **Photoelectric detector** Senses changes in light patterns that indicate someone is in the area. The photoelectric device emits a beam of light, which, when disrupted, sounds an alarm.

- **Infrared detector** Senses changes in the heat patterns of an area that indicate the presence of an intruder.

- **Sound detector** Senses sounds and vibrations, and can detect changes in the noise levels in an area.

Travel Advisory

The main drawback of most intrusion-detection systems is the large number of false alarms that can occur because of abnormal weather conditions, animals, and improper calibration.

Locks

The most basic and least expensive type of physical-access control is the use of a lock and key. Unfortunately, in large environments this can quickly become an administrative nightmare, because the number of keys that must be distributed for each lock can grow quickly. In addition, employees lose keys, duplicate them, and let other users borrow them. When an employee is terminated, he might not always return his keys, and then every lock has to be changed.

Depending on the environment, different types of locks can be used. For perimeter security, a simple padlock on a chained fence might suffice. For more high-security areas, electronic or mechanical locks with programmable keys can be installed. These require a combination or key code to open, instead of a physical key.

Travel Advisory

Electronic locks should be linked with the alarm system. In case of a fire or other emergency, the locks should automatically disengage to allow people to leave the building.

Access Logs

As part of an overall security plan, access logs should contain the names of all visitors to the facility and the in and out times of their visits. Most organizations have some type of policy that requires all non-employees to sign in at the front lobby of a building and indicate who they are visiting, including the times they entered and exited. This allows the organization to keep a record of all non-employees, contractors, and visitors to the building. If any security issues arise, a list is available of everyone who was in the building at that time.

Access logs are also important for highly sensitive areas of an organization such as the main server and telecommunications room that houses the primary system and networking equipment. Each administrator should record times of entry and departure of the server room to perform duties or maintenance. Any security issues that arise in regard to activities in the server room can be tracked to whoever was in the room at the time.

Most electronic badge systems automatically record this information as employees typically use their ID badges to enter and exit various parts of the building. These electronic logs can be easily obtained and scanned to determine who was at a certain location in times of a security lapse.

ID Badges

More advanced personnel-access control techniques include the use of ID badge access cards. An ID badge should provide photo identification that can immediately identify the wearer as an authorized user. ID badges should be worn at all times where they can be seen by other employees. The card should identify the person and his job function. By listing job function, that person's access clearance into a certain part of the facility can be quickly determined. Simple ID badges, however, require the use of security guards and security-conscious employees. The most common method of personnel access control used today is the access card. Typically, each employee receives a card with a magnetic strip that contains her access information. These cards are swiped in magnetic card readers that are stationed outside important access points, such as doors and elevators. The information on the card is then compared with the security access of the area the person is about to enter. If she doesn't have access to that particular area, the door won't open.

Travel Advisory

Magnetic access cards should include no company identification. If a card is lost or stolen, the unauthorized user would have no idea from which company or facility the card came.

Another type of access card system is the proximity reader, which doesn't require the physical insertion of a card. The reader can sense the card if it's within a certain minimum distance. The information is read through an electromagnetic field.

> ### Exam Tip
> ID cards should be complemented with access codes or PINs. In case the card is lost or stolen, it can't be used for access if the proper corresponding PIN is not keyed in.

Man-trap

A *man-trap* describes a two-tier physical access control method with two physical barriers, such as doors, between the person and the resource he is trying to access. A person must be authenticated to be able to get in the first door, and then when that door is closed, the person is physically caught between doors and must pass an additional form of authentication to gain entry through the second door. In high-security environments, the person is effectively trapped if he cannot be properly authenticated by the second door. The first door will be locked down and he will not be able to leave until security arrives to examine his credentials.

A more basic example of this is a bank whose cash machines are located in a lobby between the outside doors and the internal bank doors. To access the first door, the person must swipe his card for that bank. Once inside, the person must use his bank card in conjunction with a PIN to access the ATM.

Network Infrastructure Security

Physical access to special network and computer equipment rooms should be secured as carefully as access to company facilities. These rooms are the brains of company operations, concentrating a variety of critical functions, such as network communications, database servers, and backup systems. If an unauthorized user gains access to the central network room, the damage she can cause could be considerable.

The main door to the network or server room should be secured with some type of lock, preferably with some sort of card access system, as described earlier. Only those employees who need to be in the room to perform their job functions should be allowed access. Inside, servers and other sensitive equipment should be housed inside a lockable cage or rack and not left running in an open area where they could be accessed or accidentally damaged. Many types of networking equipment servers come with their own locks that require keys to open them for access. Cabling should be carefully laid out so it can't be easily disturbed by people walking through the room. Cables should either be run under the floor or around the perimeter of the room in special cable trays.

Personal Computers and Laptops

It's easy for an unauthorized user to walk by an unattended desk or system rack and quickly remove expensive equipment. Not only does the stolen equipment need to be replaced, but the sensitive data saved on that equipment must be recovered. If the item was stolen for the purpose of corporate espionage, the results of the theft can be devastating.

Any expensive or sensitive equipment—especially portable items such as laptops, PDAs, networking equipment, and small computer devices—should be kept out of sight or locked up when unattended. Device locks are available for both desktop computers and portable laptops. A desktop computer can be housed in a lockable cage that would require a great deal of effort to open. Also, alarm cards, which will sound a loud alarm whenever the computer is moved, can be installed in computers. Peripheral devices attached to a computer can be protected with cable traps that prevent their removal. Laptop computers should be fitted with special cables and locks that can securely attach it to a current work area. If the user will be away from a laptop for an extended period of time, it should be locked inside a desk or cabinet.

Social Engineering

Social engineering is the use of subterfuge to trick a person into revealing personal or confidential information. Most often this comes in the form of an unauthorized user posing as an authority who requires access to that information. In the context of physical security, social engineering could involve deception in allowing an unauthorized user to gain access to a facility. For example, an unauthorized individual might arrive at the front gates of a secured facility claiming to have forgotten his access card at home. Distracted by the user's friendly manner and banter, an unsuspecting security guard or receptionist might let him through without checking his credentials.

Fake or stolen identification could also be used to gain access to a facility that uses photo ID or a magnetic swipe access card. If the security guard gets only a passing glance at the photo, she might not realize the person wielding the card is someone who only vaguely resembles the photo. All employees must be advised never to let strangers access any secured areas of the facility without proper identification or security access. Often an unauthorized user will try to "tailgate" in behind an employee who has just unlocked a door using her own authentication.

Employees should never let another user borrow identification or access cards or give out passwords without the consent of management and security.

CHECKPOINT

✔**Objective 6.01: Explain Identification and Authentication**   Identification ensures that a user (which could also be an application program or process) is who he claims to be. The user must then pass the authentication phase using his logon user name or account number and a password. If these two criteria are matched with the global database of login user names and passwords stored on the network, the user is granted access to the network. Finally, when a user tries to access a resource, the system must check to see if that user ID is authorized for that resource and what permissions or privileges the user has when accessing it.

✔**Objective 6.02: Identify Authentication Models**   Single-factor authentication uses only one item, such as a password, and is the simplest but weakest form of authentication. Two-factor authentication builds upon single-factor by combining two single-factor authentication types, such as something the user knows (a password or PIN) and something the user possesses (a magnetic swipe card or token). Three-factor authentication is the strongest form of user authentication and involves a combination of physical items such as a smart card, token, or biometric factor, and non-physical items such as passwords, passphrases, and PINs.

✔**Objective 6.03: Deploy Authentication Models**   Remote access via VPN is typically the most secure method as it encrypts communications while ensuring that users are authenticated before being granted access. Biometrics systems identify people through a unique physical attribute, such as a fingerprint, voice scan, or retinal scan; it offers the most complete and technologically advanced method for securing access to a facility.

✔**Objective 6.04: Apply Physical Access Security**   Physical access control security includes video surveillance and monitoring, ID badges, locks, man-traps, and access logs. ID cards should be complemented with access codes or PINs. In case the card is lost or stolen, it can't be used for access unless the user keys in the corresponding PIN.

REVIEW QUESTIONS

1. You finished working on your laptop and you're going out for a one-hour lunch. What should you do before leaving?

   A. Tell a co-worker to keep an eye on your laptop.

   B. Log out of the laptop.

   C. Shut it down and close the lid.

   D. Secure the laptop to your desk or lock it away in a cabinet.

2. Which of the following access control methods is the most secure?

   A. Access list

   B. ID badge

   C. Biometric scan

   D. Door locks

3. Which of the following access control methods provides two different challenges to a user for authentication?

   A. Laptop password

   B. Camera scan

   C. ID badge

   D. Man-trap

4. After a user is identified and authenticated to the system, what else must be performed to enable the user to use a resource?

   A. Authorization

   B. Authentication by token

   C. Encryption of network access

   D. Biometric scan

5. Which of the following is an example of a two-factor authentication model?

   A. User name and password

   B. Biometric eye scan

   C. Access token, password, and fingerprint scan

   D. Smart card and PIN

6. Which of the following is the first step when allowing a user access to a network and granting her access to a resource?

   A. Authentication

   B. Authorization

   C. Identification

   D. Privilege management

7. You are setting up an IPSec VPN between two branch offices that will communicate over the public Internet. Which IPSec mode should the VPN run in?

   A. Tunnel mode

   B. Transport mode

   C. SA mode

   D. Secure mode

8. Which of the following is the standard protocol used for wireless network authentication?

   A. RADIUS

   B. 802.1X

   C. PAP

   D. Kerberos

9. Which of the following authentication models would be the most efficient for enterprise networks with a large number of resources?

   A. Single sign-on utilizing LDAP

   B. Two-factor authentication with smart card and PIN

   C. Three-factor authentication with smart card, PIN, and fingerprint scan

   D. User name and password for each resource

10. Which of the following types of authentication protocols utilizes symmetric keys and tickets servers?

   A. CHAP

   B. PAP

   C. Kerberos

   D. RADIUS

REVIEW ANSWERS

1. **D** A passerby can remove a laptop from an area in the blink of an eye. To prevent theft, the laptop should be always locked in place or stored away out of sight if you're going to be away for any length of time.

2. **C** Biometric access controls offer the most complete and technologically advanced method for securing access to a facility. Biometrics offers the ability to identify someone through a unique physical attribute, such as a fingerprint, voice scan, or retinal scan.

3. **D** A man-trap is a two-tier physical access control method with two physical barriers, such as doors, between the person and the resource she is trying to access.

4. **A** Although a user has been given access to log in to the network, she still needs to be authorized to use a particular resource.

5. **D** To pass the two-factor authentication, the user must insert her smart card and then enter her PIN into a keypad. This ensures that the smart card or the PIN alone would not grant access, since the two must be used together.

6. **C** The user must initially identify herself as a valid user for that network. This is usually provided through the form of a login user name or account. Identification is the step that makes sure a user is who she claims to be.

7. **A** IPSec uses two types of encryption modes: transport and tunnel. In transport mode, IPSec encrypts only the data portion of each packet, but not the header. This can be used only in host-to-host communications. Tunnel mode encrypts both the header and the data of the network packet. This is used to host VPN gateway communications, which is the most common form of VPN.

8. **B** The IEEE 802.1X standard is an authentication mechanism for wireless networks. Its goal is to provide a centralized authentication framework for wireless LANs, which include both wireless clients and the access points that connect them to the network.

9. **A** For large networks, it is most efficient to control authentication using a single network sign-on for all resources and authenticate to a central Lightweight Directory Access Protocol (LDAP) server that contains the authentication credential information.

10. **C** Kerberos is an authentication system that uses a special key ticket assigned to the client, which is embedded in all network data to identify the client to other clients on a non-secure network. Kerberos uses symmetric key cryptography, where the same key used to encrypt a message is the used to decrypt the message.

Assessments and Audits

Risk and
Vulnerability Assessment

CHAPTER 7

	NEWBIE	SOME EXPERIENCE	EXPERT
ETA	3 hours	2 hours	1 hour

To protect their assets from security risks inherent with the Internet, companies must audit their security practices to identify the risks and threats to assets and protect themselves in the most cost-efficient way. Security measures are justified based on a valuation of the assets to be protected (in terms of physical hardware and the sensitive data it contains) and an evaluation of effective countermeasures to protect against identified risks.

A variety of tools are available to the network administrator and security professional to test networks and systems for vulnerabilities and weaknesses; unfortunately, these tools are also available to unethical hackers who use them to exploit specific vulnerabilities. By proactively monitoring your network for vulnerabilities and taking immediate steps to rectify them, you ensure that hackers using the same tools will not find vulnerabilities to exploit. You must routinely scan your network for vulnerabilities, whether they be unpatched operating systems and application software (such as web servers and database servers), or unused open ports and services that are actively listening for requests.

This chapter describes how to conduct risk assessments and implement risk mitigation, and provides an overview of vulnerability testing tools, such as port scanners, network mappers, and protocol analyzers, that can aid in identifying vulnerabilities in your network. The importance of penetration testing is also discussed, including how it differs from and complements vulnerability assessments.

Objective 7.01
CompTIA Security+
Objective 4.1

Conduct Risk Assessments

Risk assessment and mitigation deals with identifying, assessing, and reducing the risk of security breaches with company assets. By assessing the probability of a risk and estimating the amount of damage that could be caused as a result, you can take steps to reduce the level of that risk.

Suppose, for example, that your company file server contains confidential company data. The file server asset is considered extremely valuable to the company, its clients, and its competitors. A considerable amount of financial damage would be incurred by the company in the event of loss, damage, or theft of the server. The risks and threats posed to the server could be physical—such as damage caused by a natural disaster or a hardware malfunction—to nonphysical—such as viruses, network hacker attacks, and data theft if the server is easily accessible through a network. To help reduce these risks, you can take several actions:

- Use multiple hard drives and power supplies for fault tolerance.
- Implement a good backup scheme.
- Protect the server through physical security such as door access controls.
- Install anti-virus software.
- Disable unused network services and ports to prevent network attacks.

The costs associated with reducing these risks are mitigated by the potential costs of losing data on the file server.

To identify the risks that pose a security threat to your company, you can perform a risk analysis on all parts of the company's resources and activities. By identifying risks and the amount of damage that could be caused by exploiting a system vulnerability, you can choose the most efficient methods for securing the system from those risks. Risk analysis and assessment can identify where too little or even too much security exists, and where the cost of security is more than the cost of the loss because of compromise. Ultimately, risk analysis and assessment is a cost/benefit analysis of your security infrastructure.

Risk analysis and assessment involves three main phases:

- **Asset identification**   Identify and quantify the company's assets.
- **Risk and threat assessment**   Identify and assess the possible security vulnerabilities and threats.
- **Identify solutions and countermeasures**   Identify a cost-effective solution to protect assets.

Asset Identification

Company assets can include physical items such as computer and networking equipment, and nonphysical items such as valuable data. *Asset identification* involves identifying both types of assets and evaluating their worth. Asset values must be established beyond the mere capital costs—acquisition costs, maintenance, the value of the asset to the company, the value of the asset to a competitor, what clients would pay for the asset or service, the cost of replacement, and the cost if the asset were compromised should also be considered. For example, a list of a company's clients can be easily re-created from backup if the original is lost or destroyed, but if the list finds its way into the hands of a competitor, the resulting financial damage could be devastating. Ultimately, the value of the assets you're trying to protect drives the costs involved in securing that asset.

Vulnerability and Threat Assessment

You must perform an assessment for each asset in its current state to ascertain risks. All possibilities, both physical and nonphysical, should be assessed. Data can be stolen from a file server by someone physically stealing the system or by a hacker accessing the data through a network security vulnerability.

Identify the following when performing a risk and threat assessment:

- **Vulnerability** The aspect of the asset that is vulnerable to a threat, such as lack of anti-virus software, unpatched operating system and application software, no fire prevention mechanisms, weak physical security, or ineffective network access controls.

- **Threat** The origin of the problem, such as a fire, flood, virus, malicious hacker, employee, or intruder.

- **Risk** The actual risk of a vulnerability being compromised by a threat. If a worm infects a web server that has no anti-virus protection, for example, the result could be lost or damaged data.

- **Impact** The result of damage or theft of assets or systems availability to the company, customers, employees, and others. If your company's main web server is attacked and taken offline, for example, it results not only in a downed server, but tens of thousands of dollars of revenue can be lost while the site is unavailable to customers.

- **Probability** The chances of certain threats being more likely to occur than others. For example, the probability that a malicious hacker will attempt to attack the network is greater than the chances that a natural disaster will occur.

Vulnerabilities

A *vulnerability* is a security weakness that could be compromised by a particular threat. An operating system (OS) might be vulnerable to network attacks, for example, because it was not updated with security patches. A file server could be vulnerable to viruses because no anti-virus software is installed. Web servers and database servers might have vulnerabilities that allow cross-site scripting and SQL injection attacks.

Physical vulnerabilities affect the physical protection of the asset. Physical assets, such as network servers, should be protected from natural disasters, such as fire and flood, by storing the equipment in special rooms with protective mechanisms to prevent damage from these threats.

Nonphysical vulnerabilities usually involve software or data. Software security vulnerabilities can be created because of improper software configuration, unpatched or buggy software, lack of anti-virus protection, weak access and authentication controls, unused open network ports, and misconfigured or nonexistent firewalls.

Threats

A *threat* creates the possibility of a vulnerability being compromised. A variety of threats can pose security risks, including the following:

- **Natural disasters**   A natural disaster is a fire, flood, or other phenomenon that causes physical damage to company assets—usually the facilities and the equipment within them.
- **Equipment malfunction**   Electronic equipment is vulnerable to normal wear and tear that can result in failed components—from a failed power supply fan to a failed hard drive.
- **Employees**   Assets face both malicious and nonmalicious threats from employees. The source of the threat could be human error, such as someone deleting a directory of files by mistake, or theft, vandalism, and corporate espionage.
- **Intruders**   An unauthorized person can compromise the access controls of a facility to gain access and perform theft, vandalism, or sabotage.
- **Malicious hackers**   A threat by malicious hackers is a nonphysical threat that involves a hacker's ability to compromise network security to access or damage assets on a company's network.

Travel Advisory

Although many companies make great efforts to secure their networks and facilities from external users, often little is done to protect against attacks from the inside by disgruntled employees.

Risk Assessment

After threats and vulnerabilities have been identified, your next step is to assess the risk of a threat compromising a vulnerability—such as what can happen in a security breach. For example, a combination of the lack of anti-virus software protection (a risk) and the introduction of a virus (a threat) would result in a virus-infected server, which could damage or delete sensitive data. Or an unused open network port could be a target for a denial-of-service (DoS) attack that renders the server unable to respond to legitimate network requests.

A *risk assessment* reflects the worst possible scenario of a security compromise and should be quantified with a direct financial value for losses and potential losses. A company should reflect on the amount of damage to reputation and financial security if a hacker were to launch a successful DoS attack on the company's web servers. A loss of service—even for a few hours—can severely damage a company; consider, for example, the case of a company that offers stock-trading services. On top of immediate costs for equipment or data loss, the potential loss of prolonged downtime must be factored into the equation.

Once the potential loss is calculated for each type of risk, the results can be used to create solutions and countermeasures that are cost-efficient, depending on the risk situation.

Exam Tip

The risk assessment should reflect the worst possible scenario of a security compromise and be quantified with a direct financial value for losses and potential losses.

Solutions and Countermeasures

After you've assessed and defined risk and management procedures, you'll have collected the following information:

- **Asset identification**   A list of your assets, including physical assets such as server hardware and hard disks, and nonphysical assets such as the valuable customer data stored on the hard drives.
- **Threat profiles**   A list of every possible threat against your assets.
- **Risks**   An evaluation of the potential risk of each threat—such as the risk of a malicious hacker being able to compromise a database server. If the server itself is compromised, but the valuable and confidential data on the database server is leaked by the hacker, the risk is far greater for this asset.
- **Potential loss**   The potential loss in the event your assets are attacked or compromised by threats, including the asset's capital value (such as hardware cost), plus how much it will cost to replace that asset, especially lost customer data. A failed hard drive can be a relatively low cost to recoup, but if you have no backup of customer data that was stored on that hard drive, you might have lost tens of thousands of dollars' worth of data.

Each risk scenario should be ranked by *impact* and *probability*: The risks more likely to occur are ranked toward the top of the list to indicate where solution efforts should be most concentrated. For example, within a company that already practices strict physical security and access control methods, the priority of risk scenarios could be geared toward nonphysical threats, such as viruses and network hackers.

Once this process is complete, a list of solutions and countermeasures to protect against each threat should be reviewed and documented. Examine your solutions with respect to what current security measures are in place and what needs to be done to make them more effective. Ensure that the functionality and effectiveness of the solution is sufficient to reduce the risk of compromise. Purchasing a fire extinguisher for the server room could seem like a fire-prevention solution, for example, but only an automatic fire detection and suppression system can fully protect a room full of servers from a large, out-of-control fire that occurs in the middle of the night. Similarly, buying a firewall to protect your servers from outside Internet traffic is a great idea for network security, but if the network administrator hasn't been trained to configure it properly, the firewall might not be effective at all.

Any solutions must be cost-effective to ensure that the benefits of the solution are in line with the actual value of the assets. For example, there's no point in spending $100,000 on a security solution to protect data that's worth only $40,000 to the company if it's lost or damaged. Ongoing maintenance also needs to be factored into the final calculations. Although a large initial cost is incurred for a tape backup solution, costs of purchasing new tapes as they're needed will be ongoing, and you'll pay for offsite storage of used tapes.

Exam Tip

The cost of the risk management solution shouldn't exceed the value of the asset if it's lost. For example, if a file server and its data are valued at $35,000 and the proposed security solution to protect it costs $150,000, then it doesn't make sense to implement the proposed solution.

Security is always an ongoing primary concern: To protect the network and infrastructure from new threats, the company must make sure that the current security mechanisms can effectively deal with new risks. After implementation, security solutions should be regularly tested and reevaluated to ensure their functionality and reliability, as well as their costs and benefits.

Perform Vulnerability Assessments

Vulnerability assessment and network scanning programs are important tools for a network administrator who routinely runs preventative security scans on the network. These programs provide detailed information about which hosts on a network are running which services. They can also help identify servers that are running unnecessary network services that create security risks, such as a file server running FTP or HTTP services that could provide unauthorized access to data.

Common tools, such as network mappers, port scanners, vulnerability scanners, protocol analyzers, and password crackers, are used by network administrators to identify and prevent such attacks. Unfortunately, these same tools are major weapons in the malicious hacker's arsenal. Attackers can use them to determine what systems are running on your network, what services and open ports they are running, what operating system and application software they are running, and what vulnerabilities can be exploited. Due to their simplicity, these tools are commonly used to probe and scan networks, even by amateur hackers who have no knowledge of networking protocols.

Network Mappers

A *network mapper* program scans a network and uses network IP packets to determine which hosts are available, what operating systems are running, and other types of information about a network host. Most network mappers use the ping utility to perform Internet Control Message Protocol (ICMP) sweeps of entire ranges of IP addresses looking for hosts that respond. The response contains a lot of information about the host and its place on the network (such as whether it's behind a router or firewall on a subnetwork). Hackers who already know the address of a specific target can also use a network mapper to analyze the host for open ports, services, and OS specifics.

When used against an entire network, a network mapper program can determine how many hosts are running on the network, on which subnetworks they reside, and what services and ports are running. This information offers a virtual map of the entire network for a malicious hacker who can narrow his scope of attack to specific systems, or for the network administrator who needs to find and correct weaknesses on a network.

One of the most popular tools used for network mapping is an open source and publicly available utility called *Nmap* that is used by hackers to scan and map networks and used by administrators to audit their networks for security weaknesses. The Nmap command-line utility uses simple text commands with switch options to perform tasks. For example, to perform a ping sweep on a system with Nmap, you'd enter the following:

```
nmap -sP 192.168.1.128
Host 192.168.1.128 appears to be up.
MAC Address: 00:B1:63:3F:74:41 (Apple)
Nmap done: 1 IP address (1 host up) scanned in 0.600 seconds
```

To perform a scan to identify the OS of a system, you'd enter this:

```
nmap -O 192.168.1.128
MAC Address: 00:B1:63:3F:74:41 (Apple)
Device type: general purpose
Running: NetBSD 4.X
OS details: NetBSD 4.99.4 (x86)
Network Distance: 1 hop
```

Travel Assistance
The Nmap tool can be downloaded from www.nmap.org.

Other popular tools include Cheops, a network mapper for Linux, and hping2, an advanced ping program that uses TCP to perform powerful and diverse scans.

Port Scanners

After an attacker has determined what systems are on a network and identified IP addresses that respond with acknowledgements of a live system at that address, his next step is to discover what network services and open ports are running on the system. By using a *port scanner*, an attacker can determine which ports on the system are listening for requests (such as TCP port 80), and then he can decide which service or vulnerability in the service can be exploited.

For example, if an attacker sees that SMTP port 25 is open and listening for requests, he knows that an e-mail server is operating and can launch more probes and tests to determine what mail server software is running and whether vulnerabilities can be exploited to relay spam through the server. The following example shows a listing of a port scan from the Nmap application:

```
nmap -sT 192.168.1.128
Interesting ports on 192.168.1.128:
Not shown: 1709 closed ports
PORT       STATE SERVICE
21/tcp     open  ftp
53/tcp     open  domain
554/tcp    open  rtsp
10000/tcp open  snet-sensor-mgmt
```

A standard set of ports, including 65,535 TCP ports and User Datagram Protocol (UDP) ports, are available for running network services on a computer system. The first 1024 ports are *well-known* ports, which means they make up the most common types of network ports, such as DNS (53), SMTP (25), HTTP (80), HTTPS (443), and FTP (21). Beyond these first 1024 ports are tens of thousands of port ranges that are used by third-party applications, services, and networking devices. Table 7.1 lists the most common well-known protocols and services and their corresponding TCP/IP ports.

Travel Advisory

Many of these ports also listen on UDP as well as TCP. For example, Domain Name System (DNS) uses TCP port 53 for zone transfers and UDP port 53 for DNS queries.

A port scanner will send probing network packets (sometimes called a *port sweep*) to each of the 65,535 ports (both TCP and UDP) and listen for a response. If the system port does not respond, the attacker knows it is either disabled or protected (behind a network firewall or proxy server, for example). When it does respond, this service is running on the target system, and the at-

TABLE 7.1	TCP/IP Services and Port Numbers
Service	**TCP/IP Port Number**
HTTP	80
FTP (Data)	20
FTP (Control)	21
DNS	53
DHCP	67
SMTP	25
SNMP	161
Telnet	23
POP3	110
IMAP	143
NTP	123
NNTP	119
SSH	22
LDAP	389

tacker can then use more focused tools to assault that particular port and service. For example, a SQL server may be listening on port TCP/UDP 1433. If a port scanner receives a response from this port, the attacker knows that this system is running a SQL server, and he can then direct his attacks against specific SQL vulnerabilities.

The following are different types of port scanning methods that can be used to detect open ports on a system:

- **TCP scanning**   A TCP scan uses the TCP and commands to connect to a port and open a full TCP connection before breaking off the communication. For example, when scanning a system for Telnet port 23, the port scanner will fully connect to that port on the destination host. If no response is received, the port is deemed closed or protected by a firewall.

- **SYN scanning**   A SYN scan uses small, basic IP packets to scan a host and does not open a full TCP connection to the destination host. The SYN scan will break off the communication before the handshake process is complete. This is often called *stealth* scanning and is less intrusive than a TCP scan, which opens a full connection to receive its information.

- **UDP scanning**   The UDP scan is not as effective as other scans, since UDP is a connectionless protocol. This scan gets its open port information by detecting which ports are not returning acknowledgements to requests, since a UDP request will receive a "host unreachable" message via ICMP in response. If no response is received, the port is open and listening for requests. However, this method is not foolproof, because if the port is blocked by a firewall, the user/attacker will receive no response and might assume the port is open.

Port scanners are often built into popular network mapping and vulnerability assessment tools, such as Nmap, because they provide the foundation for determining what services and open ports are on a system, which then leads to a specific vulnerability scan against those services and ports.

Vulnerability Scanners

When an attacker has ascertained which systems are available on the network, his next step is to probe these systems to see what vulnerabilities they might contain. At this point, he has an idea of what systems are alive and which network ports are open and listening for requests.

A *vulnerability scanner* is a software program specifically designed to scan a system via the network to determine what services the system is running and whether any unnecessary open network ports, unpatched operating systems and applications, or back doors can be exploited. Network administrators can use the same vulnerability scanner software to take preventative measures to close vulnerabilities that exist on their systems.

Travel Advisory

Nessus (available at www.nessus.org) is a popular, free, UNIX-based vulnerability scanner that scans systems for thousands of vulnerabilities and provides an exhaustive report about the vulnerabilities that exist on your system. Another popular tool, GFI LANguard (www.gfi.com), is a commercial software network security scanner for Windows systems.

Vulnerability scanners can include a number of scanning and security assessment abilities, such as port scanning, network scanning and mapping, and OS and application server scanning. The vulnerability scanner contains a database of known OS weaknesses and application program vulnerabilities (such as web and database servers), and it scans the target system to determine whether any of the vulnerabilities listed in its database exist. For example, a database server and front-end web application can be scanned to determine whether they are vulnerable to specific database and web server attacks. By determining the OS of a system, such as Windows or UNIX, and then using the database of known vulnerabilities and weaknesses for that OS, the attacker can target his attacks.

Protocol Analyzers

A *protocol analyzer* (also often called a *network sniffer*) is a device or software program that can intercept, log, and analyze network traffic. Each individual network packet can be analyzed to decode its header information (the packet's origin and destination) and its contents.

Because of the massive amount of data that flows on a network, protocol analyzers are often used to troubleshoot specific network segments or traffic to and from a specific host on the network. Administrators can use the analyzer to track specific network protocols as they send out queries and receive responses and to narrow down sources of communications issues (such as blocked network ports). Protocol analyzers can also be used by hackers to intercept clear-text communications (such as user account and password information) that are transmitted over unsecured protocols. For example, HTTP web traffic is transmitted in clear text, and any information transmitted to a web site in clear text, such as a login ID and password, is not encrypted and can be easily viewed by a hacker using a protocol analyzer. Confidential information can also be captured from sensitive e-mail messages passed over the network.

To protect against unauthorized sniffers, network switches can keep network broadcast traffic isolated on its own network segment; hackers would need access to the specific network segment to get at the data stored there. In addition, any sensitive data should be transmitted over the network using secure protocols that encrypt their contents.

Exam Tip

To prevent network traffic from being intercepted by a protocol scanner, use secure protocols such as Hypertext Transfer Protocol over Secure Socket Layer (HTTPS) instead of HTTP for web traffic, or Secure Shell (SSH) instead of Telnet for remote access.

OVAL

Open Vulnerability and Assessment Language (OVAL) is a security standard that provides open access to security assessments using a special language to standardize system security configuration characteristics, current system analysis, and reporting. OVAL is not a vulnerability scanner, but it provides a language and templates that help administrators check their systems to determine whether vulnerabilities, such as unpatched software, exist.

OVAL uses Extensible Markup Language (XML) schemas as its framework, with three schemas geared toward specific parts of the security standard (system characteristics, current system definition, and reporting the assessment results). These XML files can be fed through an OVAL interpreter program that examines the system, compares it to public databases of known vulnerabilities, and generates the test results that indicate any open vulnerabilities on the system.

Local Lingo

XML Extensible Markup Language is a markup-language specification that allows structured data to be shared across different computers and platforms. XML uses custom property tags to ensure data is stored and communicated properly, but does not define how the data is displayed, which is typically a function performed by HTML.

This information relies on repositories of publicly available security content that contain a collection of security definitions provided by the security community, which continually adds to the collection and drives OVAL development and evolution. This process provides a comprehensive testing and reporting standard supported by the security community that creates a baseline and checks for known vulnerabilities on computer systems.

> **Travel Assistance**
>
> More information about OVAL can be found at http://oval.mitre.org.

Password Crackers

Password cracker programs (also referred to as *password auditing tools*) are used by hackers to attack a system's authentication structure (such as its password database) and attempt to retrieve passwords for user accounts. The programs are also used by security administrators to proactively audit their password database to look for weak passwords.

Passwords crackers use a variety of methods:

- **Dictionary attack**   This type of attack relies on a dictionary of words that contain common passwords that are tried against the authentication database. Because users often use known dictionary words as passwords, this attack can succeed in cracking many passwords.

- **Brute-force attack**   This attack uses a calculated combination of characters in an attempt to guess the password. The brute-force method will keep trying every single combination until it gets the password right.

- **Hybrid attack**   Many programs use a combination of dictionary and brute-force attacks to add numbers and special characters (such as the @ symbol for *a*) on to the dictionary words in an attempt to crack more difficult passwords.

> **Travel Advisory**
>
> Examples of password cracking programs include LC4 and Cain & Abel.

After the attacker cracks a specific password, he will be able to access that user account. The administrator account for a system is most commonly attacked because it has full access privileges.

Many older computer authentication schemes stored the passwords in clear text, making it easy for a hacker who is able to access the password database file to crack an account. Most modern operating systems at the least provide some type of one-way hashing function to protect the password database. If the password database file is accessed by a hacker, it will be of no use because the contents are encrypted. However, many sophisticated password-cracking programs are able to analyze the database and attack weak encryption methods repeatedly to crack passwords over time. For example, the LM hash used in older Windows-based systems to protect passwords was weak and could be cracked fairly easily if the hacker could gain access to the password database.

Protecting against password-cracking programs relies on a strong password policy, as discussed in previous chapters. Setting maximum login attempts will lock out an account if the password has been unsuccessfully entered a set number of times.

Exam Tip

Know what constitutes a strong password to protect against dictionary attacks. Remember that a lockout countermeasure allows only a specific number of login attempts before the account locks to protects against brute-force attacks.

Protecting the password database is also a primary concern. Although a maximum login attempt policy will prevent most online brute-force attempts from guessing a password, if a hacker manages to access the database itself, he can run a cracking program against it offline for many days and weeks to crack the passwords in the database. One method of protecting the password database (other than using traditional security methods such as access permissions) is called *salting*, which refers to adding a suffix of random characters (called a *salt*) to the password before it is encrypted. Each password has its own salt, which is different for every password in the database, even identical passwords. Salting makes it difficult for a hacker to use brute-force methods to crack the password database. The longer the salt added to the password, the less likely it is to be cracked. Early implementations used 12-bit salts; however, 32- to 128-bit salts are recommended.

Travel Advisory

Windows does not use salting in its password databases; however, modern versions of UNIX and Mac OS (10.4 and greater) do use salting.

UNIX-based systems also protect their hashed password databases by using a *shadow password database.* The normal password database (located in /etc/passwd) contains the hashed passwords, but the whole file itself is readable by users other than the root user. In password shadowing, the hashed passwords are removed from the main password database and stored in a file (/etc/shadow) that is not available to unprivileged users; hackers cannot access the shadow password database to take it offline and run cracking programs on it.

Objective 7.03
CompTIA Security+
Objective 4.3

Penetration Testing and Vulnerability Scanning

The preceding section discussed the use of *vulnerability scanning* to examine your network systems for unnecessary running services and open ports, unpatched operating system and application software, or any other types of network vulnerabilities that can be exploited by a hacker. A similar preventative measure can be performed by a network administrator who wants to test the vulnerability of a system. *Penetration testing* evaluates the security of a network or computer system by actively simulating an attack. Attacks are performed using the same types of tools and exploits that malicious hackers use to compromise system security. These tools can be used to test network and system resiliency to a real attack scenario and test the effectiveness of existing security measures implemented after a vulnerability assessment. While a vulnerability scan can identify security risks and vulnerabilities, it cannot simulate the effect of real attacks.

Although vulnerability scanning and assessments are important in identifying weaknesses in system security, any countermeasures implemented to mitigate these vulnerabilities require testing, and the best way to do this is using a penetration test that simulates an actual network attack.

Exam Tip

A vulnerability scan is used to identify specific weaknesses in current systems and networks, but it cannot simulate real attacks. Penetration testing is used to simulate an actual attack on a system and can be used to test your security countermeasure and resiliency to an attack.

One of the drawbacks to penetration testing is that it can disrupt a live production system. To lessen the effects of the simulated attack, you should perform penetration testing after regular work hours at a time when any disruption to the network will not affect many users. Because of the disruptions tests can cause, many network administrators are able to perform only vulnerability assessments on their networks and systems; they cannot go a step further and perform actual penetration testing.

> **Travel Advisory**
>
> Check with your company's security policies to determine whether you are allowed to perform penetration testing before you start such a process.

Penetration tests are often performed by outside vendors who are allowed access to the network by upper management—in some cases, without the network administrator's knowledge. This ensures the testing scenario is as close to a real, unsuspected attack as possible, and provides a detailed analysis of any weaknesses in network and system security that still remain, even after vulnerability assessments have been performed.

CHECKPOINT

✔**Objective 7.01: Conduct Risk Assessments** Perform asset identification to identify and quantify assets, including full potential loss. Identify and assess risks and threats to those assets. Identify a cost-effective solution and countermeasures to reduce the risks of a security compromise. The cost of the solution should not be greater than the cost of the loss of the asset.

✔**Objective 7.02: Perform Vulnerability Assessments** Vulnerability assessment tools can be used by network administrators to find and mitigate vulnerabilities, but malicious hackers have access to the same tools to find vulnerabilities to attack. Perform port scanning to determine what services and open ports are running on your systems, and disable those that are not required. Protocol analyzers can capture and analyze individual network packets, including any clear text data sent within them. Use vulnerability scanners to determine whether your operating system and application software is up to date with the latest updates and patches. Ensure that password databases are protected via limited access rights and encryption to prevent attacks from password-cracking programs.

✔**Objective 7.03 Penetration Testing and Vulnerability Scanning**   Penetration testing evaluates the security of a network or computer system by simulating an actual attack. Vulnerability testing and assessments are helpful at identifying existing vulnerabilities and weaknesses, but only penetration testing can determine the effectiveness of the countermeasures used by the network administrator to fix these vulnerabilities.

REVIEW QUESTIONS

1. To be beneficial to a company, which of the following is the most practical relationship between a security risk and its countermeasure?

   A. The cost of the countermeasure should be less than the potential cost of the risk.

   B. The cost of the countermeasure should be greater than the potential cost of the risk.

   C. The cost of the countermeasure should be less than the cost of the asset.

   D. The cost of the countermeasure should be greater than the cost of the asset.

2. Which of the following is the most dangerous threat to a fault-redundant file server located on the network administrator's desk and fully secured with an anti-virus program, strict authentication, and access controls?

   A. Equipment failure

   B. Virus

   C. Hacking

   D. Theft

3. Which of the following vulnerabilities of a server room would be the most at risk from the threat of a natural disaster?

   A. Lack of anti-virus software

   B. Network firewall not properly configured

   C. Lack of a fire detection and suppression system

   D. No lock on the server room door

4. Which of the following tools would be able to capture and view network packets that were transmitting passwords in clear text?

   A. Vulnerability scanner

   B. Password cracker

   C. Network mapper

   D. Protocol analyzer

5. Which of the following is the most effective countermeasure against a brute-force password attack?

   A. Using dictionary words as passwords

   B. Minimum password lengths

   C. Login lockout policy

   D. LANMAN hash

6. Which of the following provides access-control protection for a UNIX password database?

   A. Salting

   B. LANMAN hash

   C. Shadow password file

   D. OVAL

7. A port scanner has reported that your web server running with a supporting SQL database is listening on TCP ports 80, 443, 21, and 1433. Which of these ports is unnecessary and should be closed to prevent hacking attempts?

   A. 80

   B. 21

   C. 1433

   D. 443

8. Which of the following web server characteristics would be flagged as a risk by a vulnerability scanner?

   A. Operating system not updated to latest patch level

   B. HTTPS server listening on port 443

   C. Network packets being sent in clear text

   D. HTTP server listening on port 80

9. After a security audit and vulnerability assessment, several servers required operating system updates, and several unused open ports needed to be disabled. Which of the following should be performed after these vulnerabilities are fixed to ensure that the countermeasures are secure against a real attack?

   A. Advertise the system's IP address publicly.

   B. Put systems back into live production.

   C. Perform port scanning.

   D. Perform penetration testing.

10. New management has decided to test the security of the existing network infrastructure implemented by the current network administrators. Which of the following should be performed?

    A. Hire a real hacker to attack the network.

    B. Perform third-party penetration testing.

    C. Perform penetration testing by the network administrators.

    D. Initiate a denial-of-service attack.

REVIEW ANSWERS

1. **A** To provide an adequate cost/benefit comparison, the cost of the countermeasure or solution to the risk should be less than the potential cost should that risk occur. The protection you implement should not cost more than the worth of the asset you're trying to protect.

2. **D** Because the file server isn't stored in a secure location, anyone walking by the area could steal it. All the other protections are for network-based threats.

3. **C** Although the server could be protected from networking attacks or physical th eft, the lack of a fire detection and suppression system leaves the server vulnerable to a fire.

4. **D** A protocol analyzer can intercept, log, and analyze network traffic. Each individual network packet can be analyzed to view the content of the packet if it is unencrypted.

5. **C** A brute-force attack will try multiple permutations of password characters to try to guess the password. By limiting the number of incorrect logins (such as three attempts), the system will automatically lockout the account to prevent any further attempts at cracking the password.

6. **C** UNIX-based systems protect their hashed password databases by using a shadow password file. In the shadow file, the hashed passwords are removed from the main password database and are stored in a location that is unavailable to unprivileged users.

7. **B** Port 21 is used by FTP, which is not required for your web/database server. This service and port should be disabled to prevent hackers from connecting to the server via FTP. Ports 80 and 443 are used by HTTP and HTTPS, respectively, and port 1433 is used by the SQL database.

8. **A** A vulnerability scanner is designed to scan a system via the network and determine what services that system is running and whether any unnecessary open network ports or unpatched operating systems and applications exist. In this case, HTTP listening on port 80 and HTTPS listening on port 443 are normal operating parameters for a web server. Unless you are using HTTPS, web network packets are always sent in clear text. The vulnerability scanner will detect that the system is not running the latest operating system patches and advise you to update the system.

9. **D** Penetration testing evaluates the security of a network or computer system by simulating an actual attack. This helps test a network's and system's resiliency to a real attack and to test the effectiveness of existing security measures implemented after vulnerability assessments.

10. **B** Penetration tests are often performed by third parties who are allowed access to the network by upper management—in some cases, without the network administrator's knowledge. This ensures the testing scenario is as close to a real, unsuspected attack as possible, and provides a detailed analysis of existing vulnerabilities.

Monitoring and Auditing

	NEWBIE	SOME EXPERIENCE	EXPERT
ETA	3 hours	2 hours	1 hour

With massive amounts of network information being collected every minute, every hour, and every day, administrators can find it difficult to stay abreast of current issues and find time to examine and analyze monitoring and logging information for anomalies that indicate possible security problems. Small issues can quickly escalate into serious breaches and attacks against your systems. A denial-of-service (DoS) attack on an Internet server might be noticed immediately on the network, but other security issues are not so easy to detect, such as unauthorized access of files, users with improperly assigned rights and permissions, and Trojan horse programs installed and running silently on workstations.

The administrator can use several proactive tools to detect suspicious behaviors that have passed the thresholds for normal system and network operation. From specialized intrusion detection systems (IDSs) to general utilities such as system and performance monitors and logging applications, these tools must be customizable by the administrator, who must also employ proper procedures and methodologies that maximize their benefits.

This chapter describes the various monitoring, logging, and auditing procedures, as well as monitoring methodologies and tools, that aid the administrator in monitoring a network and systems for security-related anomalous behavior.

Objective 8.01
CompTIA Security+
Objective 4.4

Monitor and Detect Security-Related Anomalies

Several monitoring tools can help administrators collect data on system and network performance and usage, and compare these statistics against measured baselines of typical system and network behavior. By analyzing performance trends over time, administrators can discover anomalies in the behavior of the system that differ greatly from the performance baselines; such anomalies can indicate a security issue such as a network attack or virus/worm infections. The following sections describe some of the common tools used to monitor systems and networks for security-related anomalies.

System and Performance Monitoring

System and performance monitors examine how much CPU, memory, disk input and output, and network bandwidth is being consumed at any particular time or during a specified time period. Administrators can examine the resulting data for trends that might indicate anomalous behavior.

For example, if a web server is infected with a virus or worm, it can be unresponsive to client requests or fail to respond in a timely manner. Several unrecognized processes might be running on the system and taking up most of the CPU processing time (with levels of 90 percent or more), memory usage might be unusually high, and network usage may have jumped as the worm tries to replicate itself to other servers. In other cases, excessive network usage (especially a large amount of network connections from external systems) often indicates a DoS attempt.

> ### Exam Tip
>
> Recognize what types of performance behaviors can indicate security issues when using system and performance monitors. High processor usage and network usage could indicate potential DoS attacks or virus and worm activity.

Performance Baselines

You can establish performance baselines and then track performance data to look for thresholds that surpass the baselines. This information allows you to recognize anomalous system behaviors and perform a closer examination to discover the source of the anomalies that affect system performance. To establish a good performance baseline, you must measure your system activity for 24 hours a day for at least 7 days. Data will be collected during working hours, nonworking hours, and weekends to provide an accurate view of your system performance at different times of day and days of the week. Simply sampling performance data for a few hours during the day will not provide an adequate overview of system performance trends. Likewise, measuring performance for only a few days during the week will not produce a sufficient baseline for activity during off-work hours and weekends.

The performance baseline should indicate that most primary activity occurs during normal working hours, with lighter activity during nonworking hours. Occasional spikes in activity in off-hours can also indicate normal behavior; system backup or archiving processes, for example, will increase CPU, memory, disk, and network activity during the times the processes are taking place. Your baseline will include this information as well, so that you can anticipate that performance spike. Performance spikes that you cannot account for can indicate unauthorized activities or other security-related issues.

Notification Systems

After you have recorded a system baseline, many performance monitors allow you to set alarm thresholds for parts of the system. For example, the system can notify you when CPU or memory usage exceeds a specific threshold (such as 90 percent). Take care when setting thresholds, however, to be sure that you don't receive alarm notifications for slightly above-average behaviors or for very short spikes in activity. For example, you might set your performance monitor to send an alert when CPU usage exceeds 90 percent for at least 30 minutes; this ensures that each momentary processing spike will not generate an alert, and that prolonged usage at a high rate will generate a notification.

Protocol Analyzers

A *protocol analyzer* is a device or application that can intercept, log, and analyze network traffic. Each individual network packet can be examined to decode its header information (which contains the packet's origin and destination) and its contents. Figure 8.1 shows a typical protocol analyzer display from Wireshark, which shows each inbound and outbound network packet and the exact details of each packet's contents.

> **Travel Assistance**
>
> More information on Wireshark can be found at www.wireshark.org.

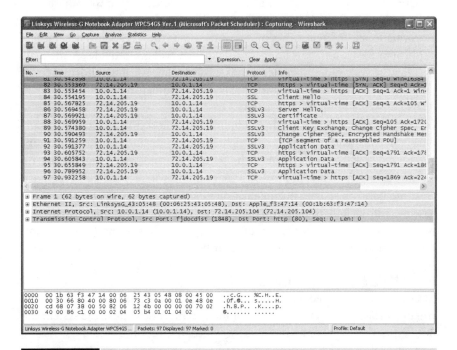

FIGURE 8.1 Wireshark protocol analyzer

Protocol analyzers are not used continually to monitor every packet that passes through the network. Because of the huge amounts of data flowing across a network, this would be an impossible task. Instead, they are used to troubleshoot specific network segments or traffic to and from a specific host on the network. Administrators can use an analyzer to track specific network protocols as they send out queries and receive responses; this helps narrow down sources of communications issues.

In terms of monitoring for security issues, protocol analyzers are very useful for viewing within specific network packets the source, destination, and content of the packet. For example, a network administrator might suspect that a specific workstation on the network is infected with some kind of Trojan horse program that is communicating data from the workstation to an attacker's computer over the Internet. By using the protocol analyzer, the administrator can watch every single network packet that leaves the workstation and narrow down the search using the ports specifically used by Trojan horse programs. The examination of the workstation will show communications to and from these ports to a specific external IP address on the network. At this point, the administrator can confirm the type of Trojan horse program being used and attempt to clean it off the infected workstation. The external IP address to which the Trojan horse program is communicating can also be blocked at the firewall to prevent any future occurrences of data being transmitted to that address.

Protocol analyzers and similar network monitoring tools can also be used to track general trends in networking bandwidth. For example, suppose you hear complaints from users that a specific web server is too slow to respond. By enabling the protocol analyzer to analyze network packets going to and from the web server, you discover massive amounts of network traffic originating externally from the network. By analyzing the network packets, you discover ping messages from multiple IP addresses. This indicates that your web server could be suffering from a distributed denial-of-service (DDoS) attack in which multiple computers on the Internet are sending a flood of ping requests to the web server in an effort to slow it down or crash it. You can then take steps to mitigate the attack, such as disabling the ping service on the web server.

Network Monitor

Network monitoring applications allow the administrator to take a real-time view of current network activity on the entire network. Network monitors will display a map of the network and indicate bandwidth usage and network trends, similar to how a traffic congestion map would depict a major expressway. Network monitors are usually located in full view of the administrator so that she can constantly monitor the health of the network with a quick glance.

Administrators can be alerted if a specific section of the network has lost connectivity due to a failed switch or network cable. The display will indicate that section of the network in a warning color (such as red) that can be noticed immediately by the monitoring administrator. Alerts can also be sent via e-mail, text message, and pager to notify the administrator of critical network errors.

Beyond general network troubleshooting issues, network monitors can be a valuable resource for alerting the administrator to network problems that might be due to security-related issues. For example, if one of the organization's Internet web servers is experiencing a DoS attack, the network monitor will indicate severe network congestion on the network between the primary router/firewall and the web server. In many cases, the network monitor can show the web server as completely unavailable, as it cannot respond to the diagnostic queries from the monitor due to the attack. Abnormal network activity can also be detected by the monitor on specific hosts on the network that could be infected with a worm, virus, or Trojan horse program that is trying to replicate itself to other systems on the network. This allows the administrator to pinpoint the source of the anomalous network activity quickly and take immediate steps to shut down the server or workstation and run diagnostics and anti-virus scans to try to clean the infected host.

Intrusion Detection and Prevention Systems

An *intrusion detection system* (IDS) can monitor the network and host systems for suspicious behavior that can indicate a malicious hacker is trying to break in to or damage the system. Because it proactively monitors the system, the detection system can immediately notify an administrator through an e-mail, instant message, or pager, of the intrusion. Some detection systems (also called *intrusion prevention systems* or *IPSs*) can repair the problem and either disconnect suspicious network connections or turn off network services that are being attacked.

A network-based IDS/IPS analyzes network traffic going in and out of your network and in between devices on the network. It can detect suspicious behavior that can indicate unauthorized access or network attacks against network hosts. A network-based IDS can examine network patterns, such as an unusual amount of requests destined for a particular server or service, like a web server. The headers of network packets can be analyzed to determine whether they were changed in transit or contain suspicious code that indicates malformed packets. Corrupted packets, malformed data, and specific code to exploit vulnerabilities can crash a web server or result in unauthorized access to its data.

A host-based IDS/IPS protects one specific host or device. By analyzing incoming and outgoing network activity, detecting suspicious system behavior, and logging user logins and access, it can spot possible attempts to compromise security.

When an intrusion is detected, the system works in either an active or a passive way to alert the administrator of the problem. A passive system will send warnings and alarms through log files, e-mail, instant message notification, and paging. An active system (an IPS) tries to fix the problem through shutting down certain services or preventing connections from a suspicious host.

When using IDSs, make sure your database of signatures is up to date. To protect against the latest threats, you must have the latest signatures for your IDS software. During monitoring, IDS systems can generate a lot of false positives, which is legitimate behavior that has been detected by the IDS as malicious. IDSs must be constantly fine-tuned to the specifics of your network to ensure that regular network behavior will not generate alarms. Typically, this is performed by adding your trusted system addresses to an "allowed" list of systems that can perform any type of network activity without triggering an IDS alarm.

Travel Assistance

IDSs and IPSs are discussed in more detail in Chapter 4.

Compare Monitoring Methodologies

Objective 8.02
CompTIA Security+
Objective 4.5

Monitoring applications such as IDS/IPS are used to monitor and analyze network traffic and system activity to detect security threats such as network-based attacks (DoS, ping sweeps, and port scans) and system issues (viruses, Trojan horse programs, and unauthorized access). When a security threat is detected, the system will log the event and notify the administrator, or it might even take immediate steps to mitigate the incoming threat. Different types of monitoring methodologies can be used to detect intrusions and malicious behavior. The following sections describe these monitoring methodologies and their benefits and weaknesses.

Exam Tip
Understand the differences between signature, behavioral, and rule-based monitoring methodologies, including their strengths and weaknesses.

Signature-based Systems

Signature-based monitoring systems are similar to anti-virus programs and contain predefined signature databases of known attacks that have appeared previously. Each type of attack can be recognized by its unique characteristics, and a signature is created for that type of attack. For example, signature-based systems can detect attempts to exploit a popular buffer-overflow vulnerability in which the network packets contain additional information intended to attack a web server. The signature (if available) can detect this exact information in the network packet and generate an alert to the administrator. These databases are continuously added to and maintained, and the monitoring program must be continually updated to ensure it has the latest signatures to identity the latest types of threats.

Signature-based systems are powerful and efficient because they rely on the collective knowledge of security vendors, who analyze and collect information on Internet security threats and trends and who update their databases quickly when new threats arise. However, signature-based systems are unable to detect very new attacks whose signatures are not yet available. In this respect, signature-based systems are often used in conjunction with behavior-based systems.

Behavior-based Systems

Behavior-based monitoring systems (also referred to as anomaly-based or statistical-based systems) do not use a predefined database of signatures but start from a baseline of normal system behavior and then monitor traffic based on these system performance profiles to recognize behavioral anomalies that exceed the thresholds of the normal baseline. The system becomes more effective over time as baseline activity is recorded, allowing the system to detect aberrations to these baselines more efficiently. For example, a sudden burst of incoming connections that is out of character for this system will trigger the monitoring system to generate alerts of the activity and in some cases to take proactive steps to mitigate the anomalous behavior (which could be a DoS attack) by blocking the attempted connections.

The primary benefit of behavior-based systems is that they easily and quickly adapt to the current environment and can detect new variants of attacks that a signature- or rule-based monitoring system might not recognize. The monitoring system is actively looking for behavior that is inconsistent with the current system baseline profile; therefore, even new types of attacks will be recognized immediately and action can be taken. New attacks are often referred to as *zero-day* attacks, and signature-based monitoring systems might not recognize them as threats.

Exam Tip

A zero-day threat is a type of attack that has rarely or never been encountered, such as an unknown virus or a malicious program that takes advantage of previously unknown weaknesses and vulnerabilities in a software program or operating system. As the attack is new, no existing defense or signature has been created to detect it.

The disadvantage of a behavior-based system is that it takes some time to build the baseline profile, and until the system learns enough information about the current system, it cannot accurately detect exceptions to that profile; efficiency is built over time. False positives can occur, in which normal behavior is flagged as anomalous, because the system has not had time to build its baseline profile to recognize it as normal behavior. Also, the anomalous behavior detected can generate an alert, but the behavior-based system can only warn the administrator that the thresholds have been exceeded; the administrator must determine whether an actual attack is taking place and what steps to take to mitigate it. The behavior-based system doesn't always recognize the type of specific attack, only its symptoms.

Rule-based Systems

Rule-based security monitoring takes more work to match the efficiency and effectiveness of other types of monitoring methods such as signature- and behavior-based systems. Similar to firewall access control rules, a rule-based security monitoring system relies on the administrator to create rules and determine the actions to take when those rules are transgressed. For example, a rule can be created that will block connections from an IP address if more than 100 connections are attempted from the same IP address within a certain time period, such as 30 seconds. This could indicate a DoS attack, and when the rule thresholds are exceeded, the offending connection will be blocked to contain the threat.

Rule-based systems require significant manual initial setup and constant maintenance to keep the rules current and up-to-date with the latest threats. These factors are handled automatically by a signature-based system, which already contains an up-to-date database of the latest security threats and compares these threats to the behaviors the system is experiencing. The system will then take action as appropriate.

Objective 8.03
CompTIA Security+
Objective 4.6

Execute Proper Logging Procedures

Each aspect of a computer system or device, whether it is the operating system, an application, or a system service, generates log files. Log files are used to track informational notifications, warnings, and critical errors within each of these critical system components and services. These logs contain information vital to the system's health and security, and they must be analyzed by the security administrator on a regular basis to monitor for behaviors and anomalies that are inconsistent with regular system operation.

The following sections describe some of the most important log files to examine on a system or network and cover how to analyze their contents properly to identify security threats.

System Logs

System logs record information such as warnings, notifications, and critical error messages on a variety of system processes, such as kernel processes, application processes, memory and disk warnings (such as low disk space), and just about any service running as part of the core operating system. Many types of services and applications have their own logs outside the primary system log, but most of the critical information about the primary operating system is stored in the system log.

Although security issues are more likely to be discovered using an external log analyzer and IDS/IPS that can automatically detect anomalies, smaller organizations without an expensive security infrastructure can rely on manual examination of the system logs for any security issues.

In many cases, the log files are not in a format that is easily readable by the administrator, and an external log viewer is required. Due to the great amount of information that is stored in the system log, administrators must be able to parse and search the log files for pertinent information. For example, if you know the name of a specific process for troubleshooting, you can load the log file into a log analyzer program and search the file using the name of the process, such as *smtp*, to display only log entries specific to the Simple Mail Transfer Protocol (SMTP) e-mail server process. From here you can analyze each mail server connection and response and more easily troubleshoot the issue you are experiencing.

It is also important that you configure the system logs to record and display only the information you need; many logging subsystems can be configured to show only warning or critical error messages, while not logging each and every minor occurrence on the system. This will make logs easier to search and analyze and decrease the amount of resources (especially disk space) required to process and store the logs. However, certain logs, such as access logs, should display all information for tracking all system logins and logouts.

Performance Logs

Performance monitors examine how much CPU, memory, disk input and output, and network bandwidth is being consumed at any particular time or over a specified time period. From this information, administrators can examine the *performance log* data for trends indicating anomalous behaviors. The log tracks performance trends against a baseline of normal behavior. Several system characteristics can be tracked (such as CPU, memory, disk usage, network usage, and so on) and compared to the baseline over time. Figure 8.2 shows an example of the Windows Performance Monitor screen that is monitoring CPU, memory, and disk usage.

Performance logs provide data spanning over minutes, hours, days, and weeks, and performance trends can be mapped based on this data to indicate any anomalous trends or spikes in behavior. For example, the administrator might notice from the performance log data that CPU usage spikes for a few hours starting at midnight until 2 A.M. However, this is the time that the server runs its daily backup routines, so the CPU spike appears in the performance report every day at this time. This is a baseline behavior for this system. CPU spikes that occur for large periods of time at other times of the day, especially during nonworking hours, could indicate that the server is under attack or that a Trojan horse program is sending out data at specific times.

Access Logs

Access logs provide information on user logins and logouts from specific servers and network resources. Access logs are a valuable audit tool, as they provide information on when a specific user has logged in or out of the network. If secu-

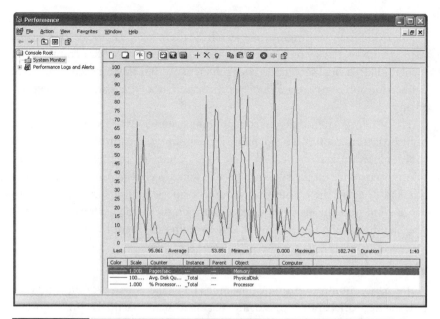

FIGURE 8.2   Windows Performance Monitor

rity anomalies occur during a certain time period, you might be able to narrow down what users were logged in at the time of the incident.

Access logs also record failed attempts at logging, and patterns of behavior can be detected by checking the access logs for numerous attempts at trying to access an account. For example, suppose the access logs show that someone has tried to access the administrator account over the network during nonworking hours. After several attempts at guessing the password, the account was locked out to prevent further brute-force attempts. The access logs will show the IP address from which the attempted logins originated, and the administrator can determine whose workstation is the source of the attempted unauthorized access.

A typical access log can display information similar to the following:

```
08:33 Login: admin 192.168.1.110 Success
08:52 Logout: admin 192.168.1.110
10:45 Login: admin 192.168.1.110 Success
11:50 Logout: admin 192.168.1.110
15:20 Login: admin 192.168.1.110 Success
17:10 Logout: admin 192.168.1.110
23:11 Login: admin 192.168.1.99 Failure
23:57 Login: admin 192.168.1.99 Failure
23:59 Login: admin 192.168.1.99 Failure
```

This indicates normal login and logout behavior for the admin user from his or her workstation during normal work hours. However, starting at 11:11 P.M., a user attempted to log in as the admin user from a different workstation on the network and failed three times. In most cases, if automatic account lockout is enabled, the admin user account can be locked out after the third unsuccessful attempt, depending on the configuration.

DNS Logs

DNS logs typically contain information on DNS queries to the server, including the source IP address of the request and the domain name of the destination IP address that the DNS server will return in the response. DNS logs can also contain error messages and notifications for regular processes such as failed zone transfers that occur when the DNS server cannot update zone information to another system.

This information can help administrators track the source of possible DNS poisoning attempts, in which the DNS tables of IP addresses and hostnames are compromised by replacing the IP address of a host with another IP address that resolves to an attacker's system. If authentication measures are in place to protect against DNS poisoning attacks, you might see a number of failed attempts to update the zone information on your DNS server in the DNS logs. These logs can help you track down the IP address of the attacker's server, which will be indicated in the DNS queries.

In a DoS attack, DNS logs will indicate that a specific host is sending large amounts of queries to your DNS server. If you determine the IP address source of the queries, you can take steps to block that address from connecting to your DNS server.

Travel Advisory

Typically, DNS logging is enabled only while you're trying to troubleshoot an issue. If the DNS server is logging every single query from clients, the massive amounts of DNS lookup queries that can occur in a large organization can cause performance issues.

Firewall Logs

As all inbound and outbound network traffic passes through the network firewall, the firewall logs are a critical resource when examining network trends and analyzing for anomalous behavior. A firewall is the first line of defense at the network's perimeter, and network attacks are often first detected and discovered in the *firewall logs*. For example, when new worms infect Internet servers and then try to spread to other Internet servers, the connections have to pass through an organization's firewall. The network administrator monitors the firewall and is first to notice and report these worm outbreaks. The administrator will notice hundreds of denied connections to servers on the network, as the firewall is blocking these connections from entering. DoS attacks are also detected in a similar manner.

The most common types of anomalous network behaviors that can be detected at the firewall are port scans. Hackers often use port scanning software to scan a specific network address to probe for open ports, or to perform a scan of all IP addresses on the network to see which systems respond. Hackers can then use this information to target systems they know are alive on the network and listening for requests on specific ports. Firewalls (if they are implemented properly) will protect the details of the internal network and will not allow port and IP scanners to glean any information from the network.

Firewall logs can be scanned for patterns of port scanning behaviors, such as a single network address trying to connect to consecutive port numbers on the same system from port 1 to 65525, or an IP range scan in which a single network address is scanning banks of IP addresses such as 192.168.1.1 to 192.168.255.255. For example, the following log trace shows behavior of a port scan from a specific IP address:

```
Source: 172.16.1.12 Destination: 192.168.1.128 TCP Port 21
Source: 172.16.1.12 Destination: 192.168.1.128 TCP Port 22
Source: 172.16.1.12 Destination: 192.168.1.128 TCP Port 23
Source: 172.16.1.12 Destination: 192.168.1.128 TCP Port 24
Source: 172.16.1.12 Destination: 192.168.1.128 TCP Port 25
Source: 172.16.1.12 Destination: 192.168.1.128 TCP Port 26
Source: 172.16.1.12 Destination: 192.168.1.128 TCP Port 27
```

The port scan will continue until it reaches port 65525 in an effort to find open ports that can be accessed and potentially attacked.

Exam Tip

Recognize different types of attacks based on the details of firewall log messages.

Firewall logs (including personal software firewalls) are also an important tool for exposing Trojan horses or other types of malicious software installed on client computers that are trying to communicate through the firewall back to the hacker's computer. The administrator can see the source and destination IP address of the request and identify which computers might be infected on the network, and then take immediate steps to clean the Trojan horse program.

Anti-virus Logs

Anti-virus logs are generated by anti-virus software running on server and client systems. They contain important information on the number and types of viruses that have been detected, quarantined, or cleaned on the system, and they also provide diagnostic information on the anti-virus signature updates. In many cases, client logs can be coalesced on the central anti-virus server for more efficient log monitoring and auditing.

Administrators can analyze anti-virus logs to gather information about computers on the network that have been attacked by viruses, computer files that have been quarantined or cleaned, or, more important, computer files that are infected and cannot be cleaned. This information can alert the administrator to clients on the network that are continually infected or attacked, which can indicate that the user's anti-virus program is not working properly or the user is involved in risky Internet behaviors, such as unauthorized downloading of files or receiving viruses via instant message chats.

Anti-virus programs use signature files, databases of patterns of known viruses that are continually updated and downloaded by anti-virus programs at scheduled intervals. If this update process breaks down, and the anti-virus program cannot communicate with the anti-virus signature file server (after being blocked by a firewall of if the signature server is unavailable, for example) your system will not be protected from the newest virus threats. By regularly analyzing the anti-virus logs, administrators can ensure that they are regularly updating their signature files, and that no communications issues exist between the anti-virus program and the signature update server. If the update fails at each scheduled interval, the administrator can troubleshoot the network path to determine what is blocking the updates from being downloaded.

Security Logging Applications

Because a specific system or network device can contain log files for a variety of operating system processes, system services, and application programs, several different log files might need to be analyzed by the security administrator. Many of these logs are extremely large and can generate megabytes of data within a single day of operation. It would be very difficult for the administrator to be proactive and manually monitor and analyze each of these logs every single day.

For Unix-based systems, the *syslog* (system logger) functionality allows all systems on a network to forward their logs to a central syslog server. The syslog server stores these log entries in one large log file. The administrator can perform simple text and pattern searches on this log to pinpoint specific information required from all the server logs on the network.

Windows-based systems rely on the Event Viewer (shown in Figure 8.3), an application that provides a centralized location to view application, system, and security logs. Log entries are typically divided into different categories such as Error, Warning, and Information that allow the administrator to sort and scan the logs for critical errors and warnings, while ignoring more informational log entries. Security logs typically contain entries indicating Success or Failure, such as when a user accesses a specific file or directory.

Several more advanced types of third-party security logging applications can coalesce information from several log sources into one database that can be easily searched and analyzed using the logging application, and they can generate reports on log entries for specific services or overall trends in the logging data. Some logging applications can even actively scan the log files and generate notifications and alerts of specific critical errors to the administrator. This allows the administrator to fine-tune the results of the logs to view and report only on serious or critical errors. Informational data, such as general notifications or low-level warnings, are usually ignored.

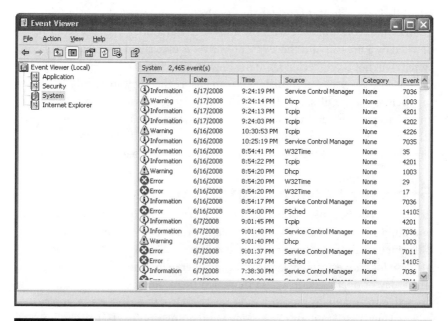

FIGURE 8.3   Windows Event Viewer

Conduct System Audits

Objective 8.04

CompTIA Security+
Objective 4.7

No matter how many security procedures you have in place, an active community of hackers and crackers will invent new ways to circumvent them. Fully effective security policies and procedures must be audited on a regular basis to test and assess their efficiency. *Auditing* also ensures that both users and network administrators are conforming to security procedures. Auditing can be general in nature, where logs of the most common activities are analyzed for any suspicious behavior. More advanced and detailed techniques can involve proactive monitoring of as many systems as possible, even down to the desktop level. Auditing is, ultimately, a way of ensuring accountability and preventing small problems from escalating into large security breaches.

System Baselines

The goal of any type of auditing is to create a baseline of current activity and then measure future activity against this baseline for changes from preexisting thresholds. Creating a security baseline involves analyzing user activity, such as physical entrance and exit from the facility, recording logins to systems, and recording file and application access. The amount of information that can be collected is daunting, and the security administrator must balance the time needed to analyze all this activity versus the security risk levels they represent.

Information recorded from user activity can be organized into several areas.

System-Level Events

System-level events include events specific to a certain system or a network of systems, including the following:

- **Login and logout times**   The logs of users that entered and exited a system can be helpful in determining which user was accessing the system at the time a security event occurred.
- **Login attempts**   If a user seems to be trying to access an account too many times with the wrong password, this could indicate someone is trying to hack into that account. Many network operating systems can limit the logon attempts by disabling the account if too many unsuccessful logins occur.
- **Password and account changes**   By analyzing account and password changes, you can monitor whether a user has suddenly gained privileges he or she never had before and that weren't entered by the network administrator.

User-Level Events

User-level events can be recorded to monitor activities performed by users. Like application-level events, a large list of activities can be recorded. The following are the most common user-level events that should be recorded:

- **Use of resources**   The administrator can record what resources the user accessed during a login session—files, servers, printers, and any other network services. This will help indicate whether users are accessing information to which they should not have access or information that is inappropriate to their job and security level.

- **Command and keystrokes**   At a granular level, the keystrokes and commands used by a user while logged in can be recorded and analyzed for unusual activity. This sort of logging can be the most time-consuming to analyze.

- **Security violations**   Each time a user attempts to access a resource for which he doesn't have the necessary privileges, an entry can be written to a log. Too many attempts at inappropriately accessing resources can indicate attempted unauthorized activity.

Application-Level Events

These events happen at the *application level*—a user is using an application to view or manipulate data. The amount of information that can be collected with this type of monitoring can be overwhelming, so only certain key elements should be recorded:

- **File access**   The application logs can record which files were accessed and whether they were modified to monitor what time a certain file was modified from its original form. Monitoring critical system files for this type of activity is especially important.

- **Error messages**   By recording error messages that occur during the use of an application, you can analyze whether the user is intentionally trying to use the application in a manner for which it wasn't designed.

- **Security violations**   Any attempts at using an application to compromise access permissions should be recorded. Repeated security violations of the same resource can indicate improper behaviors.

Exam Tip	
Know what types of networking and system activities beyond everyday use can be considered suspicious.	

User Access Rights Review

Beyond monitoring and auditing system log information for security breaches and anomalous behavior, security administrators must also regularly review the access rights and permissions granted to users on the network. Evidence of a user having inappropriate access privileges can be gleaned from an audit log that identifies specific files being accessed by a user who should not be granted access. Realistically, many users can have access permissions they don't require. Analyzing user security rights and policies on a regular basis is critical to ensuring that existing security holes in user policies can be repaired before a user accesses or damages data to which he or she should not be allowed access.

Group policies are often the most common source of users gaining inappropriate rights and privileges. Network administrators who lack knowledge about how to use these policies can assign inappropriate access rights to several users in a group. A specific user typically has access only to the files in his or her own private home directory. When group permissions and policies are applied to that user, he or she gains the additional rights allocated to the group. A user can belong to several groups, each with its own set of security rights. For example, suppose a user was transferred from one department to another (such as from sales to marketing). When analyzing the user's security rights, an administrator realizes that she still has access to the sales department's files, in addition to those granted to the marketing department. The administrator can remove the user from the sales group to remove her access rights to sales directories and files.

Group policy management software systems can aid the administrator in managing an organization's group policies to ensure that policies such as group policies, domain policies, and individual user policies do not give a user inappropriate access rights. Group policy management software can accurately determine the final policy applied to a user, which helps the administrator determine what access rights a user has when all policies are applied.

Reviewing Audit Information

Simply recording and collecting information isn't helpful unless the information is reviewed and analyzed. The auditing information can be viewed manually or forwarded by an automatic system—either way, you must construct meaningful information from the data before it can be useful.

Reviewing all this information can be a daunting task, but many tools and reporting applications can translate the raw data into something coherent and useful. To maximize the efficiency of your reporting procedure, only data perceived as beyond normal operating thresholds should be included. For example, unless a specific incident occurs, you'd have no need to analyze logs of which users logged in and out at certain times. Instead, you might choose to see only those users who logged in after normal working hours to look for suspicious activity.

Auditing the Administrator

In most corporate environments, the network administrator analyzes and audits network activity. In high-security environments, an independent auditor can be asked to analyze the log information. The network administrators have full access to all systems in the company, and their activities must also be recorded and monitored, along with that of regular users. High-level functions, such as user account creation, modification, and deletion, as well as changes to system configuration files, should be monitored and analyzed on a regular basis by a security professional.

Storage and Retention Policies

Security administrators have the task of regularly examining audit data such as system and network intrusion logs. In most cases, this information is automatically collected and saved to a specific location to be retrieved and analyzed by the administrator. Data storage and retention policies that are applied to typical company information such as user data files and e-mail messages should also apply to auditing information. This policy ensures that the audit information can be stored and retained for a sufficient amount of time so that it can be analyzed properly and preserved as legally required for evidence in investigations of security incidents.

CHECKPOINT

✔ **Objective 8.01: Monitor and Detect Security-Related Anomalies** Anomalous behaviors can be detected by performing a baseline of normal system operation and then analyzing data that goes beyond the thresholds of the baseline. Baseline data should be collected for an entire week to provide an accurate view of your system performance at different times and days of the week. Use system, network, and performance monitors for collecting and monitoring data, and intrusion detection and prevention systems to provide more specialized and proactive monitoring solutions.

✔**Objective 8.02: Compare Monitoring Methodologies** Signature-based monitoring systems contain predefined signature databases of known attacks, but they are unable to detect the newest attacks that do not yet have signatures available. Behavior-based monitoring systems start from a baseline of normal system behavior and then learn from these system performance profiles to recognize behavioral anomalies that pass the thresholds of the normal system baseline. The disadvantage of behavior-based systems is that it takes some time to build the baseline profile, and they can initially cause false positives. Rule-based security monitoring systems rely on the administrator to create rules and define the actions to take when those rules are transgressed. Rule-based systems require a lot of manual initial setup and constant maintenance to keep the rules current and up-to-date with the latest threats.

✔**Objective 8.03: Execute Proper Logging Procedures** Configure your logs to display only the information you require to reduce resource usage and allow more efficient log searching. Performance logs can indicate security issues via behaviors that stray from the system baseline. Access logs provide an audit trail of who has logged in and out of the system. Firewall logs can track all network packets coming in and out of the network and often provide the first indication of attacks. Check anti-virus logs for problem computers that are infected more often than others, and ensure the anti-virus signature database is updating properly at its scheduled intervals.

✔**Objective 8.4: Conduct System Audits** Security logs should be audited for suspicious behaviors. Regular review allows for proactive monitoring of network and system utilities. Create a baseline of normal activity, and then measure all future activity against the baseline. System, user, and application events should be recorded for auditing.

REVIEW QUESTIONS

1. Which of the following collected data is considered a good indication of a system performance baseline?

   A. Network bandwidth usage per hour for a 24-hour period

   B. CPU processing trends measured during typical working hours

   C. CPU, memory, and network usage data collected for an entire week

   D. Concurrent connections during the busiest server times

2. A signature-based monitoring system has failed to detect an attack on one of your web servers. Which of the following is the most likely cause?

   A. Misconfigured firewall

   B. Signature-based systems scan only outbound traffic

   C. The administrator did not properly implement an access rule for that attack

   D. This new attack has no signature available yet

3. Which of the following types of scanning methodologies checks for anomalous behavior on a system that differs from its routine baseline performance?

   A. Behavioral-based

   B. Rule-based

   C. Signature-based

   D. Role-based

4. Which of the following tools would be able to capture and view network packets to look for anomalous network activity from a specific system?

   A. Intrusion detection system

   B. Performance monitor

   C. Access logs

   D. Protocol analyzer

5. Which of the following logging procedures would reduce the amount of time examining and analyzing several different logs on a system?

   A. Disabling logging

   B. Logging only minor errors

   C. Logging only warning and critical errors

   D. Enabling verbose logging of all errors

6. Which of the following can indicate a security issue when scanning a system performance log?

   A. Disk space free at 70 percent

   B. Memory usage at 45 percent

   C. CPU usage at 99 percent

   D. Network bandwidth usage at 50 percent

7. During routine examination of the firewall logs, the administrator notices that a specific host is attempting to connect to the same internal IP address starting at port 1 and continuing to port 65525. Of which of the following could this be evidence?

    A. Ping sweep of a server on your network

    B. Port scanning of a server on your network

    C. Normal behavior for network diagnostics

    D. DNS requests for name resolution

8. Which log would an administrator check to find out which users were logged in during the time a confidential file was accessed without proper authorization?

    A. Access log

    B. DNS log

    C. Performance log

    D. Firewall log

9. After a security audit, which of the following items would *not* be considered anomalous behavior?

    A. Several unsuccessful attempts to log in as the administrator

    B. A ping sweep on the firewall for the IP range 10.10.0.0 to 10.10.255.255

    C. Error messages in the system's log that indicate excessive disk usage

    D. A member of the sales group accessing the sales shared file directory

10. During an audit of a server security log, which of the following entries would be considered a possible security threat?

    A. Five failed login attempts for user jsmith

    B. Two successful logins with the administrator account

    C. A 500K print job sent to a printer

    D. Three new files saved in the accounting folder by user finance

REVIEW ANSWERS

1. **C** To establish a performance baseline, you must measure your system activity for 24 hours per day for at least 7 continuous days. This ensures that you have data for an entire week's worth of activity, including working hours, nonworking hours, and weekends. Simply sampling performance data for a few hours during the day will not provide a sufficient indication of performance trends.

2. **D** Signature-based systems are powerful and efficient because they rely on the collective knowledge of security vendors who analyze and collect information on Internet security threats and trends and are able to update their databases very quickly when new threats arise. However, they are unable to detect very new attacks that do not have signatures available yet.

3. **A**   Behavior-based monitoring systems start from a baseline of normal system behavior and then learn from these system performance profiles to recognize behavioral anomalies that pass the thresholds of the normal baseline of the system.

4. **D**   A protocol analyzer is a device or software program that can intercept, log, and analyze network traffic. Each individual network packet can be analyzed to decode its header information (packet origin and destination) and content.

5. **C**   To reduce that amount of minor and informational types of messages in the logs, administrators should configure their logging systems to log only warning and critical error messages. This reduces the amount of resources required to store logs and reduces the time required to analyze them, as only the most important data is logged.

6. **C**   A system running with its CPU usage at 99 percent for a long period of time can indicate that some anomalous process (such as a virus, Trojan horse, or worm) is causing CPU processing to spike beyond the normal system operating baseline.

7. **B**   A host system that is scanning a server for any open ports using the entire port range indicates that a port scanning program is being used to determine which services are running and which ports are open and available. A malicious hacker might be trying to find vulnerabilities and attack your system.

8. **A**   Access logs provide valuable audit tools because they provide information about when a specific user has logged in our out of the network. If security anomalies occur during a certain time period, you might be able to narrow down which users were logged in at the time of the incident.

9. **D**   A member of a group accessing the shared files for the group to which she belongs does not constitute anomalous behavior; however, ping sweeps against the firewall, disk error messages in the system's log, and several attempts to access the administrator account are all security issues that should be carefully examined.

10. **A**   A large amount of unsuccessful logins for one user is unusual. Either the user has forgotten his password, or someone is trying to guess the password to hack into the account.

Cryptography

Cryptography and Encryption Overview

CHAPTER 9

	NEWBIE	SOME EXPERIENCE	EXPERT
ETA	3 hours	2 hours	1 hour

Cryptography is the conversion of communicated information into secret code that keeps the information private. The protection of sensitive communications has been the basis of cryptography throughout history. Modern cryptography performs essentially the same function, but with some added functionality to accommodate today's computerized world, such as *authentication* and *data integrity.*

The central function of cryptography is *encryption,* the transformation of data into some unreadable form. Encryption ensures privacy by keeping the information hidden from those for whom the information is not intended. *Decryption,* the opposite of encryption, transforms encrypted data back into some intelligible form. Even though someone might be able to read the encrypted data, it won't make any sense until it's been properly decrypted.

The encryption and decryption process involves taking data in *plain text,* which is readable and understandable text, and manipulating its form to create *ciphertext.* Once data has been transformed into *ciphertext,* the plain text becomes inaccessible until it's decrypted. The entire process is illustrated in Figure 9.1.

This process enables the transmission of confidential information over an insecure communications path, greatly decreasing the possibility of the data being compromised. In a file storage system, data is protected by *authentication* and *access controls* that prevent unauthorized users from accessing some files. When this data is transmitted over a network, these controls no longer exist, and the data becomes vulnerable to interception. If the information or the communications channel itself is encrypted, the chance of someone intercepting and deciphering the data is extremely slim.

This chapter details the subjects of cryptography and encryption, including mathematical algorithms, public key infrastructure systems, and encryption standards and protocols.

Objective 9.01
CompTIA Security+
Objective 5.1

Explain General Cryptography Concepts

Today's cryptography involves more than hiding secrets with encryption systems. With the world using more technological means to perform business and legal functions, such as purchasing items from a web-based store, con-

| Plaintext | Encryption | Ciphertext | Decryption | Plaintext |

FIGURE 9.1 Encryption and decryption

ducting online banking, and digitally signing documents, the need for strong and secure encryptions systems to protect these transactions has become vital.

Information Assurance

Information assurance is a method of protecting information and information systems by providing confidentiality, integrity, authentication, and nonrepudiation.

Confidentiality

Confidentiality is the concept of ensuring that data is not made available or disclosed to unauthorized people. Processes such as encryption must be used on the data, network infrastructure, and communication channels to protect against data interception and disclosure.

Integrity

Data *integrity* is the protection of information from damage or deliberate manipulation. Integrity is extremely critical for any kind of business or electronic commerce. Data integrity guarantees that when information has been stored or communicated, it hasn't been changed or manipulated in transit.

Authentication

Authentication is the concept of uniquely identifying individuals to provide assurance of an individual user's identity. It is the act of ensuring that a person is who he claims to be. Typical physical and logical authentication methods include the use of identification cards, door locks and keys, and network logins and passwords. For modern e-commerce and legal applications, this type of authentication needs to be tightly controlled. Encrypted digital certificates are used to identify users electronically on a network. Encrypted forms of authentication can also be used in smart cards, which are a more secure medium than a typical ID badge.

Nonrepudiation

Nonrepudiation is the term used to describe the inability of a person to deny or repudiate the origin of a signature or document, or the receipt of a message or document. For example, a user could legally prove that an electronic document or transaction did not originate with her. The user could have digitally signed a contract that was transmitted through e-mail, but if the data or transmission wasn't considered secure because of the lack of encryption, the user might legally claim it was tampered with and call its integrity into question. By implementing nonrepudiation processes, a cryptographic system can be considered secure for business and legal transactions.

> **Exam Tip**
>
> A specific type of encryption scheme, algorithm, or protocol could cover only certain parts of the information assurance objectives. For example, certain encryption protocols concern themselves only with authentication, while others cover all the objectives of confidentiality, integrity, authentication, and nonrepudiation.

Algorithms

A system that provides encryption and decryption services is called a *cryptosystem*. The cryptosystem uses a mathematical encryption *algorithm*, or *cipher*, to turn data into ciphertext. An algorithm is a complex mathematical formula that dictates how the encryption and decryption process takes place. Because these mathematical algorithms are usually publicly known, the cryptosystem is strengthened with the addition of a secret key, as shown in Figure 9.2.

A *key* is like a password that's combined with an algorithm to create the ciphertext. The encryption can't be deciphered unless the key is used to decrypt it. No one can simply unravel the algorithm to decode the message, because the key is also needed. Depending on the encryption mechanism used, the key might be used for both encryption and decryption, while for other systems, different keys might be used for encryption and decryption.

The strength of the key depends on the algorithm's *keyspace,* which is a specific range of values—usually measured in bits—that's created by the algorithm to contain keys. A key is made up of random values within the keyspace range. A larger keyspace containing more bits means more available values exist to use for different keys, effectively increasing the difficulty for someone to compromise the system. The smaller the keyspace, the greater the chance someone can decipher the key value.

The strength of the cryptosystem lies in the strength and effectiveness of its algorithm and the size of the keyspace. Most attackers use some method of

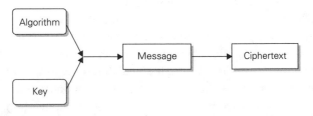

FIGURE 9.2   Cryptosystem using algorithms

brute-force attack to figure out the cryptosystem by processing large numbers of values to subvert the algorithm. No matter how strong the algorithm, it will be rendered useless if someone obtains the key, so the key must be protected, and one of the methods is by encryption protocols such as Secure Sockets Layer (SSL) for secure key delivery.

> ## Travel Advisory
>
> Most attacks on encryption center on the interception of keys rather than on attempts to subvert the algorithm, which requires large processing resources.

Two main types of cipher encryption can be used:

- **Substitution**   In its most simplified form, a *substitution* cipher takes plain text and substitutes the original characters in the data with other characters. For example, the letters *ABC* can be substituted by reversing the alphabet, so the cipher form will read *ZYX*. Modern substitution encryption ciphers are much more complex, performing many types of substitutions with more than one alphabet.

- **Transposition**   In a *transposition* cipher, the characters are rearranged through mathematical permutations. When used with difficult mathematical formulas, these ciphers can be extremely complex.

Most modern ciphers use a combination of long sequences of substitution and transposition schemes. The data is filtered through an algorithm that performs these complex substitution and transposition operations to arrive at the ciphertext.

Two main types of encryption use key values and complex algorithms: *symmetric* and *asymmetric*.

Symmetric Keys

In a *symmetric* encryption scheme, both parties use the same key for encryption and decryption purposes. Each user must possess the same key to send encrypted messages to each other, as shown in Figure 9.3. The sender uses the key to encrypt the message and then transmits it to the receiver. The receiver, who is in possession of the same key, uses it to decrypt the message.

The security of this encryption model relies on the end users to protect the secret key properly. If an unauthorized user were able to intercept the key, he or she would be able to read any encrypted messages sent by other users by

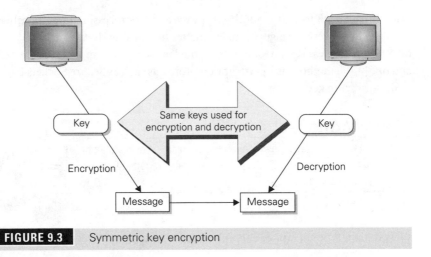

FIGURE 9.3 Symmetric key encryption

decrypting the message with the key intercepted. It's extremely important that a user protect the key itself as well as any communications in which he transmits the key to another user.

One of the main disadvantages of symmetric encryption schemes is that it doesn't scale well with large numbers of users. A user needs different keys depending on the person with which he is communicating—with a large number of users, the number of keys that need to be distributed and tracked can become enormous. Another disadvantage is that the system needs a secure mechanism to deliver keys to the end users. Symmetric systems can offer confidentiality only through encryption; they offer little in the way of authentication and nonrepudiation.

Symmetric systems, however, can be difficult to crack if a large key size is used. A symmetric system is also much faster than asymmetric encryption because the underlying algorithms are more simple and efficient.

Two main types of symmetric encryption can be used:

- **Stream cipher** A *stream cipher* encrypts data 1 bit at a time, as opposed to a block cipher, which works on blocks of text. Stream ciphers, by design, are fast compared to block ciphers. The encryption of any plain-text data with a block cipher results in the same ciphertext when the same key is used. With stream ciphers, each bit of the plain-text stream is transformed into a different ciphertext bit. A stream cipher generates a key stream that's combined with the plain-text data to provide encryption.

- **Block cipher**   A *block cipher* encrypts entire blocks of data, rather than smaller bits of data as with stream cipher methods. A block cipher transforms a particular block of plain-text data into a block of ciphertext data of the same length. For many block ciphers, the block size is 64 bits.

Popular symmetric algorithms include Advanced Encryption Standard (AES), Data Encryption Standard (DES), Blowfish, International Data Encryption Algorithm (IDEA), and RC5.

Asymmetric Keys

In an *asymmetric* encryption scheme, everyone uses different, but mathematically related, keys for encryption and decryption purposes, as shown in Figure 9.4.

Even though the keys are mathematically similar, they can't be derived from each other. An asymmetric scheme is the basis for the *public key* system. Two keys are created for encryption and decryption purposes: One key is the public key, which is known to all users, while the private key remains secret and is given to the user to keep private. To use this system, a user will encrypt a message or file with the intended receiver's public key. To decrypt this message, the receiver will use a private key that only he possesses. No one else can decrypt the message without this private key. Public keys can be passed directly among users or found in directories of public keys.

The advantage of this system over symmetric schemes is that it offers a level of authentication. By decrypting a message with a sender's public key, the re-

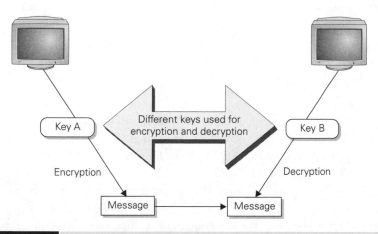

FIGURE 9.4   Asymmetric key encryption

ceiver knows this message came from the sender. The sender is authenticated because, to be decrypted with a public key, the private key had to be used to perform the initial encryption.

Exam Tip

Recognize how the different combinations of key-pair encryption methods can provide different kinds of functionality such as authentication, confidentiality, and integrity.

The main disadvantage of asymmetric encryption is that it can be much slower than symmetric schemes. Unlike symmetric systems, however, asymmetric schemes offer confidentiality, authentication, and also nonrepudiation, which prevents a user from repudiating a signed communication. Asymmetric schemes also provide more manageable and efficient ways for dealing with key distribution.

Popular asymmetric algorithms and applications include RSA (named for creators Rivest, Shamir, and Adleman), Elliptical Curve, Digital Signature Standard (DSS), and Diffie-Hellman.

Exam Tip

In a symmetric encryption scheme, both parties use the same key for encryption and decryption purposes. In an asymmetric encryption scheme, everyone uses a different but mathematically-related key for encryption and decryption.

Steganography

Steganography does not involve algorithms to encrypt data; it is a method of hiding data in another type of media that effectively conceals the existence of the data. This is typically performed by hiding messages in graphics images such as bitmap (BMP) files or other types of media files such as WAV digital music files. Many companies hide a watermark (a hidden image) within a company image to be able to prove it is owned by the company in the event it is being used by another company or person. Unused sectors of a hard disk can also be used in steganography. These types of files contain insignificant data bits that can be replaced by the data to be hidden without affecting the original file enough to be detected.

Public Key Cryptography and Key Management

Traditional cryptography methods based on symmetric key cryptography describe the use of the same secret key between the sender and the receiver of a transmission. The key the sender uses to encrypt the message is the same key used to decrypt the message. The disadvantage of this type of scheme is that it can be difficult to transmit this secret key securely from one user to another. If an unauthorized user intercepts the key en route, she can use that key to decrypt, read, forge, and modify all messages encrypted or authenticated. Key management issues in such systems are difficult, especially in systems that serve large numbers of users.

Public key cryptography was introduced in 1976 by Diffie and Hellman, whose public key protocol was created to solve the key management problem. In public key cryptography, each user receives two keys: the public key and the private key. The private key is kept secret, and the public key can be published for any user to see or use. The problem faced using symmetric keys is solved because no need exists to share a secret key. All transmissions involve only the public keys; no private key is ever transmitted or shared. The sender encrypts the message with the receiver's public key. The receiver then decrypts the message with his own private key, as shown in Figure 9.5. The security mechanism is safe as long as the private keys aren't compromised.

Public Key Infrastructure (PKI) is a standard infrastructure consisting of a framework of procedures, standards, and protocols, based on public key cryptography. PKI is a hybrid of asymmetric and symmetric key algorithms and provides the full range of the information assurance objectives for confidentiality,

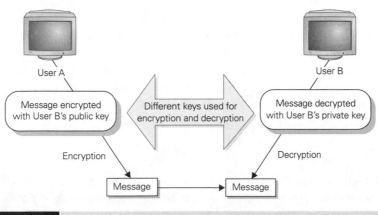

FIGURE 9.5   Public key cryptography

integrity, authentication, and nonrepudiation. The asymmetric keys are used for authentication, and, after this is successfully accomplished, one or more symmetric keys are generated and exchanged using the asymmetric encryption. A message is encrypted using a symmetric algorithm, and that key is then encrypted asymmetrically using the recipient's public key. The entire message (symmetrically encrypted body and asymmetrically encrypted key) is sent together to the recipient. The message might also be digitally signed through the use of digital certificates.

Exam Tip

Public key cryptography uses a hybrid of symmetric and asymmetric encryption systems. A message is encrypted using a symmetric algorithm, and that key is then encrypted asymmetrically using the recipient's public key. The entire message (symmetrically encrypted body and asymmetrically encrypted key) is sent together to the recipient.

Digital Certificates

A *digital certificate* is a credential required by PKI systems that can securely identify an individual, as well as create an association between the individual's authenticated identity and public keys. A trusted third party, called a *certificate authority* (CA), is used to sign and issue certificates. The CA is responsible for verifying the identity of a key owner and binding the owner to a public key. This enables users who have never met to exchange encrypted communications, because the authentication is performed by the third-party CA. Each certificate contains a unique serial number, identity, and public key information of the user, and the validity dates for the life of the certificate.

Certificate Authorities

A CA is an organization or entity that issues and manages digital certificates. The CA is responsible for authenticating and identifying users who participate in the PKI. This service doesn't necessarily involve a third party; it can be internal to an organization. A CA server can be set up to act as the manager of certificates and the user's public keys. Third-party CAs are special organizations dedicated to certificate management, such as VeriSign and Entrust.

Exam Tip

A certificate authority (CA) is an organization or entity that issues and manages digital certificates. The CA is responsible for authenticating and identifying users who participate in the Public Key Infrastructure (PKI).

Some of the actual authentication and identification services for certificates are managed by other organizations called *registration authorities* (RAs). These organizations offload some of the work from CAs by confirming the identities of users, issuing key pairs, and initiating the certificate process with a CA on behalf of the user. The RA acts as a middleman between the user and the CA, and doesn't issue certificates on its own.

To verify a user's identity, the CA and RA usually require some form of identification, such as a driver's license, Social Security number, address, and phone number. Once the identification is established, the CA generates a public and private key for the user. A certificate is then generated with the identification and key information embedded within it. Once the user is registered and receives a certificate, she can begin using the certificate to send encrypted messages. When the receiver gets the message, her software can verify the certificate to make sure that the message is from the stated sender. Certificates can also be revoked if the certificate's original subscriber information has changed, has been compromised, or is no longer valid.

Exam Tip
A certificate contains the authenticated identification of a user and his or her public key information.

Trust Models

Trust models define how users trust other users, companies, CAs, and RAs within the PKI. These models provide a chain of trust from a user's public key through the root key of a CA. The validated chain then implies authenticity of all the certificates. Following are the most common trust models used in PKI.

Web of Trust

The *web of trust* is a simplistic trust model that relies on each user creating and signing his own certificate, as shown in Figure 9.6. This is the basis for encryption applications, such as Pretty Good Privacy (PGP), in which no central authority exists. With this model, each user is responsible for authentication and trust, and anyone can sign someone's public key. When User A signs User B's key, User A is introducing User B's key to anyone who trusts User A. Each user is considered a trusted introducer in the model.

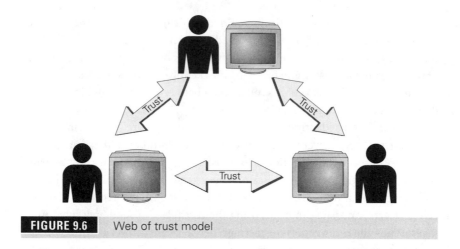

FIGURE 9.6   Web of trust model

Third-party (Single Authority) Trust

A *third-party central CA* signs a given key and authenticates the owner of the key. Trusting that CA means, by association, that you trust all keys issued by that CA, as shown in Figure 9.7. Each user authenticates the other through the exchange of certificates. The users know the CA has performed all the necessary identification of the owner of the certificate and therefore can trust the owner of the message.

Hierarchical Model

The *hierarchical model* is an extension of the third-party model, where root CAs issue certificates to other lower-level CAs and RAs, as shown in Figure 9.8. Each user's most trusted key is the root CA's public key. The trust inheritance can be

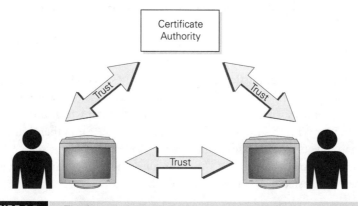

FIGURE 9.7   Third-party single authority trust model

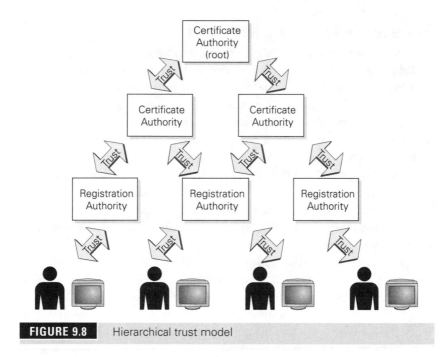

FIGURE 9.8 Hierarchical trust model

followed from the certificate back to the root CA. This model allows enforcement of policies and standards throughout the infrastructure, producing a higher level of overall assurance than other trust models. A root certificate is trusted by software applications on behalf of the user. For example, web browsers will create trusted connections to secure servers using SSL with root certificates that indicate to the user that this web site and its certificate are trusted.

Digital Signatures

A *digital signature* is an encrypted hash value used to ensure the identity and integrity of a message. The signature can be attached to a message to uniquely identify the sender. Like a written signature, the digital signature guarantees the individual sending the message is who he claims to be. The sender runs a hash function on his message, takes the resulting hash value, encrypts it with his private key, and sends it along with the message. When the receiver gets the signed message, he first decrypts the encrypted hash with the corresponding public key (verifies the sender) and then performs his own hashing function on the message. The calculated hash is then compared against the unencrypted hash, and if they are the same, the receiver knows the message hasn't been altered in transmission.

Trusted Platform Module

A *trusted platform module* (TPM) is a special hardware chip that is typically installed within a computer system or device, such as on the system motherboard of a PC or laptop. This module provides authentication by storing security mechanisms such as passwords, certificates, and encryption keys that are specific to that system hardware. The chip itself contains a built-in RSA key that is used for encryption and authentication. In the past, hardware-based passwords on PCs and laptops were typically stored in clear text and therefore vulnerable to unauthorized access. With the advent of TPM, any system passwords are now stored and encrypted on the TPM chip. The TPM provides greater security benefits over software-based solutions as it runs in a closed hardware subsystem that mitigates external threats. TPM-based systems are compatible with most popular operating systems.

Laptops are especially prone to physical theft because of their portability, and if the hard drive contents are not encrypted, an unauthorized user can easily access these files. TPM allows contents of the hard drive to be encrypted; the user simply generates a key that is stored on the TPM chip. When the user needs to access the hard drive, she uses operating system software, such as Windows, to send the key to the TPM chip for authentication. This prevents an unauthorized user from accessing the hard drive contents of equipment.

Whole Disk Encryption

In *whole disk encryption*, the entire contents of a computer system's hard drive are encrypted, typically by encrypting the disk volume that contains all the operating system data; this does not include the booting instructions located in a boot volume or Master Boot Record (MBR). By encrypting all files, including temporary and swap space files, no unauthorized user can access this data if the system is compromised or stolen.

Many operating systems come with whole disk encryption mechanisms, such as the BitLocker Drive encryption feature in Windows Vista or Mac FileVault that encrypts and decrypts data on the fly as the user is operating the computer. The BitLocker software encrypts a system's operating system volume on the hard drive and provides authentication for the boot process (which cannot be encrypted). It is critical that disk encryption systems use some form of authentication for the boot process, such as a locked-down mini–operating system or a TPM mechanism whose only function is to authenticate the user before booting the system. Otherwise, an authorized user can still boot the system and access user files as if he were the original user. To authenticate the user, a combination of passwords, passphrases, PINs, or hardware tokens can be used before allowing access to the encrypted disk volumes.

Explain Basic Hashing Concepts

A *hashing* value is used in encryption systems to create a "fingerprint" for a message. This prevents the message from being improperly accessed on its way to its destination. In the overall information assurance model, hashing is used to protect the integrity of a message and is most often used with digital signatures.

The most commonly used hashing function is the *one-way hash*, a mathematical function that takes a variable-sized message and transforms it into a fixed-length value referred to as either a *hash value* or a *message digest*. This function is *one-way* because it's difficult to invert the procedure, and the procedure is never decrypted. The hash value represents the longer message from which it was created. This hash value is appended to the message that's sent to another user. The receiver then performs the same hashing function on the message and compares the resulting hash value with the one sent with the message. If they're identical, the message was altered.

Attacks against one-way hash functions can be prevented by longer hash values that are less susceptible to brute-force attacks. A good minimum starting point for the size of a hash value is 128 bits. The most common problem with weak hashing algorithms is the possibility of *hash value collisions* that occur when two hashed messages result in the same hashing value. When these collisions are discovered, they can be used to reveal the underlying algorithm. *Birthday attacks,* a class of brute-force attacks, are often used to find collisions of hash functions. The birthday attack gets its name from this surprising result: The probability that two or more people in a group of 23 share the same birthday is greater than one half. Such a result is called a *birthday paradox*. In encryption terms, if an attacker finds two hashed values that are the same, she has a greater chance of cracking the algorithm with this information.

The following sections describe some of the common hashing algorithms in use today.

Message Digest Hashing

Message digest hashing algorithms are used for digital signature applications when a large message must be hashed in a secure manner. A digital signature is created when the digest of the message is encrypted using the sender's private key. These algorithms take a message of variable length and produce a 128-bit message digest. Three versions of the message digest algorithm, discussed next, are commonly in use.

Exam Tip

Remember that a digital signature is created when the digest of the message is encrypted using the sender's private key.

Message Digest 2

Message Digest 2 (MD2) is a one-way hashing algorithm that can produce a 128-bit hash. Developed in 1989, MD2 is optimized for 8-bit machines. In the MD2 algorithm, the message is first padded so its length in bytes is divisible by 16. A 16-byte checksum is then appended to the message, and the hash value is computed on this resulting message.

Message Digest 4

Message Digest 4 (MD4) is a one-way hash function that produces a 128-bit hash message digest value. Developed in 1990, MD4 is much faster than MD2 and is optimized for 32-bit machines. The message is padded to ensure its length in bits plus 448 is divisible by 512. Next, a 64-bit binary representation of the original length of the message is added to the message. The message is then processed in 512-bit blocks, and then each block is processed in three rounds. Over time, MD4 has been shown to be easily broken.

Message Digest 5

Message Digest 5 (MD5), developed in 1991, is a slower but more complex version of MD4. MD5 is popular and widely used for security applications and integrity checking. For example, downloaded software usually includes an MD5 checksum that the user can compare to the checksum of the downloaded file. MD5 produces a 128-bit hash value using a hexadecimal 32-character string. Its complex algorithms make it much more difficult to crack than MD4. The algorithm consists of four distinct rounds that have a slightly different design from that of MD4. Vulnerabilities have been found in MD5 in which techniques are used to reverse-engineer the MD5 hash, and Secure Hash Algorithm (SHA) hash functions are often considered better alternatives to MD5 hashing.

Secure Hash Algorithm

SHA was developed by the US National Security Agency (NSA) for use with digital signature standards and is considered a more secure successor and alternative to MD5.

Travel Assistance

The NSA website (www.nsa.gov) provides an excellent overview of the history of cryptography for American national security.

SHA produces a 160-bit hash value that is run through the Digital Signature Algorithm (DSA), which adds the signature for the message. The sender encrypts the hash value with a private key, which is attached to the message before it's sent. The receiver decrypts the message with the sender's public key and runs the hashing function to compare the two values. If the values are identical, the message hasn't been altered. Other variants of basic SHA (sometimes called SHA-1) exist, such as SHA-224, SHA-256, SHA-384, and SHA-512, which indicate their larger bit values. SHA is used in several popular security applications such as PGP, Transport Layer Security (TLS), SSL, and Internet Protocol Security (IPSec). SHA is considered fairly secure, although published theoretical attacks have been able to break the hash.

Exam Tip

Be aware of the different types of hashing algorithms available and their strengths and weaknesses.

LANMAN Hash

The Windows LANMAN (LAN Manager) hash is used by older versions of Windows servers (such as Windows NT) for encrypting user passwords for authentication purposes. The hashing system used is easily subverted via a brute-force attack in which a password can be cracked in only a few hours. LANMAN's hashing method includes converting all characters in the password to uppercase, truncating longer passwords and splitting then into two even 7-byte halves, and then using DES to encrypt the halves separately, creating a ciphertext hash. This made it susceptible to cracking because the two smaller halves could be cracked separately.

LANMAN has been replaced by NTLM (NT LAN Manager) in Windows NT 3.1 servers and later, although LANMAN is still enabled for backward compatibility. In the Windows Vista operating system, LANMAN is completely disabled, but it can be enabled manually. In general, LANMAN should be disabled if all of your systems are running Windows 2000 or later.

NTLM

NTLM (NT LAN Manager) was created as an improvement to the original Microsoft LANMAN implementation and combines challenge/response authentication with message digest-hashed passwords that are transmitted between the clients and authenticating servers. NTLM version 1 uses MD4 hashing, while version 2 (introduced in Windows NT Service Pack 4) uses keyed-Hash Message Authentication Code (HMAC)–MD5 hashing and is more secure than version 1.

Since Windows 2000 and the growth of Active Directory–based implementations, Microsoft has implemented Kerberos authentication, but NTLM is still used for authentication purposes in cases where Windows networks are run without Active Directory domains or any other type of third-party authentication service.

<table>
<tr><td>Objective 9.03</td></tr>
<tr><td>CompTIA Security+
Objective 5.3</td></tr>
</table>

Explain Basic Encryption Concepts

In a symmetric encryption scheme, both parties use the same key for encryption and decryption purposes. Each user must possess the same key to encrypt and decrypt messages sent to each other. In an asymmetric scheme, two keys are created for encryption and decryption purposes: one key is the public key, which is known to all users, while the private key remains secret and is kept private by the user to which it is assigned. Asymmetric encryption schemes are widely used in public key cryptography systems.

Symmetric Encryption Algorithms

The following sections describe examples of symmetric-based algorithms.

DES and 3DES

The Data Encryption Standard (DES) is a block cipher defined by the US government in 1977 as an official standard. The actual encryption system used was originally created by IBM. DES has become the most well-known and widely used cryptosystem in the world. This symmetric cryptosystem uses a 64-bit block size and a 56-bit key. It requires both the sender and receiver to possess the same secret key, which is used both to encrypt and decrypt the message. DES can also be used by a single user for encrypting data for storage on a hard disk or other medium.

After DES was used for many years, the government ceased to authorize it as a standard and moved on to more secure methods of encryption, such as Triple DES (3DES) and the AES standard. Using the same standard with a weak 56-bit key for so long increased the chances for the encryption scheme to be broken.

Travel Advisory

Despite being criticized for published weaknesses, DES-based encryption such as 3DES is still in wide use today.

Over time and after tests with multi-CPU systems proved the standard could be broken through brute force, DES encryption was considered insecure. A Double-DES encryption scheme was created that contained a key length of 112 bits, but its susceptibility to being cracked wasn't considered much different from the original DES.

3DES is a 168-bit encryption standard that's resistant to cryptanalysis because it uses 48 rounds of cryptographic computations. 3DES is considered 2^{56} times stronger than DES. The main disadvantage of 3DES is that encryption and decryption is much slower than that of DES by almost three times. Nevertheless, 3DES is considered powerful enough to be implemented in many banking and financial applications.

AES

Advanced encryption standard (AES) (also often called Rijndael) is the government-defined encryption standard created to replace DES, which was considered vulnerable. The new standard uses a symmetric-block cipher supporting variable block and key lengths, such as 128, 192, and 256 bits. In 2003, the US government stated that the AES encryption standard could be used for nonclassified documents, while AES using 192–256 bits was required for top secret purposes.

AES itself has not been compromised, but a number of speculative theoretical attacks have been published. Some attacks, called "side channel attacks," have compromised AES encrypted data, but only because the implementation of the encryption scheme itself was weak, not the encryption algorithm. These cases are rare, and they typically involved attacking an application server using AES that had weaknesses in its timing and caching mechanisms that accidentally leaked data, which led to discovery of the AES key.

Blowfish

Blowfish is a symmetric block cipher that uses 64-bit blocks of data. Its key length is 448 bits and it uses 16 rounds of cryptographic computations. Blowfish was designed specifically for 32-bit machines and is significantly faster than DES.

IDEA

International Data Encryption Algorithm (IDEA) is a symmetric block cipher that uses 64-bit blocks of data, with a key length of 128 bits. The data blocks are divided into 16 smaller sections, which are subjected to eight rounds of cryptographic computation. The speed of IDEA in software is similar to that of DES. IDEA is the cipher used in the popular encryption program Pretty Good Privacy (PGP).

RC5

RC5 is a symmetric block cipher patented by RSA Data Security. It uses a variety of parameters to offer data block sizes such 32, 64, and 128 bits. The number of computational rounds can range from 0 to 255. The key can be anywhere from 0 bits to 2048 bits in size. Such built-in variability provides flexibility in levels of security and efficiency.

Asymmetric Encryption Algorithms

The following sections describe examples of asymmetric-based algorithms.

RSA

RSA, one of the most popular asymmetric public key algorithms, is the main standard for encryption and digital signatures and is widely used for electronic devices, operating systems, and software applications. The acronym RSA stands for Rivest, Shamir, and Adelman, the inventors of this technique. RSA is also used in many web servers that use SSL, and its algorithm is based on the factoring of prime numbers to obtain private and public key pairs. RSA is used primarily for encryption and digital signatures.

Elliptic Curve Cryptosystems

Elliptic Curve Cryptosystems (ECC) provides functionality similar to RSA, such as encryption and digital signatures. The ECC cryptosystem uses complex mathematical structures to create secure asymmetric algorithms and keys. ECC was created for devices with smaller processing capabilities, such as cell phones, PDAs, and other wireless devices. ECC uses smaller keys than the similar RSA; larger keys need more processing power to compute.

Diffie-Hellman

Diffie-Hellman isn't an actual encryption algorithm: it's a key agreement protocol that enables users to exchange encryption keys over an insecure medium.

The Diffie-Hellman protocol depends on the discrete logarithmic formulas for its security. The main vulnerability with the basic protocol is that the key exchange doesn't authenticate the participants. Further enhancements to the Diffie-Hellman protocol allow the two parties to authenticate each other through the addition of digital signatures and public-key certificates. This system is used in the PKI.

DSA (Digital Signature Algorithm)

The *Digital Signature Algorithm* (DSA) was published by the National Institute of Standards and Technology (NIST) in the Digital Signature Standard (DSS), which is a part of a US government project. The DSS was selected by NIST, in cooperation with the NSA, as the digital authentication standard of the US government. DSA is based on discrete logarithms and is used only for authentication. The algorithm is considered secure when the key size is large enough. DSA was originally proposed with a 512-bit key size and was eventually revised to support key sizes up to 1024 bits. Because of DSA's lack of key exchange capabilities, relative slowness, and public distrust of the process and the government involvement that created it, many people prefer RSA for digital signatures and encryption, but both standards are used widely.

Pretty Good Privacy

By default, a mail server doesn't encrypt e-mail messages. This means anyone who might have access to your account, who has hacked the system, or who is capturing the unprotected network traffic can read your private e-mail messages. E-mail messages, once sent, can relay among a large number of e-mail servers until they arrive at their destination. If any one of these servers is insecure, e-mail could be captured and viewed. Users can protect themselves with encryption products or through the use of digital certificates. Once the e-mail is encrypted, there's no way for an unauthorized user to view the contents of the e-mail. The destination user must also have the matching encryption key, so he or she can unlock the message when it arrives.

PGP is one of the most common encryption tools used to protect messages on the Internet, because it's both easy to use and effective. PGP uses its own decentralized type of digital certificates using an RSA-based public-key encryption method with two keys: One is a public key you give to anyone with which you share messages, and the other is a private key you use to decrypt messages you receive. A passphrase is used to encrypt the user's private key, which is stored on the local computer. Each PGP user distributes her own public key, creating a "web of trust" with other users. Each user keeps a collection of other user's public keys on a *key ring*. PGP is different from a centralized certificate authority, where one authority is used to authenticate users; using PGP, users rely on each other to establish trust between other users and their keys.

Travel Assistance

For detailed information on PGP, see www.pgp.com.

One-time Pad

A *one-time pad* is a type of encryption scheme that, when implemented correctly, is considered secure and theoretically impossible to compromise. The pad is generated from random values and uses a mathematic function called an *exclusive-OR (XOR)* to encrypt the plain-text message into ciphertext. Several rules make the one-time pad secure:

- *The pad must be used only once (hence its name).* Using the pad multiple times will increase the possibility that its patterns will be recognized and broken.
- *The pad must be as long as the message it is encrypting.* If it is not, patterns in the pad will be repeated to cover the entire message and can introduce the risk of it being recognized and broken.
- *The communications of the pad must be secure.* If the pad itself is discovered in transit, messages encrypted with the pad can be easily decrypted.
- *The pad's values must be completely random.* The introduction of patterns in the pad (because even some random number generators have been discovered not to be completely random) can cause the pad to be broken.

One-time pads are difficult to implement within computerized environments, as not all of the requirements can be successfully met, and they are often used as a manual backup encryption method for extremely high security areas such as military and government environments.

Transmission Encryption

The following encryption protocols and techniques are specifically designed for the security of wireless communications.

Wireless Encryption Protocol

For wireless networks, the *Wireless Encryption Protocol* (WEP) security protocol provides encrypted communication between the wireless clients and access points. WEP uses a key encryption algorithm to encrypt communications between devices. Each client and access point on the wireless LAN must use the same encryption key. The key is manually configured on each access point and each client before either can access the network. Basic WEP specifies the use of up to 64-bit keys (40-bit key plus a 24-bit initialization vector); however, 64-bit WEP encryption has been proven to be vulnerable to attack because of a weak algorithm. Most devices now support up to 128-bit encryption (104-bit key plus a 24-bit initialization vector); however, this has also been proven to be crackable. If your wireless access point supports only WEP, you should use 128-bit WEP encryption in conjunction with the MAC address filtering and network identifier methods described previously.

WPA and WPA2 Security

Wi-Fi Protected Access (WPA) is the most recent and secure form of encryption for wireless networks. It was created to fix several weaknesses in the WEP standard.

WPA can use a pre-shared key, or it can use an authentication server that distributes the keys. In the pre-shared key method (also called Personal WPA), all devices on the wireless LAN must use the same passphrase key to access the network. The authentication server method (also called Enterprise WPA) is more suited for environments with hundreds of clients, where using a single passphrase key for each device is not scalable, and the authentication server takes care of key management between the wireless devices on the network.

Using WPA, data is encrypted using a 128-bit key that is actually routinely changed during sessions using Temporal Key Integrity Protocol (TKIP). With WPA, a single session key cannot be hacked by the time the protocol changes keys. WPA also provides for improved integrity checking of the data traversing the wireless network to make sure that data cannot be intercepted and changed on the way to its destination. This provides much more protection than the original WEP.

The strength of a WPA network, however, is only as strong as the passphrase used. A WPA passphrase can be from 8 to 63 characters and should be as strong as possible and not based on known dictionary words: it should include numbers, uppercase and lowercase characters, and special characters such as the @ symbol. All devices on the WPA network must share the same passphrase, including all access points.

WPA2 is the most recent version of WPA and adds Robust Security Network (RSN) support that includes added protection for ad-hoc networks, key caching, pre-roaming authentication, and the Counter Mode with Cipher Block Chaining Message Authentication Code Protocol (CCMP) that uses the AES cipher to replace TKIP. All currently manufactured devices support WPA2 in addition to WPA. If your network devices support WPA2, they should use this type of encryption. However, many older devices do not support WPA2, and you will have to use WPA or some other common encryption method, such as WEP, that can be supported by all your clients.

Exam Tip

You should use the highest level of encryption available for wireless networks, such as WPA2. Older levels of encryption, such as WEP and WPA, have proved to be vulnerable.

Objective 9.04
CompTIA Security+
Objective 5.4

Explain and Implement Protocols

Securing communication between systems is an important part of security that prevents malicious users from capturing data in transit. The following sections outline some of the various encryption protocols and their implementations in communications security.

Secure Sockets Layer/Transport Layer Security

Although the data on a server might be secured from unauthorized access, the communications pathways between the server and client systems might not be. The SSL protocol enables communication between systems to be encrypted.

Many web sites have both secured and unsecured areas. The secured areas might provide access to a financial bank account or a database of personal information, for example. This secured area of the site usually requires user authentication to proceed. To increase security when switching from the unsecured public part of a web site to a secured area, SSL encryption is invoked. SSL must be supported by both the web server and the client browser to function. SSL is also often used in e-mail systems to secure the message communications between mail servers and mail clients.

In an SSL communication, a process known as a *digital handshake* occurs. The handshaking phase begins when the server sends a message to the client indicating a secure session must be set up. The client then sends its security information and encryption key to the server, which compares the credentials with its own to find the right match. Next, the server sends authentication information, so the client knows the web server with which it is communicating is the correct one. This is an important step, because it's possible, through redirection or other methods, that a user can be switched from one web site to another without the user's knowledge. So, for example, as you enter your user name and password, you might be entering the information into a bogus web site that collects this information to perform unauthorized activity with your accounts. This handshake confirms that you are not only who you say you are, but that the site with which you're connected is the actual site you expect it to be. The SSL protocol uses public key cryptography in the handshake phase to securely exchange symmetric session keys that are then used to encrypt communications for the duration of the session. When the client moves to another web site, the encrypted session is closed.

TLS is the next generation of the SSL protocol. Although the two protocols are similar, TLS builds on the strong security of SSL with more enhanced encryption and authentication techniques. Unfortunately, TLS and SSL aren't compatible because a TLS-secured communication cannot interoperate with an SSL communication.

HTTP/HTTPS/SHTTP

Hypertext Transfer Protocol (HTTP) is used by the World Wide Web. HTTP runs on the Internet's networking protocol, TCP/IP, and forms the communications protocols that allow web browsers to connect to and retrieve content from web servers. When a user clicks a web hyperlink, HTTP tries to connect with the associated Uniform Resource Locator (URL). The browser sends an HTTP request to the corresponding web server hosting that URL. The web server returns the content of the web site to the browser through HTTP. HTTP is a *stateless protocol,* meaning that with each communication, the link between the browser and the server is created, and then it's broken when the communication is finished. All HTTP communications are sent in clear text, so no messages are secure, and they can be easily viewed using a protocol analyzer. This makes HTTP unusable for communications requiring security and privacy, such as web-based banking and other online financial transactions.

Hypertext Transfer Protocol over Secure Socket Layer (HTTPS) is a secure means of communicating HTTP data between a web browser and web server. HTTPS protects the communication channel by using SSL and certificates to provide encrypted and protected communications. When connecting to a web site that uses a secured channel, the URL begins with *https* instead of *http,* such as *https://secure.website.com.* HTTPS is typically used in banking and online shopping transactions, where the transfer of credit card and personal information must be encrypted to prevent an unauthorized user from stealing the information while it's in transmit between the client and the server. When a client connects to the secure site, the web server sends a certificate to the web browser to establish its identity. If the browser accepts the certificate and finds no validation issues with the certificate, SSL is activated between the server and client. This ensures that the web site is genuine (who it says it is), and that the client is not connecting to a *rogue* site. In many web browsers, a secure site is indicated by a small padlock icon in the application taskbar. HTTPS uses TCP port 443 for communications.

Secure Hypertext Transfer Protocol (SHTTP) is an alternative to HTTPS for encrypting web communications, although over time it has lost popularity, and most applications use HTTPS for secure HTTP communications using SSL. HTTPS provides the same authentication and encryption functionality as SHTTP, but HTTPS can encrypt all data being sent between web client and server, while SHTTP encrypts only the HTTP-specific messages. One advantage that SHTTP has over HTTPS is that it uses only symmetric keys and does not require public key certificates for the clients, which means that private transactions can occur without requiring that clients have an established public key.

Exam Tip

Remember that HTTP and SHTTP use TCP port 80, and HTTPS uses TCP port 443.

S/MIME

Multipurpose Internet Mail Extension (MIME) is a specification for transferring multimedia and attachments through e-mail. This specification offers a standard way for all mail clients and mail transfer systems to handle certain types of attachments. For example, if a user sends an audio clip to another user through e-mail, the MIME header will include information on the attachment. When the audio clip reaches the destination user, the user's computer will understand what type of file it is and what application can be used to open it.

Secure MIME (S/MIME) is an extension of the MIME standard that is used for digitally signing and encrypting e-mail using certificates. S/MIME is used for sending confidential e-mail that needs to be secured so other users can't capture the message and read its contents. By encrypting the e-mail, an unauthorized user will be unable to decipher the contents of the message and its attachments. S/MIME requires the use of public key certificates for authentication and provides message confidentiality and integrity via the user's encryption and hashing algorithms.

Point-to-Point Tunneling Protocol

Point-to-Point Tunneling Protocol (PPTP) is a Microsoft implementation of secure communications over a virtual private network (VPN). Because PPTP is an extension of the Point-to-Point Protocol (PPP), it has become one of the most widely used tunneling protocols. It allows network packets to be encapsulated within PPP communications for transfer over another network, such as the Internet through a dial-up, cable, or DSL connection. Tunneling protocols allow users connected to a public network to create their own private VPN connections to corporate large area networks (LANs).

PPTP decrypts and encapsulates PPP packets to create the VPN connection. The security mechanisms within PPTP include authentication and encryption of data. PPTP connections are authenticated with Microsoft Challenge Handshake Authentication Protocol (MSCHAP) or the certificates-based Extensible Authentication Protocol (EAP)–TLS. One major security problem with PPTP is that when a connection is negotiated, the communication is transmitted in clear text. This data can therefore be captured by an unauthorized user to try to hack the connection.

Over time, PPTP has been replaced by Layer 2 Tunneling Protocol (L2TP) and IPSec, which provide more advanced security mechanisms and point-to-point encryption capabilities.

Layer 2 Tunneling Protocol

L2TP is a tunneling protocol like PPTP, but it combines the best features of PPTP with the Layer 2 Forward (L2F) protocol created by Cisco Systems. L2TP is most often used with other media technologies, such as Frame Relay. The main difference between L2TP and PPTP is that L2PT can run on top of and tunnel through other network protocols, such as Internetwork Packet Exchange (IPX) and Systems Network Architecture (SNA), while PPTP can run only on top of IP networks. L2TP, however, doesn't provide any type of native encryption, so it must be combined with another encrypted protocol such as IPSec. Unlike PPTP, L2TP supports TACACS+ and RADIUS for authentication.

IP Security

IPSec is a standards-based suite of protocols that provide privacy, integrity, and authenticity to information transferred across IP networks. IPSec works on the IP network layer to encrypt communications between the sender and receiver. IPSec is most often used to secure VPN communications over an open network such as the Internet; however, because IPSec operates at lower levels than most application security protocols (such as SSL), it offers greater flexibility in its implementation, as applications do not need to be aware of IPSec to make use of its benefits. IPSec ensures that communications cannot be read by a third-party, that traffic has not been modified in transit, and that messages received are from a trusted source.

IPSec uses two types of encryption modes: transport and tunnel. In *transport* mode, IPSec encrypts the data portion of each packet, but not the header. This can be used only in host-to-host communications. *Tunnel* mode encrypts both the header and the data of the network packet. This is used to host VPN gateway communications, the most common form of VPN. The receiver of the packet uses IPSec to decrypt the message. For IPSec to work, each communicating device needs to be running IPSec and share some form of public key. Key management is provided by the Internet Key Exchange (IKE), formerly ISAKMP/Oakley. IKE enables the receiver to obtain a public key and authenticate the sender using digital certificates.

Secure Shell

SSH is a secure form of terminal access to other systems. Like other terminal communications utilities such as Telnet, SSH lets a user log in to a remote machine and execute commands as if she were working at the console of that system. Telnet, however, is insecure because its data isn't encrypted when communicated. SSH provides a secure, encrypted tunnel to access another system remotely. SSH is sometimes used as a low-cost alternative to normal VPN communications because of its simple installation and delivery of well-encrypted, secure communications.

SSH uses public key cryptography for authentication, and when a client connects to a system using SSH, an initial handshaking process begins and a special session key is exchanged. This starts the session, and a secure channel is created to allow the access.

Vulnerabilities have been discovered in some versions of SSH, so make sure that you are using the latest version. Early versions of SSH were susceptible to man-in-the-middle attacks because a hacker could capture the headers of the handshaking phase to intercept the session key.

Exam Tip
SSH uses TCP port 22 for communications.

CHECKPOINT

✔**Objective 9.01: Explain General Cryptography Concepts** Information assurance protects information and information systems by securing their confidentiality, integrity, authentication, and nonrepudiation. An algorithm is a complex mathematical formula that dictates how the encryption and decryption process takes place. Because these mathematical algorithms are usually publicly known, the cryptosystem is strengthened with the addition of a secret key. A key is like a password that's combined with the algorithm to create ciphertext, and encrypted data can't be deciphered unless the same key is used to decrypt it. In a symmetric encryption scheme, both parties use the same key for encryption and decryption purposes. In an asymmetric encryption scheme, everyone uses different, but mathematically-related, keys for encryption and decryption purposes. In public key cryptography, each user received two keys: the public key and the private key. The private key is kept secret, while the public key can be published for any user to see or use.

✔**Objective 9.02: Explain Basic Hashing Concepts** A hashing value is used in encryption systems to create a "fingerprint" for a message. This prevents the message from being accessed and changed on the way to its destination. In the overall information assurance model, hashing is used to protect the integrity of a message and is most often used with digital signatures. A one-way hash is a mathematical function that transforms a variable-sized message into a fixed-length value, referred to as either a hash value or a message digest. Popular hashing algorithms include MD5 and SHA.

✔**Objective 9.03: Explain Basic Encryption Concepts** Use AES-256 and RSA algorithms as secure encryption algorithms. PGP is the most commonly used e-mail encryption application and uses its own decentralized type of digital certificates using an RSA-based public-key encryption method with two keys: a public key you give to anyone with whom you share messages, and a private key you use to decrypt messages you receive. A one-time pad must be used only once, must be truly random, must be communicated securely, and must be as long as the message it is encrypting. Use WPA for encrypting wireless networks as the WEP method has become vulnerable.

✔**Objective 9.04: Explain and Implement Protocols** Encryption protocols include SSL/TLS and HTTPS for secure web communications, S/MIME for securing e-mail messages and attachments, and IPSec for VPN communications. Use SSH as an encrypted alternative to Telnet or other mechanisms that use clear text in their communications.

REVIEW QUESTIONS

1. When clear text data is encrypted, what does it become?
   A. Certificate
   B. Symmetric
   C. Public key
   D. Ciphertext

2. Which of the following isn't a function of information assurance within encryption systems?
   A. Efficiency
   B. Confidentiality
   C. Integrity
   D. Nonrepudiation

3. Which encryption scheme relies on the sender and receiver of a message using the same secret key for encryption and decryption?
   A. Asymmetric
   B. Symmetric
   C. RSA
   D. Diffie-Hellman

4. Which of the following standards replaced DES as a more secure encryption scheme?
   A. DSA
   B. Elliptical curve
   C. SSL
   D. AES

5. Which encryption scheme relies on the sender and the receiver of a message to use different keys for encryption and decryption?
   A. Steganography
   B. Non-symmetric
   C. Asymmetric
   D. Symmetric

6. Which of the following encryption types would be used to encrypt an e-mail message?

   A. SSL

   B. SSH

   C. S/MIME

   D. TLS

7. If the hash values of two different messages result in the same value, what is this called?

   A. Birthday attack

   B. Collision

   C. Hash

   D. Block cipher

8. Which entity issues, manages, and distributes digital certificates?

   A. Certificate authority

   B. Registration authority

   C. Government (NSA)

   D. PKI

9. A network packet sniffer can be used to obtain user credentials in clear text from which of the following protocols?

   A. SSL

   B. SSH

   C. HTTPS

   D. HTTP

10. When a user connects to a secure HTTPS web page, which of the following actions is performed first?

    A. The username and password are sent for authentication.

    B. A digital certificate establishes the web site identity to the browser.

    C. The web page is displayed, and then authentication is performed.

    D. The client establishes its identity to the web server.

REVIEW ANSWERS

1. **D**   Clear text is transformed into ciphertext after being put through some type of cipher or encryption algorithm system. The ciphertext is unreadable unless it is decrypted back into clear-text form.

2. **A**   Efficiency is not a function of information assurance within encryption systems. The four basic functions pertaining to information assurance are confidentiality, integrity, authentication, and nonrepudiation.

3. **B**   In a symmetric encryption scheme, both parties use the same key for encryption and decryption purposes. Both users must possess the same key to send encrypted messages to each other.

4. **D**   Advanced Encryption Standard (AES) is the US government–defined encryption standard created as a replacement for DES, which was considered vulnerable to cryptographic attacks because of weaknesses in its algorithm.

5. **C**   An asymmetric encryption scheme relies on the sender and receiver of a message to use different keys for encryption and decryption. The keys are mathematically related but can't be derived from each other.

6. **C**   Secure MIME (S/MIME) is an extension of the MIME standard and is used for digitally signing and encrypting e-mail using certificates. S/MIME is used for sending confidential e-mails that need to be secured so other users can't capture the message and read its contents.

7. **B**   A collision occurs within a hashing algorithm when the hashed values of two different messages result in the same value. Collisions can be used to aid in cracking a hacking algorithm.

8. **A**   The certificate authority is responsible for identifying and authenticating a user, and then issuing a certificate with that user's credentials and public key. A registration authority is simply the middleman between the user and the certificate authority that forwards a request on behalf of the end user.

9. **D**   HTTP communications send all data in clear-text form. For secure web communications, HTTPS is a secure means of communicating HTTP data between a web browser and web server. HTTPS protects the communication channel by using SSL to provide encrypted and protected communications.

10. **B**   When a client connects to the secure HTTPS site, the web server sends a certificate to the web browser to establish its identity. If the browser accepts the certificate and finds no validation issues with the certificate, SSL is activated between the server and client. No other communication can occur between the server and client until the certificate is validated and accepted.

Public Key Cryptography

	NEWBIE	SOME EXPERIENCE	EXPERT
ETA	2 hours	1 hour	0.5 hour

Traditional cryptography methods based on symmetric key cryptography describe the use of the same secret key by both the sender (to encrypt the message) and receiver (to decrypt the message). Unfortunately, it can be difficult to transmit the secret key securely from one user to another. If an unauthorized user intercepts the key, he can decrypt, read, forge, and modify all messages encrypted using that key. Key management is a challenge for these systems, especially for systems that serve large numbers of users.

Public key cryptography was introduced in 1976 by Diffie and Hellman, whose public key protocol was created to solve the key management problem. In public key cryptography, each user receives two keys: the public key and the private key. The private key is kept secret, while the public key can be published for any user to see or use. The problem faced using symmetric keys is solved because no need exists to share a secret key. All transmissions involve only the public keys; no private key is ever transmitted or shared. With public key cryptography, *asymmetric cryptography* is used to exchange symmetric keys. The sender encrypts the message with the receiver's public key. The receiver then decrypts the message with his own private key, as shown in Figure 10.1. The security mechanism is safe as long as the private keys aren't compromised.

This chapter describes the core concepts and implementation of public key cryptography, including certificate authorities and the certificate lifecycle.

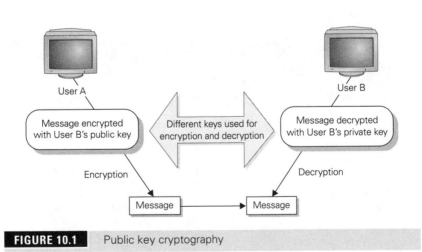

FIGURE 10.1   Public key cryptography

Objective 10.01 Public Key Cryptography

CompTIA Security+
Objective 5.5

The *Public Key Infrastructure* (PKI) is a standard infrastructure consisting of a framework of procedures, standards, and protocols, based on public key cryptography. A hybrid of asymmetric and symmetric key algorithms, PKI provides the full range of information assurance objectives for confidentiality, integrity, authentication, and nonrepudiation. The asymmetric keys are used for authentication, and then one or more symmetric keys are generated and exchanged using asymmetric encryption.

> **Travel Assistance**
>
> See Chapter 9 for detailed information on the differences between asymmetric and symmetric cryptography.

A message is encrypted using a symmetric algorithm, and that key is then encrypted asymmetrically using the recipient's public key. The entire message (symmetrically encrypted body and asymmetrically encrypted key) is sent together to the recipient. The message can also be digitally signed through the use of digital certificates.

> **Exam Tip**
>
> Public key cryptography uses a hybrid of symmetric and asymmetric encryption systems. A message is encrypted using a symmetric algorithm, and that key is then encrypted asymmetrically using the recipient's public key. The entire message (symmetrically encrypted body and asymmetrically encrypted key) is sent together to the recipient.

Digital Certificates

A *digital certificate* is a credential required by PKI systems that can securely identify an individual as well as create an association between the individual's authenticated identity and public keys. A trusted party, called a *certificate authority* (CA), is used to sign and issue certificates. The CA is responsible for verifying the identity of a key owner and binding the owner to a public key. This enables users who have never met to exchange encrypted communications because the authentication is performed by the CA. Each certificate contains a unique serial number, identity, and public key information for the user, and the validity dates for the life of the certificate.

Certificate Authorities

A CA is an organization or entity that issues and manages digital certificates and is responsible for authenticating and identifying users who participate in the PKI. This service doesn't necessarily involve a third party; it can be internal to an organization. A CA server can be set up to act as the manager of certificates and the user's public keys.

Third-party CAs are special organizations dedicated to certificate management. Some of the larger companies that offer this service, such as VeriSign and Entrust, have their functionality built in to popular web browsers to perform certificate services automatically.

Exam Tip

A certificate authority is an organization or entity that issues and manages digital certificates. The CA is responsible for authenticating and identifying users who participate in the Public Key Infrastructure (PKI).

Some of the actual authentication and identification services for certificates are managed by other organizations called *registration authorities* (RAs). These organizations offload some of the work from CAs by confirming the identities of users, issuing key pairs, and initiating the certificate process with a CA on behalf of the user. The RA acts as a middleman between the user and the CA and doesn't issue certificates on its own.

To verify a user's identity, the CA and RA usually require some form of identification, such as a driver's license, Social Security number, address, or phone number. Once the user's identification is established, the CA generates a public and private key for the user. A certificate is then generated with the identification and public key information embedded within it. Once the user is registered and receives his certificate, he can begin using his certificate to send encrypted messages. When the receiver receives the message, her software can verify the certificate to ensure the message is from the stated sender. Certificates can also be revoked if the certificate's original subscriber information has changed, has been compromised, or is no longer valid.

Exam Tip

A certificate contains the authenticated identification of a user and his public key information.

Trust Models

Trust models define how users trust other users, companies, CAs, and RAs within the PKI. These models provide a chain of trust from a user's public key to the root key of a CA. The validated chain then implies authenticity of all the certificates. The following are the most common trust models used in PKI.

Web of Trust

The *web of trust* is a simplistic trust model that relies on each user creating and signing her own certificate, as shown in Figure 10.2. This is the basis for encryption applications, such as Pretty Good Privacy (PGP), where no central authority exists. With this model, each user is responsible for authentication and trust, and anyone can sign someone else's public key. When User A signs User B's key, User A is introducing User B's key to anyone who trusts User A. Each user is then considered a trusted introducer in the model.

Third-party (Single Authority) Trust

A *third-party central certifying agency* signs a given key and authenticates the owner of the key. Trusting that authority means, by association, that you trust all keys issued by that authority, as shown in Figure 10.3. Each user authenticates the other through the exchange of certificates. The users know the CA has performed all the necessary identification of the owner of the certificate and can therefore trust the owner of the message.

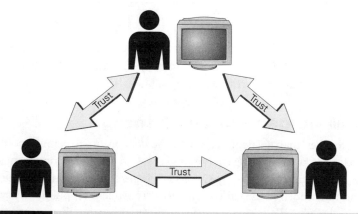

FIGURE 10.2   Web of trust model

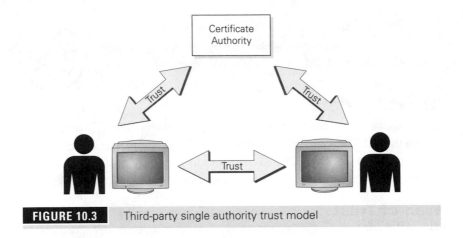

FIGURE 10.3   Third-party single authority trust model

Hierarchical Model

The *hierarchical model* is an extension of the third-party model, in which root CAs issue certificates to other lower level CAs and RAs, as shown in Figure 10.4. Each user's most trusted key is the root CA's public key. The trust inheritance can be followed from the certificate back to the root CA. This model allows enforcement of policies and standards throughout the infrastructure, producing a higher level of overall assurance than other trust models. A root certificate is trusted by software applications on behalf of the user.

Local Lingo

root certificate   A root certificate is the highest certificate in the hierarchical tree, which is used to sign other lower-level certificates. These certificates inherit the trust of the root certificate.

For example, web browsers will create trusted connections to secure servers using Secure Sockets Layer (SSL), using root certificates that identify to the user that this web site and its certificate are trusted.

Key Management and Storage

Encryption key management deals with the generation, distribution, storage, and backup of keys. Securing encryption keys is an extremely important aspect of encryption and cryptography. Once a key is generated, it must be secured to avoid an unauthorized user discovering the key. Attacks on public-key systems are typically focused on the key management system, rather than on attempts to break the encryption algorithm itself. No matter how secure or difficult a

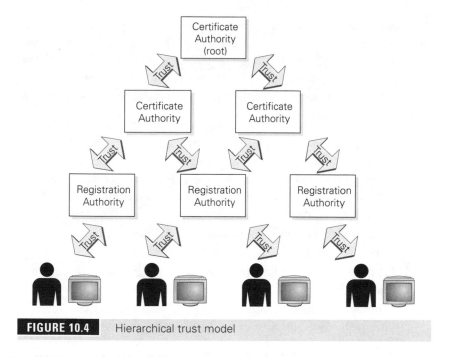

FIGURE 10.4 Hierarchical trust model

cryptographical algorithm, the entire process can be compromised by poor key management.

Centralized vs. Decentralized Storage

Keys need to be generated and securely sent to the correct user. The user must then store that key in a secure place so it can't be accessed by another user. The key can be encrypted and stored on a hard drive, a CD or DVD, a portable USB key, or a PDA. The keys should also be recoverable if they're lost or damaged, or if passwords to use them are forgotten. Key storage is an important aspect of secure key management, which can be centralized either to a particular server or a third-party service. Key storage can involve both hardware and software storage methods.

In the early days of encryption key management, cryptographic keys were stored in secure boxes and delivered to users by hand. The keys were given to the systems administrator, who distributed them from a main server or by visiting each workstation. This type of administrative overhead for key management could almost be a job in itself, and it obviously didn't scale well in large enterprise networks. In today's networks, key distribution and storage are typically performed automatically through a special key management system, such as a key management server, or through a third-party service such as VeriSign or Entrust. Key management can be an extremely time-consuming process for network administrators in a large enterprise network.

Centralized Storage   Most modern encryption infrastructures use a *centralized storage system* for key management, a single place where all key management occurs. This typically involves a centralized server on your network that takes care of key management for you. The server can issue key pairs, store and back them up, and take care of certificates. A centralized key management system offers several advantages:

- **Administration**   Managing the accounts and keys of users at one centralized location is secure and convenient, relieving the administrator and the users of administrative overhead. Signature verification is automatic because the validity information is co-located with the actual key and other account information.
- **Scalability**   Key management servers are built to scale to any size enterprise network.
- **Integrity**   Keys stored at a server can be easily backed up, eliminating the potential for the loss of a vital verification or an encryption key.
- **Security**   Unlike a decentralized storage system in which keys can be insecure because of lack of user education or operating system (OS) vulnerabilities, a key storage server is a secure environment where audited controls are required for access to the physical hardware and the keys are protected with specialized cryptographic devices.

Exam Tip

Centralized key storage solutions provide greater security and integrity of keys than decentralized solutions. They're also far more manageable and scalable.

Decentralized Storage   A *decentralized storage system* is typically used by individual users or a small network. Once the user has created her keys, her private key is stored locally on her system or some other secure device. She then sends her public key with a certificate request to a CA that, after authenticating the user, sends her a certificate, which is again stored locally.

The advantage for end users is that they're always in control of their private keys and certificates. The users trust themselves with the security, rather than trusting a server or a third-party service that might not properly protect their information or that could divulge their private keys to third parties, such as government authorities.

A decentralized storage method has many disadvantages as well. For example, if the user encrypts data on her hard drive and misplaces her private key, she won't be able to recover any information encrypted with her private key. Another concern involves users in a corporate network: After a disgruntled employee leaves an organization, he might not reveal the key needed to decrypt information that was protected on the corporate network, denying access to the information from other people who need it.

Keys can also be damaged or lost, and if the user didn't properly back them up, those keys will be permanently lost. This means the data the user encrypted will also be lost permanently, because no key exists to decrypt the information.

Travel Advisory

Decentralized methods are typically used by individual users. Centralized types of key storage are used for larger networks of users, for which individual key management would be insecure and time-consuming to manage.

Key Storage and Protection

Once a key pair has been generated, the private key must be safely stored to protect it from being compromised, lost, or damaged. The type of security used to encrypt and protect the private key should be as strong as the security used to encrypt and protect the actual message or files. A number of methods for protecting the private key can be used, including both hardware and software methods.

The most important aspect of hardware key protection is the ability to protect the hardware itself. Many users store their private keys on their computers' hard disks. Their computers might be part of a network, potentially allowing access to anyone on that network. To prevent this sort of access, private keys are usually stored on removable media that can be more easily protected and can be physically carried with the user. This hardware can be typical media, such as a CD or DVD, USB key, or a PDA. However, these small media devices can be easily lost or stolen, which is why the stored key should always be encrypted.

A private key should never be stored in its plain-text form. If an unauthorized user manages to find the file or steals the device in which the file is located, that user could uncover the private key. The simplest method of protection is to secure the encrypted private key with a password and store it locally on a disc or a USB key. The password should be as carefully crafted as your network password so it can't be guessed easily or discovered through brute-force attack methods.

> ### Exam Tip
> A private key should never be stored in plain-text form. It needs to be encrypted and protected with a password.

For enterprise-level networks, the installation of a key management system takes the burden of key storage and protection away from the user and lets the OS or application take care of storing keys on a centralized server.

An additional method of protection includes the generation of another key pair to be used to encrypt the private key. This key is usually kept with a third party using a key escrow–type service.

Key Escrow

The concept of *key escrow* has been heavily overshadowed over the years by debates between privacy groups and the government, because it concerns the issues of data privacy versus national security. Key escrow involves a third party, such as a government agency or an authorized organization, that holds a special third key on top of your private and public key pair. The third key is used to encrypt the private key, which is then stored in a secure location. This third key can be used to unlock the encrypted copy of the private key in case of loss or the theft of the original key. Although the main concern of privacy activists is the possible abuse by the government regarding individual data privacy, the main security issue for most companies is the idea of a third-party entity controlling a crucial part of the company's security infrastructure.

> ### Exam Tip
> Key escrow involves a trusted third party that holds a special key in addition to your private and public key pair. This third key is used to encrypt the private key that is then securely stored. In the event the private key is lost or stolen, the third key can be used to unlock the encrypted copy of the private key.

Another common key escrow entity is the CA, which is responsible for authorized and distributing certificates and encryption key pairs. As part of your overall security plan, the ability for the CA to protect your information is crucial. CAs are a popular target of malicious hacker attacks because of the valuable information they store. Attacks are usually targeted at the CA's own private keys.

The CA's key pairs are common targets of cryptanalytic attacks that attempt to break weak keys through brute force. CAs need to be both secure and practical because their public key might be written into software used by a large number of users. If the key needs to be changed, every user's software will need to be updated to accept the new key.

Travel Advisory

When examining a key escrow service, pay careful attention to its methods of security, including the secure storage and transfer of keys and certificates.

Key Recovery

As the main key to unlocking the encryption on a file or other critical data, the private key must be carefully protected. If the private key is lost or destroyed, nothing that's been encrypted with that key will be accessible. With the storage and backup of private keys, a balance must be maintained between the security of the key and the ability to archive it in the event of the need for recovery.

Unfortunately, the concept of key recovery has been clouded by the issue of governmental control and the possibility that the government, in the interest of national security, would require a mandatory key recovery system. Such a mandatory key recovery system might enable the government to decrypt private data through the use of key escrow and key management companies. Whatever the outcome of that debate, secure methods of key recovery are available that keep the responsibility and capability of key recovery within the end user's hands.

One method gaining in popularity is for a company to maintain protection of the backup of its private keys, but to use a third-party company, called a *recovery agent*, to store a unique key that can be used to unlock the backup of the private keys. This system prevents any of your private keys from leaving your premises and offers little room for compromising the security of those keys. The private keys are stored on your site, while the key to unlock those private keys is stored offsite.

Another method uses what is known as *M of N control*, which refers to a method of storing a private key, protected and encrypted with a separate unique key. The key used for recovery is split into different parts and distributed to various individuals, called *key recovery operators*, and is usually stored in a smart card or other memory device. To use the recovery key, a certain number of the operators must be present with their part of the key.

> **Travel Advisory**
>
> M of N control can be somewhat difficult to maintain, especially with employee turnover where new replacements must be entered into the scheme.

The term *M of N control* refers to the number of operator keys that must be present to create the recovery key, such as *2 of 3* or *4 of 7*. For example, in a 4 of 7 scheme, a recovery key is split into seven parts and only four of those parts are needed to create the recovery key that will decrypt the backup of the private key.

> **Exam Tip**
>
> M of N control refers to the number of keys that must be present to create the recovery key, such as 3 of 5.

Multiple Key Pairs

The issue of using multiple key pairs in a PKI implementation greatly increases both the security and the complexity of data encryption. Using multiple keys directly involves the problems associated with backing up certain types of key pairs for recovery.

In a typical PKI setup, a private key and a public key are generated to be used for encryption and digital signatures. These keys can be used for three basic purposes:

- **Encryption** To encrypt data to protect its contents
- **Authentication** To identify users through their public keys and certificates
- **Nonrepudiation** To make it impossible for someone to deny having signed a transaction or file

The problem with using a single key pair for these functions is that the single key pair can often conflict with the backup and recovery requirements of the organization. A key pair used for encryption should be backed up in case the private key is lost or destroyed, so it can be recovered to decrypt the locked data. The backup of the same key pair used for nonrepudiation purposes, however, could be harmful. A digital signature intended to be legally binding can be repudiated if the signer proves it could be invalid because of the existence of another copy of the private key.

To solve this conflict, a dual key pair system can be used that can satisfy all security and backup requirements. One key pair can be used for encryption and decryption, while the second key pair can be used exclusively for digital signatures and nonrepudiation needs. The key pair used for encryption can be safely backed up for recovery purposes, while the second key needn't be backed up, in conformance with nonrepudiation procedures.

Exam Tip

Know the concept of nonrepudiation and how a dual key system can resolve the conflict with key backup.

Another important concept is the problem of *key history*. When using multiple keys and discarding old keys in favor of new ones, you might have archived data protected with encryption keys that you no longer use. As part of your key backup strategy, you need to retain copies of keys for encryption still in use on your network.

Travel Advisory

Without some form of key history, you won't be able to recover data files that have been encrypted with older keys you no longer possess.

Objective 10.02 Certificate Management

CompTIA Security+
Objective 5.6

In the overall encryption trust model, all aspects, including users, administrators, the key management server, and any third-party key management company, must be able to trust one another so the keys and identities of those using the keys are secured. As part of identifying users of keys, certificates are created, so users' identities and their public keys can be fully authenticated. If the public keys corresponding to a certain certificate have been compromised, any messages or files that were encrypted might be vulnerable. The only way to ensure the validity of the key is to check the status of the certificate.

Certificates go through a lifecycle that identifies how long they're valid, how the certificate is renewed, when they can be suspended and revoked if compromised, and when they can be destroyed when no longer needed.

Certificate Lifecycle

The lifecycle protects and secures the certificate mechanism itself, because the entire key infrastructure could be undermined if it is compromised. The lifecycle of a certificate goes through the following stages, as detailed in Figure 10.5:

1. Certificate is requested.
2. Certificate is issued.
3. Certificate is published.
4. Certificate is received.
5. Certificate is suspended/revoked.
6. Certificate is expired.
7. Key is destroyed.

If the certificate is renewed prior to being revoked or suspended, the lifecyle is extended.

Exam Tip

Know the various aspects of the certificate lifecycle and what scenarios can cause certificates to be suspended or revoked.

Certificate Requested, Issued, Published, and Received

In the first steps of the certificate lifecycle, the user makes a request to a CA for a certificate. In this request, the user must submit certain identity details. A CA cannot issue a certificate without verifying the identity of the requester. As part

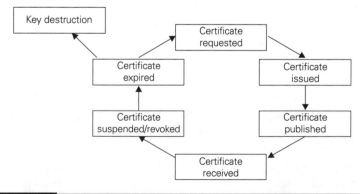

FIGURE 10.5   Certificate lifecycle

of the request, the user can generate his own public key pair when he submits his request, or the CA can perform the key generation when the user's identity is established.

If the process is followed correctly, the requester's identity is established and pubic key pairs are generated; then the CA can issue the certificate, and then publish and distribute it. The user will then receive his certificate, which authorizes him to use the certificate for its intended purpose.

Certificate Suspension and Revocation

A particular certificate can be suspended and revoked before its expiration date for a number of reasons. The most common reason for revocation is that the user who is using that certificate isn't authorized to use it anymore, as in the case of a company employee who quits his job or is fired. Alternatively, the certificate subscriber's data, such as the name of the company, might have changed, or it could have been incorrect on the certificate application. Other reasons for revocation include the problem of a key pair or certificate being compromised. If the private key is lost or compromised, the details in the corresponding certificate will no longer be valid. By immediately revoking the certificate, it can't be used for any authentication, encryption, or digital signature purposes. *Suspension* is a temporary revocation of the certificate until the problem concerning the certificate or the certificate owner's identity can be corrected. A suspension of a certificate can be undone, but a revocation is permanent.

The owner of the certificate must initiate communication with the CA to begin the revocation process. This needs to be performed in a secure way, through a signed message, in person, or via another authenticated channel. The private key corresponding to the certificate being revoked can be used to authenticate a revocation request, but if the revocation is a result of the key being compromised, the key can't be used to support authentication for a new certificate.

When a certificate is revoked, it's placed on a CA's Certificate Revocation List (CRL), which includes certificates that have been revoked before their expiration date by the CA. A CRL is used by other users and organizations to identify certificates that are no longer valid.

CRLs can be distributed in two main ways:

- **Pull model**   The CRL is downloaded from the CA by those who want to see it to verify a certificate. In this model, the user or organization is responsible for regularly downloading the latest CRL for the most recent list.
- **Push model**   In this model, the CA automatically sends the CRL out to verifiers at regular intervals.

These models can also be hierarchical in nature, in which a specific CRL of a CA is pushed to other sites, where other users and organizations can download it. CRLs are maintained in a distributed manner, but various central repositories contain the latest CRLs from a number of CAs.

Web sites and companies that deal with large numbers of secure transactions might need their own local version of a CRL that can quickly be compared to the large number of certificates accepted.

To check the status of a certificate, the CRL can be obtained from the specific CA or from a centralized database of CRLs released by a collection of authorities. To help automate this process, certificate status checks have been built into software applications, such as e-mail programs and web browsers that automatically check the status of a received certificate. Status checks can also be made manually by checking the web site of a CA and entering the serial number of a certificate.

Exam Tip	
Know the purpose of a CRL and how it can be used to verify certificates.	

Certificate Expiration

Within each certificate is a specific date for the beginning and ending of that certificate's lifecycle. Most certificates are valid for approximately one to three years. The length of time the certificate is valid depends on the type of certificate issued and its purpose. A high-security defense contractor might switch its key pairs on a regular basis, meaning the certificates it uses could be valid for a short time.

The purpose of certificate expiry is to protect certificates from brute-force attacks. The longer certificates are in use, the greater the risk that they will be cracked. This is similar to a password expiry and retention scheme for a network in which users must regularly change their passwords to prevent them from being compromised.

If you want to use a certificate after its time of validity is complete, you'll need to renew the certificate. See the section "Certificate Renewal" a little later for more information.

Exam Tip	
Once a certificate has expired, it can't be renewed. A new certificate and key pair need to be generated.	

Key Destruction

If a certificate and key pair have been compromised or are no longer in use, the key pair (the private and public key) should be destroyed to prevent further use. Because the public key has been distributed many times during its lifetime, it can obviously be difficult to destroy completely. Therefore, the destruction of the private key is essential to ensure certificates or digital signatures can no longer be created with those keys.

Some private keys, however, need to be retained—for example, if they're used for key management or data privacy, such as an encrypted file on a corporate network file server. The private key might need to be maintained as part of a key history, so items being stored with an older encryption key can be unlocked if necessary. A balance must be struck between the security need for key destruction and the need to access archived information.

Another aspect of key destruction involves the certificate that validates those keys. If the certificate is still valid, according to its creation and expiry date, then it needs to be revoked by contacting the CA, which will include the certificate's serial number in its CRL.

Destroying the private key can be a fairly simple process, but it must be thorough to ensure that the private key can't be recovered in any way. If the key is simply stored on a local hard disk, it can be deleted. The drawback to this method, however, is that many OSs don't delete the file; they delete only the file name from the disk directory, while the actual file is still stored on disk, so it can be retrieved through a data recovery program such as Microsoft Windows Recycle Bin. In some cases, such as if the computer were stolen, an unauthorized user could analyze the hard drive or send it to a special recovery lab that can restore the data still residing on the disk.

To prevent such discovery, many utilities can delete files permanently from magnetic media. Other options include the actual physical destruction of the media itself, whether it be a hard drive, floppy disk, CD, smart card, or flash memory device.

Certificate Renewal

To continue to use a certificate, it must be renewed before its expiry date. Typically, the CA will contact the owner of the certificate when the certificate's expiration date is impending. The certificate owner has the responsibility of renewing the certificate before the expiration date. If this renewal isn't performed before the expiry date, the certificate will become invalid, and anyone trusting the source of that certificate will be unable to transact or communicate with the certificate owner. For companies that rely on certificates for digital transactions, this could be fatal. In addition, a request for a new certificate will need to be issued, which might take time to process before you receive the new certificate and keys.

The policies and procedures of the CA must be examined carefully to ensure that certificates are renewed on time, especially because CAs usually need extra time before the expiry date to register the renewal properly. As a rule of thumb, you should renew certificates at least 30 days before they expire.

One important aspect of renewal is deciding whether or not to generate a new key pair to go along with the new certificate. Many CAs, in the process of renewal, merely repackage the certificate with the same public key. Because cryptographical keys can be compromised over time through sustained computational brute-force methods, the longer you keep the same key pair, the more insecure it will become. Therefore, it's extremely important for cryptographical security to generate a new key when renewing a certificate. This might not be so important for an individual who uses encryption only sparingly for personal purposes, but for companies with high-security needs, this is vital.

CHECKPOINT

✔ **Objective 10.01: Public Key Cryptography** Decentralized storage is used by individual users, and centralized storage is used for enterprise networks. Private keys need to be stored securely and, preferably, encrypted with a password. Key escrow companies can store the encryption key that can unlock the encryption on your private key, which is stored at your location. Backups need to be made of keys to prevent loss of data because of lost, stolen, or damaged keys. Keys for digital signing shouldn't be backed up because of nonrepudiation requirements. A dual-pair key system can generate separate keys for encryption and digital signing. M of N control stores different parts of a key distributed among several people, or a third-party recovery agent can be used to store your keys. Only a certain number of key parts are needed to provide the key.

✔ **Objective 10.02: Certificate Management** Certificates need to be renewed before expiry, or else a new certificate must be generated. A certificate should be suspended or revoked if the keys related to that certificate are compromised. Check the CRL for certificates that have been revoked.

REVIEW QUESTIONS

1. When you save a private key on a local hard drive, how do you ensure its security?

   A. Needs to be password protected

   B. Save the backup to a floppy

   C. Store a written copy in an envelope

   D. Store it in the same directory as the public key

2. A key management server is considered what type of storage?

   A. Local storage

   B. Centralized storage

   C. Decentralized storage

   D. Distributed storage

3. What should be stored to prevent a loss of data that was encrypted with older encryption keys?

   A. Public key

   B. Key history

   C. Expired certificates

   D. Escrow key

4. Which of the following would be the most secure way to store a private key?

   A. Save it on a hard drive in plain text

   B. Seal it in an envelope and store it in a desk

   C. Encrypt it on a smart card

   D. Store it on a portable USB device in plain text

5. In a key escrow model, what is stored offsite with a third party?

   A. Encryption key to decrypt a private key file

   B. Encryption key to decrypt a public key file

   C. Copy of a public key

   D. Copy of a certificate

6. An encryption key split into separate parts and distributed to a number of certain users to be used to create the recovery key is an example of what type of key recovery scheme?

   A. Key backup

   B. Key management server

   C. Key escrow

   D. M of N control

7. Which of the following describes the inability for someone to deny having signed a transaction or file with his or her encryption key?

   A. Nonrepudiation

   B. Authentication

   C. Encryption signing

   D. Digital signature

8. A network administrator has recently been fired from a company. What should be done with his current certificate?

   A. Renewed for the new administrator

   B. Revoked

   C. Suspended

   D. Expired

9. When a certificate is revoked, where are its serial number and information published?

   A. Certificate Destruction List

   B. Certificate Suspension List

   C. Certificate Revocation List

   D. Certificate Expiry List

10. When should a certificate be renewed?

   A. On its expiry date

   B. After it expires

   C. After it's revoked

   D. Thirty days before expiry

REVIEW ANSWERS

1. **A** To ensure the security of a private key, especially when it's stored locally on some kind of device, the private key should be protected with a password. If the key or device on which is it stored is stolen, the unauthorized user won't be able to unlock the key without the password.

2. **B** A key management server is a centralized storage system that takes care of the process of distributing, storing, and backing up keys for users of an enterprise network. The administrative overhead associated with manually managing keys for so many users would be overwhelming.

3. **B** By saving a history of keys that have been used in the past, you'll be able to decrypt archived files saved with those keys. If those keys are lost, the data can't be unlocked.

4. **C** Private keys should never be stored in plain text. If they're stolen, an unauthorized user will be able to use them to decrypt messages and files.

5. **A** In a key escrow storage scheme, an encryption key used to encrypt and decrypt the private key file is stored offsite with a third party. If access is needed to the backup copy of the private key, the encryption key needs to be obtained from the third-party company after you've been properly authenticated.

6. **D** In this key recovery scheme, a prescribed number of the key owners must be present with their parts of the key. M of N control refers to the number of operator keys that must be present to create the recovery key, such as 2 of 3 or 4 of 7. For example, if a recovery key is split into 7 parts, only 4 of those are needed to create the recovery key that will decrypt the backup of the private key.

7. **A** A person can deny having signed a transaction or file with his or her encryption by proving another copy of the private key exists. This is a drawback of some key backup and recovery models. The use of dual key pairs facilitates having a separate key for digital signing that shouldn't be backed up.

8. **B** The certificate should be revoked because the user assigned to that certificate is no longer with the company. This prevents the user from continuing to use that certificate for encryption and authentication.

9. **C** A Certificate Revocation List (CRL) is published by a CA to show certificates that have been revoked. A verifier can examine the list to check the validity of another user's certificate.

10. **D** Most certificate authorities require that a certificate be renewed a certain amount of time before the actual expiry date. This provides the CA with enough time to renew the certificate and deliver it back to the client for distribution.

Organizational Security

Redundancy and Environmental Planning

	NEWBIE	SOME EXPERIENCE	EXPERT
ETA	3 hours	2 hours	1 hour

Protecting your organization's and customers' information from corruption, lack of access, or data loss is vital in maintaining your ability to provide vital services to your organization and your customers. As part of a company's overall security and disaster preparedness plans, redundancy planning is concerned with preventing your systems from downtime caused by failed equipment, interrupted communications, and environmental issues.

The key components of redundancy planning are high availability and fault tolerance. Maintaining *high availability* is the premier goal of most businesses that guarantee access to data and provide host services and content that must be always available to the customer. *Fault-tolerance* defines how able your system is to recover from software or hardware errors and failure. For example, a server with only one hard drive and one power supply isn't fault-tolerant: If the power supply fails, the entire server will be rendered useless because there's no power to the system. Similarly, if your file server's hard drive crashes and is unrecoverable, all data on that hard drive will be lost. Fault-tolerant systems are important for maintaining business continuity.

This chapter describes the components of redundancy planning, the importance of ensuring business continuity via high availability and fault tolerance, and the importance of environment controls in an organization's security strategy.

Objective 11.01
CompTIA Security+
Objective 6.1

Explain Redundancy Planning

R*edundancy planning* is key in preventing downtime for your organization in the event of equipment or communications failure. *High availability* and *fault tolerance* are extremely important factors in redundancy planning and ensuring business continuity, and they are implemented at the system level to provide redundancy, to protect data, and to maintain system uptime.

Your system's ability to recover from a disaster is greatly dependent on the facilities and equipment available if your main facility is heavily damaged or destroyed. Backup equipment and facilities are vital elements in planning for recovery, and each should be examined for both onsite and offsite strategies.

High Availability

The ability to provide uninterrupted service consistently is the goal of maintaining a high-availability system. This initially requires that you identify systems that need to provide services at all times. Answer the following questions to help you in planning for high-availability systems:

- What is the monetary cost of an extended service downtime?
- What is the cost to a customer relationship that can occur as a result of an extended service downtime directly affecting that customer?
- Which services must be available at all times? Rank them in order of priority.

If your company hosts a number of services required by customers, these services should be given higher priority than your own systems because the service level promised to customers must be maintained at all times.

Service Levels

Many companies measure their ability to provide services as a *service level*. For example, a web server–hosting company might promise 99 percent service availability when the systems and services it hosts are available. The other 1 percent of the time, the systems might be unavailable because of maintenance, equipment failure, or network downtime.

> ### Local Lingo
>
> **service level**   Specifies in measurable terms the level of service to be received, such as the percentage of time when services are available. Many Internet service providers (ISPs) provide a service-level agreement to guarantee customers a minimum level of service. Some IT departments now provide a measured service level to the rest of the company.

The most common examples of servers and services that require high availability and high service levels include the following:

- **Internet servers**   These include Internet services, such as web and FTP servers. These types of servers usually require that the information and data stored on them be available at all times.
- **E-mail**   E-mail is the most commonly used Internet service because all users need and use e-mail. Therefore, mail servers and gateways must maintain high levels of service availability.
- **Networking**   As the backbone of all computer communications, the networking equipment that provides the infrastructure for private and public networks must be available at all times.
- **File servers**   File servers house all data and information needed by the users. Without access to this data, users can't perform their job functions.

- **Database servers**   Database servers are typically required as back-end servers to web servers and other applications that use database transactions. Data stored on database servers, such as file servers, must be available at all times.

Onsite Redundancy

Most disasters and disruptions are localized in nature and typically involve only one room or one particular piece of equipment. Failed hardware is the most common type of service interruption, such as blown power supplies, damaged network cabling, failed hard drives, and broken tape backup drives. Having spare hardware onsite to fix these small problems is vital to handling these smaller disruptions quickly. Many companies have vendor maintenance contracts that require the vendor to replace failed hardware, but in case of an emergency, the spare parts might not be delivered for many hours or even days. It's critical for hardware components that are commonly prone to failure to be switched quickly with an onsite spare.

The following spare components should be kept onsite at all times:

- Hard drives
- Redundant Array of Independent Disks (RAID) controllers
- SCSI controllers
- Hard-drive ribbon cabling
- Memory
- CPU
- Network cards
- Keyboard/mouse
- Video cards
- Monitor
- Power supplies
- Network switches, hubs, and routers
- Phone sets

It is also highly recommended that you have a contact list on hand for the manufacturers of your components in the event a replacement part needs to be ordered.

Redundant Servers   In high-availability environments such as e-commerce or financial web sites, where servers must be up and running 24 hours a day and 7 days a week, a downed server can cause a company severe financial damage. Customers will be unable to make purchases online while the server is down, and critical stock trades or financial transactions cannot take place. In these environments, redundant servers are installed that will take over in the event the primary server is unavailable. For example, an organization with a critical web server can install a secondary identical web server that can be swapped with the primary if the primary is down. In the event redundant servers are not running concurrently, having spare servers and workstations on hand means that if the primary server goes down, the failed file server hardware can be quickly replaced and the data restored from backup. This is often the preferred method for smaller organizations that do not have the resources or budget to run live redundant systems.

Exam Tip

High availability ensures that a service, such as a web or database server, is always available. Redundancy via live or spare replacement servers is a recommended method of ensuring availability.

Clustering   For more advanced high-availability purposes, the use of *clustering* technology enables you to use several servers to perform the services of one. Clustering greatly enhances load balancing, as the resources of all the servers can be used to perform the same task as one server. For fault-tolerance purposes, if one system goes down, one of the other servers in the cluster can take over seamlessly without any interruption to the clients.

Two primary types of clusters are used: active/active, and active/passive. *Active/active* means that both servers in the cluster are up and running and actively responding to requests. In the event one server is unavailable, no drop in availability occurs as the other server is still actively responding to requests. In an *active/passive* arrangement, one server is actively responding to requests, while the other server acts as a live standby. In the event the active server is unavailable, the other passive server can be triggered into becoming the active server and begin responding to requests.

For major disaster recovery scenarios, failover systems and redundant servers can be located in buildings of other company locations. For example, a company operating in Los Angeles might have another facility operating in New York. This allows the servers in New York to take over the services offered by the Los Angeles servers if LA suffers an interruption or disaster.

System Configuration Backups   The use of backups in a business continuity sense involves not only the backup of important information and data, but also backing up the system files and configuration settings of your server and network equipment.

> **Travel Assistance**
>
> See Chapter 12 for detailed information on backup and recovery concepts and best practices.

When equipment failure causes the loss of your server, you not only lose the data and services housed on that server, but you lose all your system settings and configuration. Depending on the type of server, these configuration settings can be complex and can take many hours, or even days, to restore. For example, an e-mail server is usually configured with many options and settings that are unique to your location. If the server has failed or is destroyed and needs to be rebuilt, you'll need to reinstall the OS, install your e-mail server applications, and configure the system properly before you can restore your mail files that were backed up to tape. If you didn't back up your system files, you'll need to re-call and enter your system settings manually, which can take up too much time when a high-availability server is down.

Most modern backup applications have disaster recovery options that save important elements of the OS and application configuration files that can be instantly restored in case of a disaster. If you're recovering a server, you need only install the OS and the required media device drivers for your backup media device to retrieve the rest of your server files and system configuration from the backup media.

Redundant Internet Lines   It might be surprising to learn that many organizations rely on only one Internet service provider (ISP) to host their connections to the Internet. If any communications issues occur with the Internet line, or the ISP itself, the organization's communications are instantly crippled. No users will be able to access the Internet or e-mail, and for companies that have deployed Voice over IP (VoIP) telephony applications that rely on the Internet, the telephones will not be operational. It is difficult to think that so much time and money can be spent on redundant servers and equipment, while no thought is put into communications redundancy.

It is a best practice to have two or even three completely different ISP services and connections to provide a backup line of communication or to run concurrently with your current ISP line. In the event one of the ISPs or lines goes down, you will still be able to communicate to the Internet via the redundant connection. The ISP lines must be from different companies, or else your supposedly redundant Internet lines will be going to the same point of failure at the same ISP, and if the central router fails at the ISP, both your connections to the Internet will be down.

Many organizations also use redundant ISPs to provide some bandwidth control. For example, critical applications and services can be routed to one ISP, while general company connectivity (such as e-mail or web browsing) can be directed to the second ISP to ensure critical applications receive the maximum bandwidth they require from their own dedicated Internet connection.

Alternative Site Redundancy

In the event of a physical disaster such as a fire or a flood at your main company site, you need alternative facilities to house backup equipment to get your company operational again. In some cases, your original server and networking equipment could be damaged or destroyed, and then a new infrastructure must be created at a new site. For a company with no alternative site in its disaster recovery plan, this could mean many weeks before a facility is secured and new equipment is set up in the new building. The purpose of an alternative site is to have a facility already secured and, in some cases, already populated with a network and server infrastructure to minimize downtime. The choice of alternative sites will come down to how time-sensitive your company's product or services are and how fast you need to be operational again.

Hot Site   A *hot site* is a facility that's ready to be operational immediately when the primary site is unavailable. All equipment and networking infrastructure the company requires are already in place and can be activated quickly. The equipment duplicates the setup installed in the original building. The hot site facility is usually provided by another company, which hosts your company's equipment. Hot sites should be tested frequently to ensure the switchover runs smoothly and quickly. This is an expensive solution, but for companies that offer critical services, the costs of losing money and customers during an extended downtime warrant the expense of a hot site.

Warm Site   A *warm site* is similar to a hot site, but without most of the duplicate servers and computers that would be needed to facilitate an immediate switchover. The warm site is there to provide an immediate facility with some minimal networking in place. In the event of a disaster, a company will transport its own equipment to the new facility, or if the original equipment is destroyed with the facility, new equipment can be purchased and moved there. A warm site could take several days to restore and transfer data and bring the business back to full operation, so this option makes sense for companies that don't offer time-critical services. This is the most widely used alternative site option because of its relatively lower price compared to hot sites and its flexibility. The disadvantage of a warm site is that it's not immediately available after a disaster and it isn't easily tested.

Cold Site A *cold site* merely offers an empty facility with some basic features, such as wiring and some environmental protection, but no equipment. This is the least expensive option, but this also means in case a disaster strikes, it might take several weeks before the facility and equipment are ready for operation, as almost all the networking and server infrastructure will need to be built and configured.

Exam Tip

Be aware of the advantages and disadvantages of the different types of alternative sites, depending on your environment.

Fault Tolerance

To protect your systems and network equipment and to provide redundancy for maintaining high-availability service, you must implement *fault-tolerant* systems. To make a system fault tolerant, it should contain a number of redundant components that will allow it to continue functioning if an equipment failure occurs. For example, a file server can be configured with two network cards. In case one network card fails, network communications can continue uninterrupted through the second network card. To ensure data integrity, it isn't enough to implement redundant hardware components, such as power supplies and network cards. The use of fault-tolerant RAID systems is required to allow multiple copies of the same data to be saved across multiple disk media, so data won't be lost if one of the hard drives fails.

Local Lingo

RAID Redundant Array of Independent Disks. Defines the concept of using a number of separate hard drives to create one logical drive. If one of the drives fails, the system can rebuild the information using the remaining disks.

Some fault-tolerant concepts must be understood before implementation:

- **Hot swap** Refers to the ability to insert and remove hardware while the entire system is still running. Most types of hardware require that the system be shut down before removing or inserting components. Hard drives in RAID systems are the most common type of hot-swap device.
- **Warm swap** Refers to the ability to insert and remove hardware while a system is in a suspended state. Although less flexible than a hot-swap

device, warm swap means you needn't shut the entire server down to replace hardware components. When the swap is complete, the server resumes its normal operations. Although services are shut down during the suspend period, time is saved by not having to reboot the entire system.

- **Hot spare** Refers to a device already installed in the system that can take over at any time when the primary device fails. There's no need to physically insert or remove a hot spare device.

The following sections outline the types of system components that can be made fault tolerant.

Hard Drives *Hard drives* are partly mechanical in nature. This makes them one of the most common components prone to failure on a server. The hard drives contain all the data and information, and if the hard drive fails, that data can be irretrievably lost.

Travel Advisory

If a hard drive fails or its data is corrupted, the information it contains can sometimes be retrieved by special hard-drive recovery specialists. This recovery process can be both time-consuming and expensive.

The most common method of hard-drive redundancy is to use a RAID system. RAID allows data to be spread across two or more hard drives, so if one hard drive fails, the data can be retrieved from the existing hard drives.

RAID can be implemented via hardware or software. Hardware RAID is based on a disk controller that controls the redundancy process across several physical hard drives. Software RAID relies on operating system kernel processes to control the RAID redundancy process, and while less expensive, it requires much more CPU processing power to manage the RAID process, and a software problem could put your data at risk compared to a dedicated hardware solution.

Mirroring the contents of one hard drive on another is called *RAID 1*. Several RAID levels can be implemented, depending on the number of disks you have and the importance of the information being stored. Other RAID techniques include *striping*, which spreads the contents of a logical hard drive across several physical drives and includes parity information to help rebuild the data. If one of the hard drives fails, parity information is used to reconstruct the data. Most RAID systems use hot swap drives, which can be inserted and removed while the system is still running. To increase the fault tolerance of a RAID system, redundant RAID controllers can be installed to remove the disk controller as a single point of failure. Table 11.1 describes the most common RAID levels and their characteristics.

Power Supplies   Because of their electrical nature, power supplies are another important common computer component prone to failure. As the central source of power for any computer or network device, a power supply that fails can instantly render a critical computer system useless. Most modern servers come with multiple power supplies, which are running as hot spares. In case one of the power supplies fails, another will immediately take over without an interruption in service. Some high-end servers have as many as three extra power supplies. Many network devices, such as switches and routers, now come with dual power supplies. Replacing a single power supply on such a small, enclosed device would be difficult.

Network Interface Cards   One of the most overlooked fault-tolerant–capable devices in a server system is the *network card*. Typically, little thought is given to the scenario of a failed network card. In the real world, losing connectivity to a server is the same as having the server itself crash because the server's resources can't be accessed. Many modern servers now come preinstalled with redundant network cards. Extra network cards can also be used for load balancing, as well as being available to take over if another network card fails.

CPU   Although CPU failure is unlikely, failure is still a scenario that requires fault-tolerance capabilities, especially for high-availability systems. Many large-scale server systems have multiple CPUs for load-balancing purposes to spread the processing across all CPUs. Extra CPUs, however, can also be used for fault tolerance. If a CPU happens to fail, another one in the system can take over.

TABLE 11.1   RAID Levels

RAID Level	Minimum Number of Hard Drives	Characteristics
0	2	Striping only, no fault tolerance
1	2	Disk mirroring
3	3	Disk striping with a parity disk
5	3	Disk striping, distributed parity
0+1	4	Disk striping with mirroring

Uninterruptible Power Supply   Although redundant power supplies can provide fault tolerance in a server if one of the power supplies fails, they can't protect against the total loss of power from the building's main-power circuits. When this happens, your entire server will immediately shut down, losing any data that wasn't saved or possibly corrupting existing data. In this case, a battery backup is needed. An *uninterruptible power supply (UPS)* contains a battery that can run a server for a period of time after a power failure, enabling you to shut down the system safely and save any data.

Travel Advisory

Most UPSs come with software that can configure your server to automatically shut down when it detects the UPS has taken over because of a power failure.

Objective 11.02
CompTIA Security+
Objective 6.5

Explain Environmental Controls

Security is often considered as protection against theft, vandalism, or unauthorized access to a company's computer systems. Typically, not enough thought and planning are put into the security of your actual facility, which is the first line of defense for your employees and your company's assets. Threats from unauthorized system access are a great concern, but protecting your facilities from environmental concerns, such as fires and floods, is equally important. At the minimum, the facility itself must adhere to any local and national safety standards as they pertain to building construction, fire ratings, and electrical code. Many of these issues need to be resolved before and during the time the facility is being constructed.

To protect your employees and sensitive equipment that resides inside the building, a regulated environment should be provided that controls the temperature, humidity, electrical systems, ventilation, and fire-suppression systems.

Facility Construction Issues

Before the foundation of a new company facility is laid, an incredible amount of planning goes into the construction process. Part of that process should involve the physical security and safety of the new facility. Several issues must be considered, often even before the new location is chosen. These main issues include location planning, building construction, and computer room construction.

Location Planning

When planning the location for a proposed company facility, several factors must be considered. Unless secrecy of the facility is desired, the building should be in a visible area and situated comfortably within the surrounding terrain. The building should be easily accessible from major roads, highways, or even railway or coastal ports, depending on the type of business. The building facility should have proper lighting for its entrances, both for the security of the employees and for adequate light for security camera recording. Most important, the site should be analyzed in respect to its susceptibility to natural disasters. If the building is located in a valley, could flooding occur? Is the building situated in an area prone to tornadoes, hurricanes, or earthquakes? All these factors should be incorporated into an overall site plan.

Facility Construction

After the site has been chosen, the actual construction of the facility must be carefully planned and executed. The construction materials need to be studied for their compliance with local and national safety standards, including fire and structural-strength ratings. Building security must also be a high priority during construction. The following outlines some of the key components of building construction, including some recommendations to enhance security:

- **Walls**   Must be examined for fire and strength ratings. For high-security areas, walls might need to be reinforced with stronger materials.
- **Doors**   Should be resistant to forced entry and fitted with security mechanisms, such as basic or electronic locks. Emergency doors must be carefully placed for access during an emergency.
- **Ceilings**   Should be examined for their fire rating, and materials should be made of noncombustible materials. The decision to use a drop ceiling is a balance between security and convenience. Although a drop ceiling is good for cable management, it also inadvertently provides access to other areas and rooms.
- **Windows**   Should be resistant to shattering and placed accordingly to prevent access to sensitive areas of the building. For added security, the windows can be made opaque or reflective, so no one can see into them from the outside. Computer screens should be facing away from the windows so that they cannot be viewed from the outside.

- **Flooring**   Should be carefully chosen for its fire rating and susceptibility to combustion. The flooring surfaces should be conducive to a nonconductive, nonstatic environment.

Computer Room Construction

To preserve the integrity and security of a sensitive company computer and networking equipment, these components should be housed in a separate environmentally and security controlled room. This room should not be accessible by other doors, rooms, corridors, or stairs. Only one secured doorway should exist, which employees can enter and exit.

Inside, servers and networking equipment are usually stacked in a rack or cabinet that can be secured by a lock. Cabling is typically run up to the ceiling, down through the floor, or high up on the walls using special cable management trays. This prevents people from tripping over equipment or wiring that might be strewn haphazardly over the floor.

The room should also be designed for maximum air ventilation and installed with environmental controls to regulate both temperature and humidity.

Exam Tip
Ensure that you know the special considerations for computer network room security compared to other parts of the building.

Environment Issues

Computers and electronic equipment are sensitive to environmental factors such as temperature and humidity and air and power quality. Imbalances in any of these utilities can result in severe damage to computer equipment, and they can potentially cause even greater perils to both the people and the facilities. Environmental controls must be installed and continuously supervised for proper operation.

Temperature and Humidity

Sensitive computer and electronic equipment must operate in a climate-controlled environment. To provide a proper operating environment, the temperature and humidity of a computer facility must be carefully controlled and maintained. In addition to this, computer facilities should be equipped with an industrial air conditioner to keep the entire room at a steady, cool temperature. Overheating of computer equipment can cause disruption or even total equipment failure. When devices overheat, their components expand and retract, which can eventually damage them permanently. In a computer system itself, several fans circulate the air and cool the components inside.

Humidity levels are important to the overall operating health of computer equipment because high humidity can cause corrosion of the internal parts of a system. Low humidity levels create a dry environment, where the buildup of static electricity can cause great harm to electronic equipment, so humidity levels should be set between 40 and 50 percent. Static electricity can also be minimized in the environment through the use of special antistatic mats and bands, which can be worn by technicians who regularly touch the equipment.

Ventilation

The quality of the air circulating through the computer facility must be maintained through the proper use of ventilation techniques. Without proper ventilation, a risk of airborne contaminants occurs. These contaminants could be dust or other microscopic particles that can get inside and clog such critical equipment as the fans, which need to be running to keep the system cool.

Electrical Power

Another important environmental concern is the electrical power system that runs your equipment. Electrical power must be provided with consistent voltage levels and a minimum of interference. Even small fluctuations in power can cause irreparable damage to sensitive electronic equipment. Power protection has two aspects: ensuring the consistency and quality of your primary power source and maintaining the availability of alternate power in a power outage.

Several types of fluctuations can occur:

- **Blackout**   A prolonged period without any power
- **Brownout**   A prolonged period of lower than normal power
- **Spike**   A momentary jump to a high voltage
- **Sag**   A moment of low voltage
- **Surge**   A prolonged period of high voltage

To protect your equipment against these different types of perils, you can use several devices. Simple power-surge protectors generally aren't rated for expensive types of computer equipment. Usually, these types of power bars contain some type of fuse or circuit breaker that cuts off the power in a spike or a surge. By the time the breaker cuts in, the moment of high voltage has already been reached and has possibly damaged the equipment that's plugged into the power bar. The recommendation is for most computer systems, servers, and network infrastructures to use a UPS, which works on a variety of levels as both a high-end surge protector and during a power failure. The battery normally contains enough power to run the system for a short time, so the system can be brought down properly and shut off before the battery runs out. Most modern UPSs come with software that shuts down during a power outage.

Travel Advisory
Don't plug power bars or high-load peripherals, such as laser printers, into UPS power outlets, because they can quickly overload the UPS.

To provide clean and consistent power to computer equipment, a device called a line or power conditioner can be used. It plugs directly into the power supply outlet and ensures that the power that reaches the computer equipment is free of voltage fluctuations and interference.

For large organizations with critical high-availability requirements, a more expensive option for backup power is the use of a backup power generator that runs on a battery or fuel. When using batteries, a power generator has a finite time that it can run until the battery power runs out. With fuel-based generators, the generator can be kept operational as long as it continues to be filled with fuel, and it provides electricity even for very long blackout periods as long as fuel is available.

Cable Shielding

Network cabling can be extremely sensitive to environmental electrical interference. This type of disruption can cause loss of information, network latency, and the complete disabling of the network. These types of problems are most pronounced in manufacturing environments where computers and networking cabling run side-by-side with large machines. The following are the most common type of problems that affect network cabling:

- **EMI** *Electromagnetic interference* is caused by the electrical "noise" created by motors, lighting, and any type of electronic or mechanical equipment. This interference can potentially disrupt communications on network cabling because of the noise in the line that distorts the network signals.
- **Crosstalk** *Crosstalk* is caused by the electrical signals of one wire disrupting the signals of another wire. Without proper shielding, network cabling is susceptible to crosstalk, especially twisted-pair wiring.
- **Attenuation** As an electronic signal travels, it slowly degrades over a certain distance. The longer a network cable, the more susceptible it is to this type of signal degradation. The rate of *attenuation* increases

when the type of network signaling is using higher frequencies for faster data transfer. Attenuation can also be caused by damaged or faulty network cabling.

To prevent these problems from affecting your network communications, the cabling you use should be properly shielded. Different types of cabling use different kinds of shielding methods.

Exam Tip
Be aware of the different types of interference that can affect network cabling.

Coaxial

Coaxial cabling consists of a special copper core wire that's surrounded by several layers of protection. The copper wire is insulated by PVC or Teflon-based material, as shown in Figure 11.1. This, in turn, is wrapped with a braided shielding material, and then the cable is covered with a protective outer sheath. This cabling is resistant to EMI and, most often, is installed in manufacturing environments because of the large amounts of interference that can result from nearby electrical and mechanical equipment.

Twisted Pair

Twisted-pair cabling consists of several insulated copper wires, surrounded by a protective sheath. The copper wires are twisted together to protect them from EMI and to balance the crosstalk between the individual wires. Two types of twisted-pair cabling exist: shielded and unshielded. Shielded twisted-pair (STP) cabling contains an extra layer of foil shielding for added protection, as shown in Figure 11.2.

Unshielded twisted-pair (UTP) cabling, which doesn't have this protection, is shown in Figure 11.3. UTP is the most common form of cabling because the extra shielding of STP makes it much more expensive.

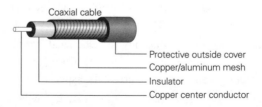

FIGURE 11.1   Coaxial cabling

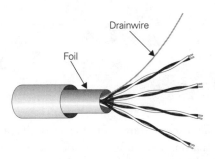

FIGURE 11.2 Shielded twisted-pair cabling

Fiber-optic

Because fiber-optic technology uses light as the medium for communication, it isn't susceptible to electromagnetic interference, crosstalk, or attenuation. Fiber-optic cabling is expensive and is typically used in large local area networks (LANs) as the backbone among smaller networks using coaxial or twisted-pair cabling. Figure 11.4 shows a cross section of a fiber-optic cable.

Wireless Networks and Cells

Although no physical wires are involved with wireless communications, wireless networks can still be disrupted in many ways. Because wireless networks use a common frequency band—typically in the 2.4 or 5.8 GHz range—they can suffer from interference from other devices that use those frequencies, such as cordless phones and microwave ovens.

Another problem is that the overlapping of *wireless cells* can cause disruptions in communications, especially when a user is tied to a specific access point. An *access point* is a wireless base station that connects the wireless clients to a

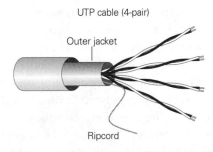

FIGURE 11.3 Unshielded twisted-pair cabling

FIGURE 11.4 Fiber-optic cabling

wired network. A *cell* is a specific area of influence of that access point or other cellular system base station. Users suffer signal degradation as they travel farther from the access point. The ranges for wireless access points are typically 500 feet indoors and 1000 feet outdoors.

> ### Local Lingo
>
> **wireless cell**   A division of wireless networks containing a certain amount of frequencies that can be used.

Fire Suppression

Although fire suppression is typically already part of the facility plans, fire suppression for a computer environment can differ from techniques used to protect building structures and their contents. The most obvious difference is this: When suppressing a fire in a computer facility that's filled with a large number of electronic servers, personal computers, laptops, printers, and network devices, the use of water can be as damaging as the fire itself. Although computer equipment–approved fire extinguishers are available, other effects of a fire, such as smoke and high temperatures, can also be damaging to computer equipment.

The key elements of fire protection are early detection and suppression. Early detection is a must in preventing fires from escalating from a small, minor fire to a raging inferno. Timing is of the essence, and you can detect a fire in several ways.

Smoke detectors are the most common form of warning device. Through the use of optical or photoelectric technology, a beam of light is emitted, and the smoke detector sets off an alarm if it detects a change in the light's intensity. As smoke filters into the unit, it senses the changes in the light pattern.

A *flame detection* unit can sense the movements of a flame or detect the energy that's a result of combustion. Flame detection units tend to be more expensive than other options, and they're typically used in high-security environments that require advanced fire-detection techniques.

Heat detector units can detect fires by sensing when a predetermined temperature threshold has been reached. Once the temperature from the fire grows to a certain level, an alarm is triggered. Heat detector units can also detect rapid changes of temperature that indicate the presence of a fire.

Once a fire is detected, a mechanism must be initiated to suppress the fire. A fire can be suppressed in several ways, each with its own positive and negative aspects, depending on the type of fire and the environment of the location.

Water

Water is the most common type of fire suppressant, but for computer facilities that contain a large amount of electrical equipment, water can be damaging. The use of water during an electrical fire can make the fire worse, causing even more damage. Water sprinkler systems usually consist of sprinkler heads that are distributed evenly throughout the area to provide maximum coverage. The detection system should be configured to shut down the electrical supply before the water sprinklers turn on. Several types of water sprinkler systems can be used:

- *Dry pipe* systems   Water isn't released into the pipe until the alarm sounds. A delayed release valve turns on the sprinklers when filled and ready. This type of system is helpful in a false alarm because the system can be turned off before water is released.

- *Wet pipe* systems   Water in the pipes is released when a predetermined temperature is reached. This is the most common method and is considered the most reliable. The disadvantage is the possibility of the pipes freezing during cold weather and the water damage that can be caused by a broken or a faulty nozzle.

- *Preaction* systems   This more expensive method combines the characteristics of the wet and dry pipe systems. Water is released into the pipes only when a predefined temperature is reached. The sprinkler system is initiated when a contact link on the nozzle has melted because of the fire and heat. This prevents water damage from false alarms or allows time to suppress smaller fires with conventional methods, such as a fire extinguisher.

Halon and Chemical-based Systems

Halon is a special fire-suppressing gas that can neutralize the chemical combustion of a fire. Halon acts quickly and causes no damage to computers and electrical equipment. This is the recommended alternative for protecting computer and server rooms. Unfortunately, because of its environmental drawbacks, including depletion of ozone and the possibility of danger to humans when used in large amounts, Halon is no longer manufactured. Halon still currently exists in some building installations, if they were installed before restrictions on Halon were put in place. Several more environmentally safe chemical-based replacements exist for Halon, such as FM-200 and Argon.

CHECKPOINT

✔**Objective 11.01: Explain Redundancy Planning** Consider using alternative sites for disaster recovery purposes. Maintain high availability of your services by implementing redundancy, data integrity protection, and fault tolerance. Use RAID for disk storage systems. Determine the level of RAID redundancy depending on the importance of the data you're protecting. Keep spare parts of common hardware on hand, so it can be replaced immediately.

✔**Objective 11.02: Explain Environmental Controls** Environmental protection involves temperature and humidity management, proper ventilation, electrical protection, and fire suppression.

REVIEW QUESTIONS

1. A facility that contains networking and server equipment and is ready to be operational immediately with no downtime is referred to as what?

   A. Warm site

   B. Hot site

   C. Cold site

   D. Offsite

2. The ability to provide uninterrupted service is referred to as what?

   A. Fault tolerance

   B. High availability

   C. Contingency planning

   D. Business impact analysis

3. The ability to insert and remove hardware while a system is still running is called what?

   A. Cold swap

   B. Suspend swap

   C. Warm swap

   D. Hot swap

4. Which RAID level defines disk mirroring?

   A. RAID 5

    B. RAID 1

    C. RAID 0

    D. RAID 3

5. In a power brownout, which of the following devices would be the most useful in maintaining proper power levels?

    A. Backup power generator

    B. UPS

    C. Line conditioner

    D. Power bar

6. Interference caused by the electrical signals of one wire disrupting the signals of another wire in a cable is called what?

    A. Crosstalk

    B. Attenuation

    C. Spike

    D. Surge

7. What is the primary purpose of an uninterruptible power supply (UPS)?

    A. To provide power supply redundancy within a network server

    B. To provide continuous power until the main power is restored

    C. To provide temporary power to allow the safe shutdown of a system

    D. To regulate and control power levels to prevent fluctuation

8. Which of the following types of network cabling is most resistant to EMI?

    A. Fiber-optic

    B. STP

    C. UTP

    D. Coaxial cable

9. Which of the following environmental issues is most likely to affect an enclosed server room?

    A. High temperatures

    B. Cool temperatures

    C. Flooding

    D. Average humidity levels

10. Which of the following fire-suppressing agents is the safest for both electronic equipment and personnel?

   A. Halon

   B. FM-200

   C. Water

   D. Sand

REVIEW ANSWERS

1. **B**   A hot site contains enough networking and server equipment to continue your business operations in case a disaster strikes your primary facility. Warm sites and cold sites contain little to no existing equipment or infrastructure.

2. **B**   The ability to provide uninterrupted service is referred to as high availability. This is important for businesses that require the services or products they offer to be available at all times.

3. **D**   A hot swap device, such as a hard drive, can be inserted or removed without the need to shut down the server. This enables you to retain the availability of the services on that server.

4. **B**   RAID 1 defines disk mirroring, a process in which a hard drive's contents are duplicated on an identical drive in the system. In case the primary drive fails, the mirrored drive will take over.

5. **C**   A line conditioner device is situated between the power source and the equipment. The device ensures that power coming from the source is at constant levels. Options such as UPSs and power bars typically don't offer this protection.

6. **A**   Crosstalk is caused by the electrical signals of a wire in a cable interfering with the signals of another nearby wire. This is most pronounced in the twisted-pair type of cabling.

7. **C**   A UPS battery typically contains only enough power to run a system for about 10 to 20 minutes. This allows enough time for the systems to be safely shut down before the power runs out. Some UPSs have software that controls this shutdown automatically.

8. **A**   Because fiber-optic cabling uses light to transfer information over the cables, they aren't susceptible to electromagnetic interference.

9. **A**   Server rooms can quickly rise in temperature with so many systems running in an enclosed area. At high temperatures, CPUs and

hard drives can shut down due to the excessive heat. Most server rooms contain air-conditioning systems that keep the temperature regulated and cooler than normal. If this air-conditioning system fails, the heat can dramatically rise within minutes.

10. **B**   Although Halon is much safer than water when extinguishing a fire near electrical equipment, it's considered dangerous to humans in high levels. Halon isn't manufactured anymore, and FM-200 or Argon is now preferred in a nonwater-based fire-suppressant system.

Disaster Recovery and Incident Response

	NEWBIE	SOME EXPERIENCE	EXPERT
ETA	3 hours	2 hours	1 hour

Disaster recovery is a subject often avoided by management personnel because of the additional costs and time required to put together a disaster recovery plan that adds little value to the company's bottom line. Unfortunately, if a company is unprepared for natural disasters such as fires, floods, earthquakes, and tornadoes, as well as unnatural disasters such as vandalism, theft, hacking, and virus attacks, and a disaster strikes, the final costs of implementing no disaster protection could prove fatal.

The most difficult task is analyzing your company's weaknesses to such risks and identifying the impact each risk will have on your business operations. When it becomes obvious that even a small-scale disaster can send your operations into a tailspin, you must begin planning an overall disaster recovery plan to prevent a disaster from fully impacting your ability to function as a business. A disaster recovery plan must be created so that representatives from each department know exactly what to do if an emergency occurs. Representatives must be trained thoroughly and the procedures documented carefully, and the plan should be tested at least once a year or when company changes require alterations to the original procedures.

Travel Advisory

A disaster recovery plan is a step-by-step plan for recovering your networks and systems after a disaster. It is essential to protect employees, the company's ability to operate, its facilities and equipment, and its vital data.

In preparing for disasters, organizations must also create policies and procedures in regard to incident response. By adjusting to the legalities of prosecuting computer crimes, most companies have trained their employees in collecting and preserving forensic evidence of computer crimes. Because the evidence is usually electronic in nature, it can easily be tampered with, causing it to be legally invalid in a court of law. Therefore, the art of computer forensics is a critical part of preventing and prosecuting computer crimes.

This chapter describes the components of disaster planning and incident response, including creating a business continuity and disaster recovery plan, initiating a backup policy and plan, and creating and practicing disaster and incident response scenarios to ensure an organization is prepared in the event of a disaster.

Implement Disaster Recovery Procedures

Objective 12.01
CompTIA Security+
Objective 6.2

Any disaster, however rare, can be fatal to a business that doesn't prepare for the emergency. Even interruptions on a small scale, such as system or network outages, can quickly incur huge financial costs and a damaged reputation. Many studies have shown that a majority of businesses that suffer a service interruption lasting more than one week are never able to recover and, consequently, go out of business.

Critical to a company's preparedness is having a proper business continuity and disaster recovery plan. Without any sort of data backup, a company risks having its entire data store wiped out forever. In most cases, this would cause the company to go under immediately or face a long rebuilding stage until it can be operational again. A well-defined business continuity and disaster recovery plan requires a strong backup strategy. Although the expense and planning requirements for such a large disaster can be costly and time-consuming because of the dedication of resources and equipment costs, it must be compared to the costs that would be incurred by losing the ability to do business for many days, weeks, or months.

Business Continuity and Disaster Recovery Plan

Although the chances of a large disaster, whatever the cause, interrupting or halting business operations are fairly slim, all companies should be prepared for disastrous events. Most management personnel pay little attention to the subject because the costs and amount of work involved in creating a *business continuity and disaster recovery plan* do little for the financial bottom line of the company. The inability to effectively recover from a disaster, however, can have dire financial consequences on a company that isn't prepared.

The overall business continuity plan is a detailed document that provides an initial analysis of the risks involved to the business because of a disaster, the potential business impacts, and a disaster recover plan for restoring full operations after a disaster strikes. The specific purpose of a disaster recovery plan is to prepare your company with a step-by-step plan to recover your networks and systems. The plan is a technologically oriented part of the overall business continuity plan, detailing specific steps to take to return and recover systems to an operational state.

The process of creating a business continuity plan includes the following phases:

- Creating a disaster recovery team
- Performing a risk analysis
- Performing a business impact analysis
- Creating a disaster recovery plan
- Preparing documentation
- Testing the plan

Disaster Recovery Team

A disaster recovery team is responsible for creating and executing business continuity activities and a disaster recovery plan that outlines the goals for restoring company operations and functionality as quickly as possible following a disaster. The team is also available to provide for the safety and support of the rest of the company's personnel and the protection of company property.

The team should include members from all departments, including management. Including all areas of the company's operations is important because each department has its own objectives and goals, depending on its function. Disaster recovery duties should be included in the job description of each department, even though these duties go over and above regular duties. Designated backup team members should also be assigned in case the original member isn't available to perform the appropriate function.

In a disaster, each team member is responsible for certain priorities and tasks, which could include coordination of other department personnel, and contact with outside emergency agencies and equipment and service vendors. The bulk of the work will be the responsibility of the IT staff that needs to coordinate the creation of a communications and networking infrastructure, as well as restore all system functionality, including the restoration of lost data.

Risk Analysis

A *risk analysis* identifies the areas of your facility and computer network that are vulnerable to certain types of disasters. The entire business operation of the company must be broken down and analyzed, so the impact of a disaster on a critical business function can be ascertained.

A risk analysis evaluates the potential outcome any type of disaster could have on your company's infrastructure. You need to analyze all possible scenarios in full. For example, in case a flood strikes the area where your main company building is located, the facility must be carefully examined for areas that would be affected by this particular disaster. Similar analysis must be made for other potential natural disasters, such as earthquakes and fire, and unnatural disasters, such as software and hardware failure, network attacks, or virus attacks. Create or obtain diagrams of the facility layout, such as building blueprints, seating plans, network cabling maps, and hardware and software inventory. The effect of each disaster scenario should be more easily ascertained with the aid of these diagrams. When you finish, you'll have a detailed document outlining the possible risks for each type of disaster that might occur. Using this information, you can formulate a business impact analysis that will show how those risks can affect your business functionality.

Business Impact Analysis

A *business impact analysis* will outline your most critical functions and how they'll be affected during a disaster. The analysis will examine the loss of revenue, legal obligations, and customer service interruption that can arise as the result of a disaster. Your most important business functions should be prioritized so that during the disaster recovery process they'll receive the attention they need to become operational before any noncritical aspects of the business.

Exam Tip

Business functions should be prioritized so that in case of a disaster they'll be made operational before other less-critical functions.

The business impact analysis should also include timelines on how long it will take to get the company operational again if a disaster occurs. The resources, equipment, and personnel required should be carefully detailed, especially the ability to recover and restore vital company information from backups.

Most important will be examining the total financial loss incurred by certain types of disasters. If the company isn't prepared, it might not survive a disaster that completely halts its operations. This information can be provided to other managers, who might help fund and organize a disaster recovery plan, based on the statistics of the impact of a disaster. Many companies don't like spending the time or money on disaster recovery, but when the cost of the impact is analyzed and calculated, the ability to be prepared for a disaster will quickly pay for itself, if and when a disaster strikes.

Types of Disasters

Many types of disasters can befall a company. Many are small and inconvenient, affecting only a certain part of the company or only one network server. They might affect only communications or software applications. Larger disasters can be devastating, causing the destruction of most or all of the company's physical facility. The following sections describe the different types of disaster scenarios that can affect an organization's operations.

Natural   The types of natural disasters that can occur depend on the location of the company facilities; natural disasters can be the most devastating emergency to affect a business. You must be aware of the types of natural disasters that can happen in your specific geographic area. A fire, flood, earthquake, tornado, or hurricane can destroy your building and its infrastructure within minutes. The only way the company can be truly protected is if its data is regularly backed up and sent to an offsite location. Your company furniture and computer equipment can be relatively quickly replaced, but sensitive company data collected over many years can't.

Human Error and Sabotage   Something as simple as a mistakenly deleted file can cause a company much grief if the data in that file is critical to the business operation. A spilled cup of coffee can render a server unusable within seconds. Human errors and mistakes can be expected and are much more common than natural disasters. Vandalism and sabotage, however, can be quite unexpected but cause great damage. Theft or malicious destruction of company equipment by a disgruntled employee can cause as much damage as any natural disaster. The need for access controls and physical security is emphasized with these types of disasters.

Network Attacks   Cybertheft and vandalism are an increasingly annoying and dangerous problem for companies, especially those whose business is Internet-related. When a company is permanently connected to the Internet, the door is open for unauthorized users to attempt to gain access to company resources. Some malicious hackers are simply trying to gain access to a system for fun. More malicious unauthorized users might cause widespread damage within the company's network if they gain access. Some attacks could come from within the network. A security professional will need to analyze threats coming from both outside and inside the network.

Viruses   Computer viruses are special programs able to replicate themselves, and they often perform malicious activities on networks, servers, and personal computers. Viruses can be extremely destructive, causing massive network outages, computer crashes, and corruption or loss of data. Once one computer is infected with the virus, the virus can quickly spread to other computers and servers on the network. E-mail–based viruses can spread quickly in a short amount of time. Protection against viruses includes the use of special anti-virus software at both the personal computer and server levels. User education about the computer viruses is also key to virus prevention.

Travel Advisory

Hacking and viruses are probably the most common disasters that befall a business. An e-mail virus can spread so fast it can overload your e-mail servers within a matter of minutes after initial infection.

Disaster Recovery Plan

As part of your business continuity plan, you should devise a disaster recovery plan so that specific tasks are defined and prioritized to aid in the recovery process. This will define clear objectives that must be met during the recovery phase.

Responsibilities must be clearly defined for those important individuals participating in the recovery as part of the disaster recovery team. Tasks should be divided and assigned to the appropriate people and departments. Each individual must be trained on the specific procedures and have them properly documented. Team leaders must be established, and central authorities can guide the recovery process through each of its critical steps.

You also need to decide which aspect of the business is the most critical and must be up and running first if a disaster occurs. Different departments in the company have unique objectives and priorities, but certain functions can be delayed if they don't immediately impact the ability of the company to function. Typically, the most important part of the company to get operational is basic communications, such as phone, fax, networking connectivity, and e-mail. Until these communication lines are functional, the company's ability to coordinate the disaster recovery effort will be greatly reduced, causing much confusion and chaos. Business-critical items should come next, such as file servers, database servers, and Internet servers that run the company's main applications or anything specifically needed by customers.

The ability for the company to restore full operations as quickly as possible depends on the efficiency with which objectives and goals, outlined in the business continuity and disaster recovery plans, are met.

Documentation

Each phase of the business continuity and disaster recovery plans should be carefully documented, and the resulting document should be readily available to all members of the disaster recovery team. The document should also be safely stored in both hard copy and software copies to reduce the potential for damage or loss. In case of a real disaster, a lack of documentation will cause nothing but chaos because no one will know how to get all aspects of the company running again, especially during a stressful and frantic time.

The disaster recovery plan must be precise and detailed, so anyone can follow the instructions without requiring further clarification. Each person on the disaster recovery team will have clear responsibilities and duties that must be performed in the most efficient manner possible.

The plan should include the following items:

- **Notification lists**   A list of people and businesses to notify in case of a disaster.
- **Contact information**   Phone numbers and contact information for employees, vendors, data recovery agencies, and offsite facilities.
- **Networking and facilities diagrams**   Diagrams and blueprints of all networking and facilities infrastructure, so it can be re-created on the new site.
- **System configurations**   Configuration information for all servers, applications, and networking equipment.
- **Backup restoration procedures**   Step-by-step information on how to restore data from the backup media.
- **Backup and licensing media**   To reinstall the servers, you will need the operating system software, appropriate license keys, and the backup media. These should be stored in a safe location so they are ready and available during the installation process.

Finally, copies of the disaster recovery plan should be stored and secured both onsite and in an offsite facility, especially any designated alternative company site. If a physical disaster strikes your main facility, the plan will be useless if it's destroyed along with the building.

Exam Tip
Be aware of the types of information that should be documented in your disaster recovery plans.

Testing

To complete your disaster recovery plan, you must fully test it to ensure all parts of the plan work as they should. Re-creating a disaster without affecting the current operations of your company might be difficult, but some form of test should be performed at least once a year.

Most disaster recovery tests involve the choice of a scenario, such as a fire in a certain part of the building. Your disaster recovery team must consult the recovery plan documentation and execute it accordingly. Depending on the size of the company, it might be feasible to involve only certain departments, but the IT department should always be included, because IT's main responsibilities are the network infrastructure and data recovery. During the testing, every phase should be fully documented through the use of a checklist. Any exceptions or problems encountered during the procedure should be thoroughly documented.

Once the test has been completed, the original disaster recovery plan should be reviewed for any procedures that didn't work correctly or that need to be modified as a result of the test. The plan should be updated with any new information as a result of the testing. Any changes to the existing facilities or infrastructure should initiate a review of the current disaster recovery procedures. Any changes should be made immediately to reflect the new environment.

Backups

Critical to a company's preparedness is having a proper backup and disaster recovery plan. Without any sort of data backup, a company risks having its entire data store wiped out forever. In most cases, this would cause the company to go under immediately or face a long rebuilding stage until it can become operational again. A well-defined disaster recovery plan is coupled with a backup strategy. Although the expense and planning for such a large disaster can be costly and time-consuming because of the dedication of resources and equipment costs, it must be compared to the costs involved with losing the ability to do business for many days, weeks, or months.

> **Travel Advisory**
>
> One of the most important aspects of a backup strategy is regularly testing backups by performing test restores. Remember that your backups are no good unless you know the information can be restored.

Planning

A good backup strategy must be clearly planned, defined, executed, documented, and tested. The first step in establishing your backup strategy is to draft a plan that covers the following points: the *type of data* to be backed up, the *frequency* in which backups will occur, the *amount of data*, and the *retention period* for the backups.

Type of Data   Your company's data must be separated into mission-critical data and more constant data that doesn't change much over time. Obviously, the most important data is the information the company requires during its daily business activities, especially if this information is something frequently accessed by customers. For example, a database company will ensure that it fully protects its customers' data. If the company loses that data without any procedure for disaster recovery, its business is essentially lost.

Frequency   Depending on the type of data your company stores, a wide range of backup frequency schedules can be implemented. For example, a transactional database used every day by customers would be considered critical data that must be backed up every day. Other files such as operating system (OS) and application program files that don't change often can be backed up on a lighter schedule—say, once a week. Backup frequency should depend on the critical nature of the data as well as the costs involved with losing and re-creating data from the same point in time. Some high-end transactional databases, for example, need to be backed up many times a day because of the high rate of transactions.

Amount of Data   The amount of data to be backed up will have a large bearing on the type of backup strategy you choose. Depending on how much information you need to save on a daily basis, you might be unable to perform a completely full backup of all your data every night because of the time it takes to perform the operation. To create a backup plan that can meet your objectives, you must achieve a balance between the type of data and the frequency with which it needs to be backed up. Instead of using full backups, you can try other alternatives, such as performing incremental or differential backups on information that has only recently changed.

Retention   You must decide how long you need to keep backed-up data. Depending on the type of business and the type of data, you might need to archive your backup data for long periods of time, so it will be available if you need to perform a restore. Other data might be needed only in the short term and can be deleted after a certain period of time.

> ### Travel Advisory
> The legal policy of some companies is to retain information for a certain period of time before the information must be destroyed. Check with your legal department to create a policy for backup tape retention.

Backup Hardware

Several types of backup hardware and devices are available to suit the needs of the backup strategies of most companies. The most common type of backup system uses magnetic tape. These can be simple devices that contain only one tape drive, to large jukebox tape libraries with robotic autoloaders. Magnetic tape drives and media are flexible and offer relatively inexpensive storage, combined with speed and ease of use. Other media storage options include optical devices, such as DVDs. These are typically used for more permanent archival purposes, however, rather than everyday backup.

Backup hardware should be routinely inspected for faults. Because of its mechanical nature, backup hardware is more prone to failure than typical electrical devices. Magnetic tape drives should be cleaned periodically with a special tape to clean the magnetic heads that become dirty over time.

Backup Types

An important part of your backup strategy is deciding what type of backup you'll perform. Depending on the size of all the data you need to back up on a daily basis, a full backup of everything every night might be impossible to do. The amount of backup media required and the time needed to perform the backup can render this option unfeasible. The goal is to achieve the most efficient backup and restoration plan possible, depending on your environment and the type of data to be backed up.

Each file on a computer system contains a special bit of information, called the *archive bit*. When a file is modified or a new file is created, the archive bit is set to indicate the file needs to be backed up. When a backup is performed, the archive bit is either cleared or left as is, depending on the type of backup method chosen.

Full Backup   A *full backup* includes all files selected on a system. A full backup will clear the archive bit of each file after every backup session to indicate the file has been backed up. The advantages of a full backup include the fact that all data you selected is saved during every session, so all your system's data is backed up in full. If you need to restore all the information back on to the server, the recovery time is much shorter because it's saved in a specific backup session and can be restored with a single restore operation. For example, if you perform a full backup on Wednesday night and the server crashes Thursday morning, your data loss will be minimal. The disadvantages of using a full backup are that, depending on the amount of data you have, the backup could take up a large amount of media, and the time it takes to perform the backup could intrude on normal working hours, causing network delays and system latency.

Incremental Backup With an *incremental backup,* only those files that have been modified since the previous full or incremental backup are stored. The archive bit is cleared on those files that are backed up. Incremental backups are much quicker to perform than full backups, and they use up much less backup media because you're saving only files that have been changed. The disadvantage of incremental backups is that to restore an entire system, you need to restore the last full backup and every incremental backup since then.

Differential Backup A *differential backup* saves only files that have been changed since the last full backup. In this method, the archive bit isn't cleared, so with each differential backup, the list of files to save grows larger each day until the next full backup. The advantage of differential backups is that to restore an entire system, you need only the last full backup and the most recent differential backup. The disadvantage is the backups will take more time and use more media with each differential backup that takes place.

Exam Tip
Be aware of the advantages and disadvantages of each type of backup method, depending on the environment.

Media Rotation and Retention
Another important factor in your backup plan is determining the length of time that backup media and its data should be retained. Theoretically, you could save every backup tape you create forever, but this increases costs because of the large amount of backup media you'll need to purchase on a routine basis. Magnetic tape media usually deteriorates over time, and if you use the same tapes over and over, they'll quickly wear out. The integrity of your backups might be compromised if you continue to use the same tapes. Media rotation and retention policies must be defined to form the most efficient and safe use of your backup media. Several methods can be used for rotation and retention, from simple to the most complex.

Son Backup Method The *son backup method* is the simplest method to use because it involves performing a full backup every day, using the same backup media each time. This method is used only for small backup requirements. The media can quickly wear out and must consistently be replaced. The son method doesn't allow for archiving, and if you need to perform a restore, you can use only the last backup as a source—so if the file you're looking for was deleted months ago, the data can't be recovered.

Father-Son Backup Method   The *father-son backup method* uses a combination of full and differential or incremental backups on a weekly basis. For example, daily tapes are used for a differential or incremental backup from Monday to Thursday, while a Friday or weekend tape is used to perform a full backup that can be archived away as a weekly backup. This method enables you to retrieve files archived from the previous week, using the weekly full backup. More tapes can be added to the strategy if further archiving is needed.

Grandfather-Father-Son Backup Method   The most common backup strategy is the *grandfather-father-son method*. This method is easy to administer and offers flexible archiving. Similar to the father-son method, daily backup media are assigned for incremental or differential backups. At the end of the week, a full backup is made, which is kept for one month. At the end of the month, a special monthly backup can be made, which is then kept for one year. This method enables you to archive data for at least a year.

Backup Documentation

Your backup plan should be carefully documented, so if the primary backup operator is unavailable, another person can perform the backup operator's functions, such as changing tapes, sending tapes offsite, performing restores, and examining backup log files. The document should outline what systems are backed up, how often they're backed up and by what method, and the location and directories of the data. The documentation should also describe any special media labeling used and contact information for any offsite storage facilities. The documentation should be constantly reviewed and updated when new hardware and software are installed. New systems with new data must be added to your backup routine immediately.

> **Travel Advisory**
>
> When adding a new system or a directory/file to a network server, ensure that it's added to your backup schedule.

Restoration

The ultimate goal of any backup system is the ability to restore lost or corrupted data from the backup media. It's amazing to think that most companies don't test the backups they've made. The only true way of testing a backup system is to perform routine test restores. Although your backup application logs might show that no problems exist and that backups have completed successfully, a hardware problem could exist with the tape drive that causes the written data to be corrupted.

When performing regular file restoration, the best practice is not to overwrite any original files of the data you're trying to restore. Create a separate directory and restore the file there. This way, the user can decide which version is required. If the original file and directory have been completely deleted, there's no need for this extra step.

All your backup media should be properly labeled, so that in case of an emergency—where time is of the essence—the correct tape containing the data can be quickly located and restored.

> **Travel Advisory**
>
> Some tape autoloader systems come with a bar-code reader, so tapes can be labeled with bar codes for easier cataloging and searching.

Offsite Storage

In the event of a disaster at your primary site, such as fire or a flood, any backup tapes stored there could also be destroyed. All the data that's saved to backup tape will be lost, and you won't have other backups available. This is why you should store copies of the backups offsite. Offsite storage is an important part of your overall disaster recovery plan. Using an offsite storage facility means after you successfully complete your backups, they're sent to a different location, which could be another office building or a special storage company facility.

> **Travel Advisory**
>
> In case you want to keep your most recent backup media onsite, you can make two copies of your full backup, and then send one of them to the offsite storage company and keep the other. However, creating the extra backup requires extra time and backup media.

When choosing an offsite storage facility, you must ensure it follows the same basic rules of facility security measures that you follow at your own site. You should visit the location where your backup media will be stored to examine the environment. For example, the storage area should be regulated for temperature, humidity, fire prevention, and static electricity prevention. Access control should be strictly enforced, so only authorized employees of your company can retrieve tapes from the facility. Depending on the type of data you're sending offsite, you should identify how quickly you'll need access to the tapes, if and when this is necessary. The storage facility should allow access at all hours in case you need a backup in an emergency.

Execute Incident Response Procedures

W hen a security incident or disaster scenario occurs, the initial incident response can make all the difference—either it quickly mitigates a threat from spreading and causing further issues, or the incident spins out of control, causing irreparable damage to your organization's ability to function. Incident response must be planned in advance to ensure that your front-line employees are prepared in the event of a disaster to quickly contain the incident, preserve any evidence in the event of a security breach, and escalate issues as appropriate to company management or third-party authorities.

After the discovery of the incident, company personnel must report the incident to the appropriate person, and this person should be identified ahead of time. The incident could have been discovered by a security guard, a late-working employee, or in many cases the network or security administrator themselves. The company's incident response policy needs to define the first responders from the incident response team that can be deployed to respond to the incident.

First Responders

A *first responder* is the first person or persons who are notified and respond to a security incident. For example, the network administrator may receive notifications from an intrusion detection system that a security breach has taken place, and therefore the network administrator is typically the first person respond to the incident. A first responder must follow several responsibilities and procedures when he or she is the first person on the scene of a security incident.

The company's incident response policy should describe the exact tasks and responsibilities of the first responder. If a computer crime occurs, an effort must be made by the first responders of the incident to contain any damage and prevent further asset or data loss. The first responders must also try to leave the original environment and evidence intact and unaltered as best they can until the authorities have been contacted. If people begin to pick apart the crime scene after a physical crime, or if the network administrator begins poking around the file system or reboots the system, the evidence could be disturbed and considered inadmissible in court. Finally, first responders need to follow an escalation policy to notify other company officials or the authorities.

Damage and Loss Control

A major initial aspect of incident response is being able to contain an incident and the damage it is causing, so as to prevent it from spreading or causing further damage. A company must create an incident response policy that indicates what can and cannot be touched if a security compromise occurs. For example, a worker at a company undergoing a denial-of-service (DoS) attack might panic and pull the plug on its Internet connection. This, of course, stops the attacks, but it brings down the entire network and no communication exists with the outside world, effectively stopping all e-mail and Internet business communications. If the business runs its operations through a web page, this can be fatal.

In other cases, such as a virus-infected server, immediately disconnecting it from the network so that it does not infect other systems might be the best response. The incident handling and response procedures will provide information on what to do in certain scenarios. In the example of the DoS attack, to prevent the entire network from going down and to preserve any evidence of the attacks, the company might let the attack continue, so the network administrator can save logs and audit trails to help trace the source of the attack. Decisions must be made on how critical specific services are, such as e-mail, file and print services, and web services. If a file server is specifically attacked, it may be less critical to take that system offline than to disconnect an e-mail service that must be running to provide communications to the organization, even though it might be under a DoS or spam attack.

Forensics

In adjusting to the legalities of prosecuting computer crimes, most companies have trained their employees from the incident and response team in collecting and preserving forensic evidence of computer crimes. Because the evidence is usually electronic in nature, it can easily be tampered with by an uneducated investigator, which would cause the evidence to be legally invalid in a court of law. Therefore, the art of computer forensics is a critical part of evidence collection necessary for prosecuting computer crimes.

Forensics is the act of collecting and preserving evidence to use in a court of law for legal proceedings. Typical forensics of crimes, such as theft or murder, includes gathering evidence to help prosecute a suspect, such as fingerprints, weapons, and even DNA samples. In the computer world, evidence of a cybercrime can be difficult to obtain, preserve, and allow into a court of law. Because of its nature, most computer crime evidence is electronic, which can easily be erased, modified, and tampered with. After a computer crime—such as a server attack—is committed, initial investigation by the network administrator can quickly ruin evidence the attacker left behind.

The following sections outline some of special procedures required when preserving and collecting evidence of a computer crime, which includes incident response policies, preserving the incident environment, and retaining a chain of custody of the evidence.

Collection and Preservation of Evidence

Collecting and preserving evidence from a computer crime usually centers around keeping and storing any logs or audit trails that detail step by step what the attacker was doing. In cases such as these, avoid panicking. If a network administrator suddenly reboots the server to ward off the attacker, she is not only disrupting access to that server for legitimate users, but she could also destroy valuable evidence in the form of audit trails and timestamps on files that might have been changed by the intruder. When computer logs are to be used as evidence, they must be collected in the regular course of business. If the log was the result of a one-time monitoring in response to an incident, it might be considered hearsay evidence, meaning the evidence is secondhand. The company must also prove the logs themselves haven't been altered in any way from the time of the original data capture, such as performing an MD5 hash of the log file immediately after the incident so that the resulting checksum can be matched to the MD5 hash at a later time. If the MD5 hash does not match, the file has been altered since the original capture.

If the crime was physical in nature, such as the theft of equipment, the evidence needed would be some type of surveillance video. If the theft took place in a secured area, it might be possible to analyze the access logs of employees who logged in to the secured area at the time. If the company uses magnetic access cards for doors, a log can be created showing who went in and out at a certain time.

Chain of Custody

When collecting evidence of a computer crime, maintaining a proper chain of custody is extremely important. A *chain of custody* requires that all evidence be properly labeled with information on who secured and validated it. This process must also occur for each individual who comes in contact with the evidence. Unfortunately, electronic evidence can be volatile, and in a court of law it can be easily dismissed because of possible tampering. Computer media can be easily destroyed, erased, or modified, so handling this evidence requires strict procedures.

If additional copies of data need to be made, reliability and integrity must be assured so the copies can be considered tamperproof. It is a good idea to perform an MD5 hash of the data so that a checksum can be created for comparison at a later time to prove the data was not tampered with. Any devices or media containing data need to be carefully catalogued and labeled, and then sealed away to prevent tampering. Magnetic media should be write-protected to prevent the data from being overwritten.

If all evidence has been properly secured, identified, labeled, and stored, then it can be considered solid and admissible in court. A clear chain of custody log ensures this process was completed without the possibility of data modification.

Exam Tip	
A chain of custody ensures that evidence has been handled with the utmost care and lists the persons who have had access to the evidence.	

Escalation Policy

An escalation policy must be enacted and followed to provide a specific list of management or other authorities that must be contacted in the event of a security incident. Depending on the department or area of the incident, one or more direct managers should be notified, as will any central security for the organization, and escalated to various executives such as directors, vice presidents, and so on, as required based on the type of incident and the downtime it has caused. For example, if a web server has attacked overnight and the attack was discovered by the network administrator in the morning, she should notify her direct manager and the security administrator.

In the event of the attacking suspect being an internal employee, the human resources department should be contacted immediately as part of the incident response policy. From there, it can be decided whether to keep the organization's investigation internal or contact the authorities and any other outside agencies to aid in the investigation.

In the event that the security threat was external, external authorities may need to be contacted if the organization warrants that the security breach or damage that it causes is serious enough to warrant notification of the police.

Reporting and Disclosure

When investigating a security incident, every single detail should be meticulously documented to ensure that every aspect of the incident, from the specific details of the security breach to every step taken during the incident response process, is recorded. This is critical during the post-incident response phase when the organization determines whether to keep the investigation and response internal or issue a public announcement to notify customers or users of the security issues.

By keeping the information of a security breach from the public, the organization can ensure that details of its internal security (or lack thereof) are not published. For example, if an organization sent out a press release that one of its web servers had been hacked using a known exploit, other hackers who heard this information might try the same exploit on the organization's other web servers if they know the servers are vulnerable.

The decision to internalize or release publicly information on a security incident becomes very sensitive when dealing with security breaches that occur in financial institutions, such as a bank or stock trading firm, and especially for medical institutions that have strict guidelines for protecting clients' data. In these cases, the decision is often regulated by the government, and any security breaches that affect the privacy of clients must be published. For example, if a hospital computer is hacked and confidential patient records are stolen or damaged, or an Internet banking system is hacked and leaks tens of thousands of their customers' bank account and credit card numbers, it is necessary or even mandatory that the company release details of the incident to ensure customers know that data has been leaked. In the case of the bank, customers should be told to contact the bank to help secure their current accounts and lock them down before they can be abused.

Reporting and disclosure are also critical issues for companies that manufacture software or hardware that are found to contain security vulnerabilities. Many companies are embarrassed by such security breaches in their products, and they quietly release patches to the product to fix the security breach in an effort to ensure the vulnerability does not become well-known. In other cases, companies try to protect the customers by not disclosing or discussing any known security issues until they have researched the issue and released a patch to deal with it. Many companies take a very proactive approach and welcome information from third parties that test their software for vulnerabilities, which actually helps the company solve the issue and prevent it from being exploited before news of the vulnerability reaches the public.

CHECKPOINT

✔ **Objective 12.01: Implement Disaster Recovery Procedures**   Create a disaster recovery plan that documents your risks, the business impact of a disaster, a contingency plan, and network and facility documentation. Implement disaster recovery procedures. Perform backups to save and archive critical company data. Full backups are recommended if time and space permit but, if not, use incremental or differential schemes. Test your backups by performing a restore on a scheduled basis.

✔ **Objective 12.02: Execute Incident Response Procedures**   Perform damage and loss control to isolate an incident and the damage it is causing to prevent it from spreading or causing further damage. To preserve evidence, leave the original system environment intact. Save audit and activity logs for evidence. Keep a chain of custody of evidence to preserve its integrity.

REVIEW QUESTIONS

1. Which of the following is a disadvantage of using an incremental backup strategy?

   A. Takes longer than other methods

   B. Uses too much backup media

   C. Restores require all incremental backups since the last full backup

   D. Resets the archive bit after backup

2. Why do backup media need to be rotated?

   A. They slowly wear out after repeated use.

   B. Full backups require media rotation.

   C. The tapes need to be relabeled after every backup.

   D. Rotation is used to reset the archive bit.

3. What is the primary purpose of storing backup media at an offsite storage facility?

   A. The facility can copy the data to CD-ROM.

   B. If the primary site is down, the offsite storage can reload your systems from backup at their facility.

   C. For proper archive labeling and storage.

   D. To prevent a disaster onsite from destroying the only copies of your backup media.

4. What is the purpose of a disaster-recovery risk analysis?

   A. To discover which network servers are most likely to fail

   B. To gather information on natural disasters in your area of the country

   C. To know which employees are most likely to be injured in a disaster

   D. To discover what aspects of your company are at risk during a disaster

5. A network administrator has discovered the company's FTP server has been hacked. Which of the following items would be the most important to collect and preserve as evidence?

   A. Server memory dump

   B. Activity log

   C. List of files on FTP server

   D. List of user accounts

6. Which of the following describes the procedures for preserving the ownership history of a piece of evidence?

   A. Screen capture

   B. Audit trail

   C. Wiretapping

   D. Chain of custody

7. As part of your organization's contingency plan in the event of a disaster, which of the following would be the primary component of the organization to make functional after an initial disaster incident?

   A. Check all file servers and make sure they are running.

   B. Retrieve all backup tapes from the offsite storage facility.

   C. Ensure basic communications such as phone and Internet connectivity are functional.

   D. Ensure that web servers are able to accept requests from customers.

8. Which of the following should be performed on a regular basis to ensure the validity and integrity of your backup system?

   A. Periodic testing of restores

   B. Multiple monthly backup tapes

   C. Offsite storage of backup tapes

   D. Updating the backup application software

9. Which of the following aspects of incident response helps contain a security incident and the potential damage it can cause?

   A. Forensics

   B. Chain of custody

   C. Damage and loss control

   D. Escalation list

10. You are the first responder to a security incident in which a database server has been compromised and has crashed. Which of the following should be performed to help preserve evidence of the incident?

   A. Restart the system to restore operations.

   B. Save access logs and a current memory dump.

   C. Perform a backup of the database.

   D. Perform a restore of the database.

REVIEW ANSWERS

1. **C** In an incremental backup scheme, only files that have changed since the last full or incremental backup are saved. To perform a restore, you need the last full backup and any incremental backups since then.

2. **A** Magnetic tape media degrade after each use. The more times they are used, the more inclined they are to failure.

3. **D** All backup plans should require backup media to be sent to an offsite storage facility. If a disaster destroys your physical location, the backup tapes will be safe.

4. **D** A risk analysis will examine what parts of your facility and infrastructure are at risk during different types of disaster scenarios. This can help you create a business impact analysis and a contingency plan to avert those risks.

CHAPTER 12 Disaster Recovery and Incident Response **363**

5. **B** The activity log will show what times the attacker was performing hacking activities and what those activities were. This evidence might be able to be used in court to help prosecute the attacker, if he is caught.

6. **D** Keeping a chain of custody requires all evidence to be properly labeled with information on who secured and validated the evidence. This can ensure the evidence wasn't tampered with in any way since the time it was collected.

7. **C** Typically, the most important part of the company to get operational is basic communications, such as phone, fax, networking connectivity, and e-mail. Until these communication lines are functional, the ability to coordinate the disaster recovery effort will be greatly reduced.

8. **A** Regularly testing your backups by performing a test restore is the only way to ensure that your backup data is valid and the data intact. If the information cannot be restored, your backup plan is not providing any benefit for a disaster recovery scenario.

9. **C** One of the initial responses to an incident is containing the incident (whether it is a security breach or physical disaster) and mitigating the damage it can cause to prevent it from spreading or causing further damage.

10. **B** Any current logs and memory dumps should be saved to ensure you have evidence of all activity during the time of the incident. If you reboot the server to get it functioning again, you can lose valuable log data or data residing in memory. Backing up or restoring data can save data that is not useful or overwrite evidence on the system.

Organizational Policies and Procedures

	NEWBIE	SOME EXPERIENCE	EXPERT
ETA	2 hours	1 hour	0.5 hour

As part of an overall company strategy, security should be officially recognized as a critical business objective just like any other important business objective. In the past, the IT department had to define security and access controls for the company network and data. In today's Internet world, corporate management adapts the legalities of the business world to computer networks by ensuring that electronic transfer of information is secure to protect both the customer and the company.

To ensure security across the organization, and to assure customers that the company can be trusted, overall security policies must be implemented to include several component policies and procedures that govern how the organization uses computer networks, protects and distributes data, and offers services to customers. Each component of the security policy defines specific security best practices for a particular topic, such as a password policy. These policies and procedures would include rules on company Internet use, customer data privacy, company structure, data retention and disposal, and HR hiring and termination practices.

For a company's security policies to be effective, they must be communicated properly to the employees to ensure companywide knowledge and compliance. Rules won't be followed if nobody knows they exist. Many companies make use of consultants to create and draft security policies and procedures, but these policies often aren't communicated to the user community and aren't used. Employees need to be aware of security issues and procedures to protect not only themselves but also the company's services and data. User education is key in preventing security issues arising from social engineering hacking techniques that are used to gain access to valuable company data.

This chapter describes the types of company policies and user education initiatives that should be in place to protect an organization, its network systems and data, its employees, and its customers.

Objective 13.01
CompTIA Security+
Objective 6.4

Explain Legislation and Organizational Policies

To provide effective security, security policy and procedure creation must begin at the top of an organization with senior management. These policies and procedures must then flow throughout the company to ensure that security is useful and functional at every level of the organization. Understanding company security must begin with an understanding of the basic laws, regulations, and legal liability issues to which the company must adhere to protect the company and its assets, as well as the employees and customers.

Security policies and procedures are official company communications that are created to ensure that a standard level of security guidelines exists across the entire organization. These policies define how the employees interact with company computer systems to perform their job functions, how to protect the computer systems and their data, and how to service the company's clients properly. The upcoming sections outline policies and procedures in the following areas:

- Network security policies
- Access control policies
- Human resources policies
- Documentation policies

Network Security Policies

Several policies provide standard guidelines for network security within a company and encompass areas such as the Internet and internal network use, data privacy, security incident response, human resources issues, and document security.

Acceptable Use Policy

An *Acceptable Use Policy* is a set of established guidelines for the appropriate use of computer networks within an organization. The policy is a written agreement, read and signed by employees, that outlines the terms, conditions, and rules of the Internet and internal network use for the company.

An Acceptable Use Policy helps educate employees about the kinds of tools they will use on the network and what they can expect from those tools. The policy also helps to define boundaries of behavior and, more critically, specify the consequences of violating those boundaries. The policy also specifies the actions that management and the system administrators may take to maintain and monitor the network for unacceptable use, and they include the general worst-case consequences or responses to specific policy violation situations.

> ### Exam Tip
> An Acceptable Use Policy is a set of established guidelines for the appropriate use of computer networks within an organization.

Developing an Acceptable Use Policy for your company's computer network is extremely important for organizational security and to limit legal liability in the event of a security issue. Acceptable Use Policies should cover the following issues:

- **Legality**   The company's legal department needs to approve the policy before it's distributed for signing. The policy will be used as a legal document to ensure that the company isn't legally liable for any type of Internet-related incident and any other transgressions, such as cracking, vandalism, and sabotage.

- **Uniqueness to your environment**   The policy should be written to cover the organization's specific network and the data it contains. Each organization has different security concerns—for example, a medical facility needs to protect data that differs significantly from that of a product sales company.

- **Completeness**   Beyond rules of behavior, your policy should also include a statement concerning the company's position on Internet use.

- **Adaptability**   Because the Internet is constantly evolving, your policy will need to be updated as new issues arise. You can't anticipate every situation, so the Acceptable Use Policy should address the possibility of something happening that isn't outlined.

- **Protection for employees**   If your employees follow the rules of the Acceptable Use Policy, their exposure to questionable materials should be minimized. In addition, it can protect them from dangerous Internet behavior, such as giving out their names and e-mail addresses to crackers using social engineering techniques.

The focus of an Acceptable Use Policy should be on the responsible use of computer networks. Such networks include the Internet—including Web, e-mail, and instant messaging access—and the company Intranet. Most Acceptable Use Policies contain the following components:

- A description of the strategies and goals to be supported by Internet access in the company
- A statement explaining the availability of computer networks to employees
- A statement explaining the responsibilities of employees when they use the Internet
- A code of conduct governing behavior on the Internet
- A description of the consequences of violating the policy
- A description of what constitutes acceptable and unacceptable use of the Internet
- A description of the rights of individuals using the networks in your company, such as user privacy
- A disclaimer absolving the company from responsibility under specific circumstances
- A form for employees to sign indicating their agreement to abide by the policy

Travel Advisory

Many company web sites contain an Acceptable Use Policy or Terms of Use statement that protects the company from any liability from users of the site.

Due Care, Due Diligence, and Due Process

Due care, *due diligence*, and *due process* are terms that apply to the implementation and enforcement of companywide security policies. A company practices *due care* by taking responsibility for all activities that take place in corporate facilities. A company practices *due diligence* by implementing and maintaining these security procedures at all times to protect the company's facilities, assets, and employees. Although many companies outline plans for security policies and standards, they often never officially implement them, or the information isn't properly shared with the employees. Without training, guides, and manuals, and without employee input and feedback, no guidance comes from management regarding the policies and their use.

By practicing due care, the company shows it has taken the necessary steps to protect itself and its employees. By practicing due diligence, the company ensures that these security policies are properly maintained, communicated, and implemented. If the company doesn't follow proper due care and due diligence initiatives, it might be considered legally negligent if company security and customer data are compromised.

Due process ensures that in the event of a security issue by an employee, the employee receives an impartial and fair inquiry into the incident to ensure the employee's rights are not being violated. If, in the course of an investigation and inquiry, the employee's rights are violated, the company may face legal ramifications via lawsuits or governmental employment tribunals.

Exam Tip

Due care is taking the necessary responsibility and steps to protect the company and the employees. Due diligence ensures these security policies are properly implemented. Due process ensures an impartial and fair inquiry into violations of company policies.

Privacy Policy

Privacy policies are agreements for protecting individually identifiable information in an online or electronic commerce environment. A company engaged in online activities or e-commerce has a responsibility to adopt and implement a policy for protecting the privacy of personally identifiable information. Organizations should also take steps to ensure online privacy when interacting with other companies, such as business partners.

The following recommendations pertain to implementing privacy policies:

- A company's privacy policy must be easy to find, read, and understand, and it must be available prior to or at the time that individually identifiable information is collected or requested.

- The policy needs to state clearly what information is being collected; the use of that information; possible third-party distribution of that information; the choices available to an individual regarding collection, use, and distribution of the collected information; a statement of the organization's commitment to data security; and what steps the organization takes to ensure data quality and access.

- The policy should disclose the consequences, if any, of an individual's refusal to provide information.

- The policy should include a clear statement of what accountability mechanism the organization uses, such as procedures for dealing with privacy breaches, including how to contact the organization and register complaints.

- Individuals must be given the opportunity to exercise choice regarding how personally identifiable information collected from them online could be used when such use is unrelated to the purpose for which the information was collected. At a minimum, individuals should be given the opportunity to opt out of such use.

- Where third-party distribution of information is collected online from the individual, unrelated to the purpose for which it was collected, the individual should be given the opportunity to opt out.

- Organizations creating, maintaining, using, or disseminating personally identifiable information should take appropriate measures to assure its reliability and should take reasonable precautions to protect the information from loss, misuse, or alteration.

Each company must evaluate its use of the Internet to determine the type of privacy policy it needs to protect all involved parties. The privacy policy will protect the company from legal issues, raising customer's comfort levels regarding the protection of their information. A privacy policy should include the following elements:

- **Information collection**   Collect, use, and exchange only data pertinent for the exact purpose, in an open and ethical manner. The information collected for one purpose shouldn't be used for another. Notify consumers of information you have on them, as well as its proposed use, handling, and enforcement policies.

- **Direct marketing**   The company can use only non–personally identifiable information for marketing purposes and must certify that the customer's personal information won't be resold to third-party marketing firms.

- **Information accuracy**   Ensure the data is accurate, timely, and complete, and has been collected in a legal and fair manner. Allow customers the right to access, verify, and change information about themselves in a timely, noncumbersome fashion. Inform customers of the data sources and allow them the option of removing their names from the marketing lists.

- **Information security**   Apply security measures to safeguard the data on databases. Establish employee training programs and policies on the proper handling of customer data. Limit the access to a need-to-know basis on personal information and divide the information, so no one employee or unit has the whole picture. Follow all government regulations concerning data handling and privacy.

Exam Tip	
Privacy policies must be easy to find and provide information on how to opt out of any use of personal information.	

Service Level Agreement Policy

A *service level agreement (SLA)* is an understanding among a supplier of services and the users of those services that the service in question will be available for a certain percentage of time. For example, a web-hosting company could have an SLA with its customers that states the web servers that host the customer's web pages will be available 99.8 percent of the time. If the service level drops below this percentage, the customer might be reimbursed for business lost during the downtime.

The SLA policy describes the policies and procedures that a company performs to support the SLA agreement, including the services performed to preserve the SLA uptime and the contingency plans and communications that must be performed if the availability of the organization's services exceeds the thresholds agreed to in the SLA.

Incident Response Policy

An *Incident Response Policy* should be part of a company's overall security policy. In the event of some form of security incident, be it physical intrusion, network attack, or equipment theft and vandalism, some form of procedure should be in place to deal with these events as they happen. Without any clear directives, the aftermath of a security breach can cause even more damage if employees don't know how to handle an incident properly. A clearly defined incident response policy can help contain a problem and provide quick recovery to normal operations.

The policy should cover each type of compromised security scenario and list the procedures to follow when they happen. For example, in case a server is hacked, procedures might be in place to deal with removing the server from the network, shutting down related network servers and services, and preserving evidence, such as audit trails and logs. The incident response policy should cover the following areas:

- Contact information for emergency services and other outside resources
- Methods of securing and preserving evidence of a security breach
- Scenario-based procedures of what to do with computer and network equipment depending on the security problem
- How to document the problem and the evidence properly

Access Control Policies

The following concepts concern access control to data, including how to increase security through proper organizational structures and data security principles.

Separation of Duties Policy

To ensure all employees and management personnel know their roles in the company, the organization's structure should be clear, with positions properly defined with formal job titles and descriptions, definitions of responsibilities, and reporting structures that define the lines of authority.

To increase security and reduce risk from security compromises, part of this effort should be directed toward both a clear organizational structure and a specific *separation of duties*. A separation of duties ensures that one individual isn't tasked with high-security and high-risk responsibilities and that users aren't accessing restricted resources because of jobs that haven't been defined properly.

To separate duties that involve high-security situations, a certain amount of collusion must take place. *Collusion* means that to proceed with a certain task, more than one person is required to allow the procedure to take place. The more people involved, the less chance of a poor security decision that could compromise security being made by one individual. For example, in a banking situation, opening the main safe might require the authorization of at least two people, because each authorized person possesses a key, and both keys needs to be used together to open the safe. This prevents a single individual from opening the safe without supervision.

Need-to-Know Principle

The *need-to-know* principle is used to ensure that users have only the access rights they need to perform their job function. This requires giving users the least amount of privileges possible to prevent them from abusing more powerful access rights. For example, a user might need access to certain files to print them for their manager. The network administrator should give the user only enough access rights to read the file and print it, without including privileges to delete, modify, or add information to the file.

The function of permission management is to decide exactly what a person needs to know or for what areas he or she requires access to complete a job assignment. The network administrator must enact the decision. When in doubt, the network administrator should err on the side of caution and allow only minimal access until someone can authorize more privileges on behalf of the user. Increased privileges should never be handed out at the request of the user who needs them.

Mandatory Vacations Policy

Mandatory vacations are a security measure that requires employees to use their vacations at specific times of year or requires that they use all of their vacation days instead of not using them and carrying over unused vacation days to a following year. This policy is most often used to detect security issues with employees, such as fraud or other internal hacking activities, as typically the employee must be present every day to continue to perpetuate or erase the evidence of malicious activities. When a user is forced to go on vacation, his or her on-the-job activities may be more likely to be noticed and detected because the user is not present to prevent its discovery. When the user is away, the person filling in for him or her will be able to audit the user's activities and reveal any suspicious behavior. For example, an unscrupulous employee in a financial institution may be performing illegal activities related to customer bank account details, and manually cleaning up log files to erase traces of her activity. When she is forced on vacation, this activity may be noticed in the logs as she is not able to cover her tracks while she is away.

Password Policy

A *password policy* document lists all the specific password policies that must be followed by all employees in an organization. Password policies ensure that all network administrators and users are aware of the rules and procedures in place for managing the user accounts and passwords that allow access to company resources. Password policies should be part of the company's overall security policy.

Typically, users create passwords that are easy to remember—such as the names of family or pets, phone numbers, and birth dates, all of which can be easily discovered by someone who knows the user or even by a complete stranger who, through simple social engineering, has to ask the user only a few questions about his or her personal life. Other types of passwords that aren't secure are those based on any word found in the dictionary. Many password-cracking programs based on dictionary attacks are available that can find out any password in a short time if it's based on a common dictionary word.

Following are some basic, but important, aspects of the password policy that should be enforced across an organization:

- **Minimum length** The minimum length for a password should be enforced for all employees. This prevents users from using small, easy-to-guess passwords of only a few characters in length. The recommended minimum password length is six to eight characters.

- **Password complexity** Password complexity must be part of your password policies to ensure that beyond a minimum length, the password is not easy to guess, such as a dictionary word, and does not contain information specific to the user, such as a birth date. Passwords should contain a mix of uppercase and lowercase characters, numbers, and symbols, and should not be based on any word that can be found in a dictionary.

- **Password rotation and aging** Most login and password authentication systems can remember a user's last five to ten passwords and can prevent the user from using the same one over and over again. If this option is available, it should be enabled, so a user's password will always be different. Also, the longer a password has been in existence, the easier it is to discover eventually, simply by narrowing the options over time. Forcing users to change their passwords regularly (password aging) prevents the discovery of a password through brute-force attacks.

Data Retention Policy

Many companies have been affected legally by archived e-mail or data that offers evidence against them during court proceedings. To prevent legal liabilities, companies have implemented *data retention* policies to help reduce the possibility of legal problems arising from past messaging communications and data.

Data retention policies should apply to electronic information, such as files, e-mails, instant messages, and traditional paper documentation. Some clash might occur between data retention policies and backup policies, where certain files are required to be archived, while others should be disposed of after a certain period of time. Only management and the legal department can define which data is covered under either policy. The data retention policy needs to be specific about your information and take into account items that could be damaging legally, as well as information that can be damaging to business if the data is lost. In the case of e-mail, the concept of data retention becomes complicated because e-mail can contain file attachments. Part of your policy might require that e-mail be retained for a certain amount of time before deletion, while the policy for actual electronic files could be different.

Hardware Disposal and Data Destruction Policy

Any policies must also include the disposal of old hardware. As the turn-around time for the life of computers is very low (three to five years), older equipment is constantly swapped out for newer, faster machines with more capabilities and resources. However, a critical security issue is apparent in regard to the proper disposal of these systems. Servers and personal computers are typically returned with their original hard drives, which could contain sensitive and classified data. System administrators must follow a specific policy for the removal and disposal of hardware to ensure that any media containing data is completely erased or overwritten.

When data is to be disposed of, the job must be done completely. When destroying paper documentation, most companies use a shredder to cut the document into pieces small enough so they can't easily be put back together. For electronic files, this process is more complicated. Merely deleting a file or e-mail from a hard drive doesn't necessarily delete the data. Many operations systems (OSs) use a special recovery method that enables you to recover deleted files easily. When a file is deleted, it usually still exists in its original location; only the locator for the file in the hard drive directory has been removed. To ensure complete destruction of data on magnetic media such as hard drives, the media should be overwritten or the drive physically destroyed. Many "shredder" utilities are available that can overwrite the contents of a hard drive with random data to ensure any information on the drive is unrecoverable. Also, a number of high-security organizations, such as the military, opt to destroy the drives physically instead of using a shredding application.

Human Resources Policies

A company's human resources (HR) department is an important link regarding company and employee security. The HR department is responsible for hiring employees, ensuring employees conform to company codes and policies during their term of employment, and maintaining company security in case of an employee termination. The following sections outline the responsibility of human resources during the three phases of the employment cycle.

Hiring Policy

When hiring employees for a position within the company, the HR department is responsible for the initial employee screening. This usually takes place during the first interview: an HR representative meets with the employee to discuss the company and to get a first impression of the employee's personality, gauging whether this person would fit into the company's environment. This interview generally is nontechnical and personality-based. Further interviews are usually more skill-oriented and are conducted by the department advertising the position. The employee could possess excellent technical skills for the position, but his personality and communications skills might not be conducive to the work environment.

During the interview process, HR also conducts background checks of the applicant and examines and confirms his or her educational and employment history. Reference checks are also performed, where HR can obtain information on the applicant from a third party to help confirm facts about the person's past. Depending on the type of company or institution, such as the government or the military, the applicant might have to go through security clearance checks or even health and drug testing.

To protect the confidentiality of company information, the applicant is usually required to sign a nondisclosure agreement, which legally prevents the applicant from disclosing sensitive company data to other companies in case of his or her termination. These agreements are particularly important with high-turnover positions, such as contract or temporary employment.

When an employee is hired, the company also inherits that person's personality quirks or traits. A solid hiring process can prevent future problems with new employees.

Codes of Conduct and Ethics Policy

The HR department is also responsible for outlining a company's policy regarding codes of conduct and ethics. The codes are a general list of what the company expects from its employees in terms of everyday conduct—dealing with fellow employees, managers, and subordinates, including people from outside the company, such as customers and clients.

This code of conduct could include restrictions and policies concerning drug and alcohol abuse, theft and vandalism, and violence in the workplace. If an employee transgresses any of these codes of conduct and ethics, he or she could be disciplined, suspended, or even terminated, depending on the severity of the infraction.

Termination Policy

The dismissal of employees can be a stressful and chaotic time, especially because terminations can happen quickly and without notice. An employee can be terminated for a variety of reasons, such as performance issues; personal and attitude problems; or legal issues such as sabotage, espionage, or theft. Or the employee could be leaving to work for another company. The HR department needs to have a specific set of procedures ready to follow in case an employee resigns or is terminated. Without a step-by-step method of termination, some areas might have been ignored during the process that compromise company security.

A termination policy should exist for each type of situation. For example, you might follow slightly different procedures for terminating an employee who's going to work for an industry-unrelated position with another company than with an employee who's going to work for a direct competitor. In the latter case, the employee might be considered a security risk if he remains on the premises for his two-week notice period, where he could transmit company secrets to the competition.

A termination policy should include the following procedures for the immediate termination of an employee:

- **Securing work area** When the termination time has been set, the employee in question should be escorted from his workstation area to the HR department. This prevents him from using his computer or other company resources once notice of termination is given. His computer should be turned off and disconnected from the network. When the employee returns to his desk to collect personal items, someone should be with him to ensure that no private company information is taken. Finally, the employee should be escorted out of the building.

- **Return of identification** As part of the termination procedure, the employee's company identification should be returned. This includes identity badges, pass cards, keys for doors, and any other security device used for access to company facilities. This prevents the person from accessing the building after being escorted from the premises.

- **Return of company equipment** All company-owned equipment must be returned immediately, such as desktops, laptops, cell phones, PDAs, organizers, or any other type of electronic equipment that could contain confidential company information.

- **Suspension of accounts** An important part of the termination procedure is the notification to the network administrators of the situation. They should be notified shortly before the termination takes place to give them time to disable any network accounts and phone access for that employee. The network password of the account should be changed, and any other network access the employee might have, such as remote access, should be disabled. The employee's file server data and e-mail should be preserved and archived to protect any work or important communications the company might need for operational or legal reasons.

> **Exam Tip**
>
> All user access, including physical and network access controls, needs to be disabled for an employee once he or she has been terminated. This prevents the employee from accessing the facility or network.

Documentation Policies

Your company produces a wide variety of documentation, from publications for internal use, to confidential papers for senior management, to publicly available documents. Without proper controls, that documentation could be used to compromise company security. The company's document control standards and guidelines must ensure all documents produced by the company are classified, organized, and stored securely to prevent their loss, damage, or theft.

To ensure control over the protection and distribution of data, it needs to be classified with a certain designation. This data *classification* indicates what type of document it is, if the information it contains is confidential or can be made public, and to whom it can be distributed. The classification also defines what levels of data retention and storage are needed for that particular document. Finally, policies must exist on the legal status of documents concerning which can be destroyed and which need to be retained.

Standards and Guidelines for Documentation

To ensure the continuity of documentation across the company as a whole, a set of documentation standards and guidelines should be introduced. These standards and guidelines can serve as templates for all documentation to ensure they have the same look and feel, and to ensure they'll all be distributed and stored securely, according to their scope or sensitivity.

The standards and guidelines should address the following topics:

- Data classification
- Document retention and storage
- Destruction

Data Classification   A company's documentation can be voluminous, comprising a variety of documents with varying value and importance. Depending on the type of document, the amount of security and procedures used in storing and distributing that document can greatly vary. Some documents might be considered public, so they can be posted in a public form or distributed freely to anyone. Other documents can be extremely confidential and contain information that only certain individuals should be allowed to see.

To aid in this effort, documents need to be assigned security classifications to indicate the levels of confidentiality of the document. Each classification requires different standards and procedures of access, distribution, and storage. The classification also sets a minimum standard of privileges required by a user to access that data. If you don't have the necessary access privileges for that classification of data, you won't be able to access it.

Several levels of classification can be assigned, depending on the type of company or organization and its activities. A typical company could have only two classifications: private and public. *Private classified documents* are only for the internal user of the company and can't be distributed to anyone outside the company. *Public documents,* however, would be available to anyone. Government and military institutions might have several levels of confidentiality, such as "Unclassified," "Confidential," "Secret," "Top secret," and so on. Each level of classification represents the level of severity if that information is leaked. For example, the lowest level, "Unclassified," means that the document is not considered confidential or damaging to security and can be freely distributed. At the highest "Top Secret" level, documents are highly restricted and would be severely damaging to national security if they fell into the wrong hands. Each document needs to be assigned a classification depending on the sensitivity of its data, its value to the company, its value to other companies such as business competition, the importance of its integrity, and the legal aspects of storing and distributing that data.

Exam Tip

The type of security protections, access controls, data retention, and storage and disposal policies to be used depends on a document's security classification.

Document Retention and Storage   Depending on the classification of a document, the procedures and policies for storing that document can be quite different. For example, a particular document might incur certain legal liabilities if it isn't properly stored, distributed, or destroyed. To ensure proper document management, depending on its classification, companies have implemented data-retention policies to help reduce the possibility of legal issues.

Certain documents are required to be archived, stored, and protected, while others should be disposed of after a certain period of time. These policies must be created by senior management and the legal department, which can define what retention policies apply to different classifications of documents. The data retention policy needs to be specific about your company's data. It also needs to take into account items that could be legally damaging and information that can be damaging to the business if it's lost or falls into the wrong hands.

To protect documentation properly, it should be stored offsite at a special document storage facility. In case of a disaster, such as a fire at the company facility, this will ensure all important documentation is secure and can be recovered.

Document Destruction   Document disposal can often be a tricky issue. In some cases, to prevent future legal or confidentiality ramifications from the existence of a certain document, it needs to be destroyed. In other cases, it's illegal to destroy certain documents that are required by law as evidence for court proceedings. Only your company's legal department can decide on retention and disposal for particular documents. Once decided, these policies need to be communicated to the employees to ensure that sensitive documents are either destroyed or retained as per their classification.

When data is to be disposed of, the job must be done completely. When destroying paper documentation, most companies use a shredder to cut the document into pieces small enough so they can't easily be put back together. Simply putting documents in the trash or recycle bin isn't acceptable because anyone can sift through the garbage or recycle containers for these documents, a practice called *dumpster diving*. As part of corporate espionage, some companies hire private investigators to examine garbage dumpsters of a target company, and these investigators try to discover any proprietary and confidential information.

Travel Advisory

To combat the problems of dumpster diving for confidential company documents, the physical security of your facility should include your garbage disposal and recycling operations.

Types of Documentation

Beyond standard company documents, such as policies, procedures, guidelines, and training manuals, some specialized document sets require added attention regarding security and storage. Network architecture diagrams, change logs, and system logs and inventories are all documents created and managed specifically by the company's IT department. Because these documents can contain specific information on system and network devices such as logs, audit trails, network addresses, and configuration data, they are usually accessible only by authorized persons within the IT department and aren't accessible by other employees in the company.

Systems Architecture The IT department should always have current diagrams of your overall company network architecture on hand. When troubleshooting network problems or security issues, engineers who have network diagrams are ready to identify devices and overall data flow within the company's network.

A variety of diagrams is needed to show different aspects of the architecture. Overall diagrams should be general and show the company network as a whole. These diagrams should possibly indicate offices only by name—with wide area network (WAN) links in between them—for companies that have geographically distant offices. More detailed diagrams can be made of the internal network structure, showing all the routers, switches, firewalls, hubs, printers, and servers, as in Figure 13.1.

Each device should be clearly labeled with identifying information, such as the system name and the network address. Including end user workstations on systems architecture diagrams is rare, because too many could exist to include on a single diagram. The general network used by the end users should be indicated, however.

As a security precaution, network diagrams shouldn't be generally published because the information can be used maliciously by a hacker to give him a roadmap of the company's network, including IP addresses of the most critical network devices and servers. Network architecture diagrams should be accessed only by authorized individuals from the IT department. Printouts of diagrams should never be posted in public places, such as on a notice board or even the office of the network administrator. The diagram can be easily stolen by someone walking by the area, or a person can use a digital camera to quickly take a picture of it for later use.

Exam Tip

System architecture diagrams should never be displayed or stored in a public area, especially if they contain system IP addresses and other information hackers can use to compromise a network.

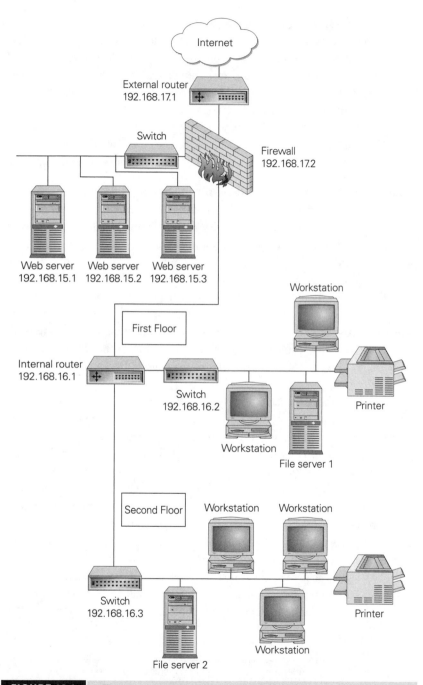

FIGURE 13.1   Example of an internal network diagram

Logs and Inventories   General application logs, audit logs, maintenance logs, and equipment inventory documentation are also important documents within an IT department. Most of this documentation is related to the maintenance and operation of the company's computer equipment, but certain logs, such as system activity logs, should be carefully archived and preserved as evidence in case of a security compromise.

System and audit logs provide snapshots of what's happening on a system at a specific point in time. These logs need to be retained for auditing in case of some security compromise. For example, the hacking of a certain server could have gone unnoticed for a long period of time. But if the logs of that system are retained and archived, they can be audited to reveal when the compromise began and how it happened. To ensure the company's backup procedures and policies are being followed, the IT department might have to retain and store copies of backup application logs, which indicate when certain data was backed up and where it's now stored. Inventories of computer equipment enable the company to keep track of its assets and know where they're located. Maintenance logs also provide important evidence for service and warranty claims.

Change Management and Control Documentation   *Change management and control documents* are used to identify current or forthcoming changes to some aspect of the company, such as the network or another critical operation. For example, the IT department might issue a change control document to the employees to notify them of a network outage because of an upgrade. More detailed change control documents for IT internal use describe the specific technical changes to the company's systems or infrastructure.

Tracking and controlling the changes to your network is important, so any unplanned changes are quickly noticed and investigated. System changes without prior knowledge or approval of management and the IT department could indicate a hacker or an intruder has compromised a system.

Objective 13.02

CompTIA Security+
Objective 6.6

Reduce the Risks of Social Engineering

The easiest way to discover someone's password often is simply to ask for it. *Social engineering* is defined as using and manipulating human behavior to obtain a required result. A user might be easily led to reveal her password or to provide personal information that might reveal her password. For example, someone might call a user on the phone, pretending to be from another department, asking for the user's password to retrieve a file. The user, thinking she knows who she is talking to, might give the unauthorized user the password without officially authenticating who the caller is or why he needs the information. The caller might make small talk with the user and trick her into revealing names of family members or her birth date, so the attacker can try out this information as a password to the user's account.

Protecting against social engineering security abuses requires user education and emphasis on the need to follow security procedures at all times, even when dealing with someone an employee knows within the company. Social engineering involves nontechnical methods of attempting to gain unauthorized access to a system or network. This typically means the hacker tricks a person into bypassing normal security measures to reveal information that can help the attacker access the network. The hacker, in effect, acts much like a con man, who tries to uncover sensitive information through manipulating someone's basic human nature.

Another typical example of this type of security breach occurs when an unauthorized user calls a help desk operator asking to reset his password. The user pretends he is a high-level manager who needs access into his account immediately. The help desk operator, if not trained properly, could instantly give this user a new password without properly identifying the user. Now the hacker can log in using the account of a high-level person who could have access to sensitive information. Other examples include questioning a network administrator for IP address information of critical network equipment, such as firewalls and routers.

To prevent against social engineering, security processes must always be followed, no matter who is requesting the information. This includes never writing down passwords in conspicuous places, never giving the password to anyone, properly logging off your system before leaving it unattended, and not letting unknown users into a secured area of the workplace.

User Education and Awareness Training

For a company's security policies to be effective, they must be communicated properly to the employees to ensure user knowledge and compliance. No one will follow any rules if they aren't aware of them. Many companies make use of consultants to create and draft security policies and procedures, but these policies often aren't communicated to the user community, and then they aren't used at all. Employees need to be aware of any security issues and procedures to protect not only themselves but also the company's services and data.

This effort must be directed from senior management and filtered throughout the company to every single employee. Different departments and divisions within a company need different security education depending on their job tasks and area of influence. The security procedures used by the financial department could be different from those used by sales or engineering, for example. Finance might need special procedures to protect confidential company and employee financial data from being exposed to other employees or companies. Engineering's security efforts will revolve around the protection and integrity of the source code or research data. Front reception could be specially trained on security practices with incoming calls or the physical security of the main entrance. Each department must interpret the company's high-level goals into the functional procedures specific to a job function.

To propagate security policies and procedures effectively to the user community, the company must make a diligent effort to communicate these policies. If no one knows about the security policies, there's no point creating them. The best methods for overall user-security awareness are though proper documentation and training.

Documentation

The first step in user awareness is creating and maintaining proper documentation of all your security policies and procedures. Policies that apply to the company as a whole should be distributed to each employee. These policies might include such areas as acceptable Internet use, employee code of ethics and conduct, and safety and emergency contact information. More department-specific policies could be distributed only to employees in that department. The HR department wouldn't publish policies for the protection of employee salary information to other departments of the company, so it wouldn't reveal or undermine any security procedures. The IT department would have different security policies because one of its main job functions is to be responsible for the security and protection of the company's network infrastructure and data.

As security policies tend to change over time, manual distribution isn't always the most efficient and timely way to communicate security information. Employees should have a way to access the most current versions of these documents in a conspicuous place, such as in a binder located outside the HR area. Another more efficient method is to publish these documents on a company intranet, so employees can easily access the most current versions. Printed versions should still be available, but, because this documentation frequently changes, only a few central copies should be created to prevent excessive paper waste. The advantages of online versions of documents are they're instantly available through the employee's computer, and they're always the most recent versions.

Exam Tip

The best place to store company documentation for easy access by employees is through the corporate intranet.

Awareness Training

Providing access to documentation is only one part of user awareness. Although printed documentation might be handed out to all employees or electronic versions could be made available online, no guarantee exists that they'll be read, understood, or implemented. To supplement the documentation and to ensure employee awareness, provide education and training sessions.

Training sessions should be mandatory for all employees and are critical for new employees. The training courses will ensure employees know the security policies and procedures the company has created and, most important, that they understand these policies and know how to enact them within their specific positions. Any policies or procedures of which employees are not sure can be discussed.

Classes can be based on overall security procedures, such as virus awareness and dealing with outside clients and inquiries. These should be attended by all employees to ensure they know how to handle security problems properly with communications media used companywide, such as e-mail or the telephone. Virus-awareness training can educate users on proper e-mail use and how to prevent viruses from infecting the company network. General security items, such as facility access control, can include training on identifying and authenticating users in the facility, so they can spot employees or strangers who are somewhere they shouldn't be. Network authentication standards, such as proper login and password management, are also applicable to all employees.

Specialized training can be presented to laptop and mobile device users who'll be traveling to ensure they protect company equipment and data when they're not on the premises. Other education initiatives can be more specific to an individual user or department, depending on their job function. The HR department can be given training on the security practices involved with hiring and terminating employees. The IT department should be given special training on specific networking security issues.

Education and training can ensure your employees are aware of and understand all company security policies and procedures, whether they apply to the company as a whole or to specific departments and job functions.

Phishing Scams

A phishing scam is a type of e-mail or web security threat that tries to use social engineering to trick an unsuspecting user into visiting a web site or replying to an e-mail with confidential personal information such as a user name and address, login and password, and banking or credit card details.

Phishing e-mails often contain logos, messages, and links to well-known trusted sites, such as a real bank or credit card company. In reality, any links in the message will actually redirect to the web site of the phishing scam operator. These web sites are often made to look just like a real bank or credit card site. The user then unknowingly enters his login and password information and personal details into the web site, when in reality it is being entered into the database of the phishing web site operator.

This activity is most commonly related with identify theft, where the unauthorized user is able to collect enough personal information about his target victim that he can perform forged credit card and banking transactions using the victim's financial and personal details.

To help protect end users, many web browsers, e-mail clients, and anti-virus software applications can detect behavior that may indicate the presence of a phishing e-mail or web site. This is typically accomplished by parsing the URL links in a message and comparing them to lists of known phishing web sites.

User education and awareness is the most important tool to protect against phishing attacks. Users must be aware that financial institutions will never ask personal details, especially bank account numbers and credit card details in an e-mail to a user. When a suspicious e-mail is received, it is also helpful to check the destination of any clickable links within the message to determine the location to which it is actually redirecting. If the destination site is not recognized, it is likely a phishing attempt. Many browsers can automatically check links for suspicious or obfuscated URL redirect links and warn the user before connecting to the site.

Travel Assistance

For detailed information and resources on phishing and best practices for reducing the risk of phishing attacks, see the Anti-Phishing Working Group web site at www.antiphishing.org.

Shoulder Surfing

End users must always be aware of their environment and the people in their surroundings when entering login names and passwords or accessing sensitive data. It is very easy for an unauthorized person to casually glance over the shoulder of an employee who is concentrating on the work at hand and watch the user as she enters user names and passwords into the computer. The person who is shoulder surfing can easily see which keys the employee is typing on the keyboard and will use the user name and password when attempting to access that account at a later time.

The issue of viewing sensitive and confidential data, such as human resources records, while other employees are present is also important. An unauthorized person can watch from behind an unsuspecting employee and view the data the authorized person is accessing on the monitor, especially today's monitors with large and wide screens.

Users must examine their surroundings before entering or viewing confidential data. If a user has her own office, she should ensure that her monitor is not easily read from a distance from the hallway and is situated in such a way so that a casual passerby would not be able to see the monitor screen. In many environments, the desk can be oriented to face away from the doorway to ensure that a monitor screen is always facing the back of the office. Special "privacy" monitor screen covers also prevent prying eyes. In open concept office spaces, this is more difficult, and it is up the user to ensure that no one is standing behind her or viewing over her shoulder while she is entering and working with sensitive data.

Hoaxes

One of the most annoying problems, hoaxes are typically some kind of urban legend users pass on to others via e-mail because they feel it is of interest. The most common types of these e-mails tell the user to forward the e-mail to 10 friends to bring the user good luck. Others claim to be collecting e-mails for a sick person. Of course, this activity merely consumes network and computer resources as the number of e-mails grows exponentially as users send them to all their friends, and so on.

Travel Assistance

See www.hoax-slayer.com for an exhaustive list of known e-mail hoaxes.

Hoaxes are generally harmless and are caused more by social engineering than maliciousness; however, some hoax e-mail messages can be phishing attempts that try to get the user to visit a link in the e-mail message that redirects to a malicious web site. The only cure for the spreading of hoax e-mails is user education to make sure that users know the typical characteristics of a hoax message and know to ignore the message and not forward it to another user.

Exam Tip

Know how to spot an e-mail hoax and how to handle it properly. The best solution is to delete it immediately and do nothing more at all.

CHECKPOINT

✔**Objective 13.01: Explain Legislation and Organizational Policies** An Acceptable Use Policy is a set of established guidelines for the appropriate use of computer networks. The company practices due care by taking responsibility for all activities that take place in corporate facilities. The company practices due diligence by implementing and maintaining these security procedures at all times to protect the company's facilities, assets, and employees. A service level agreement (SLA) is an understanding among a supplier of services and the users of those services that the service in question will be available for a certain percentage of time. A specific separation of duties ensures that one individual isn't tasked with high security and high-risk responsibilities. Users should have only the access rights they need to perform their job functions. The employee termination process includes securing the work area, returning identification and company equipment, and suspending computer accounts.

✔**Objective 13.02: Reduce the Risks of Social Engineering** For document disposal, documents must be fully destroyed to prevent dumpster diving, not simply thrown in the garbage or the recycle bin. Perform employee awareness training to educate users on the security issues of social engineering. Maintain proper documentation of all security policies and procedures, and then publish them in a conspicuous place. Ensure that no one is looking over your shoulder when you're entering sensitive data or login credentials. Educate your employees to recognize the characteristics of phishing e-mails and web sites. Ignore hoax e-mails and do not forward them.

REVIEW QUESTIONS

1. Which of the following policies concerns the use of protection and distribution of user's data?
   A. Privacy
   B. Due care
   C. Acceptable use
   D. SLA

2. Which of the following policies concerns the appropriate use of computer networks?

   A. SLA

   B. Due diligence

   C. Acceptable use

   D. Privacy

3. Which of the following policies is an agreement to provide service availability?

   A. Code of Ethics

   B. Privacy

   C. Due care

   D. SLA

4. There is a suspicion that an employee is performing illegal activities on company networks. Which of the following techniques would aid in auditing the user's activities?

   A. Password rotation

   B. Separation of duties

   C. Need-to-know

   D. Mandatory vacation

5. What should be done to prevent someone from recovering deleted files from a hard drive?

   A. Password-protect the data

   B. Overwrite the data

   C. Format the hard drive

   D. Rub it with a magnet

6. Which of the following types of data is typically protected by privacy policies?

   A. Acceptable use guidelines

   B. Anonymous web cookie tracking

   C. Nonpersonally identifiable information

   D. Personally identifiable information

7. Which of the following is the best way to assist a new employee in understanding and learning the company's security standards and policies?

   A. A training course

   B. Give them a large manual to read at home

    C. Learn-as-they-go on the job

    D. Send an e-mail with a link to online company materials

8. Which of the following is the best way to dispose of paper documentation?

    A. Ingestion

    B. Garbage

    C. Shredder

    D. Recycle bin

9. Which document classification would be considered the least secure?

    A. Secret

    B. Top Secret

    C. Confidential

    D. Unclassified

10. Which of the following IT documents should be secured in a safe place and not publicly distributed or displayed?

    A. Shift schedule

    B. System architecture

    C. Cell phone and pager numbers of IT staff

    D. Change control documents

REVIEW ANSWERS

1. **A** The privacy policy concerns the protection and distribution of users' data. A company engaged in online activities or e-commerce has a responsibility to adopt and implement a policy for protecting the privacy of individually identifiable information.

2. **C** The Acceptable Use Policy is concerned with the appropriate use of computer networks. The policy is a written agreement that outlines the terms, conditions, and rules of Internet and internal network use for the company, and it is signed by all employees.

3. **D** A service level agreement (SLA) is an understanding among a supplier of services and the users of those services that the service in question will be available for a certain percentage of time.

4. **D** When a user is forced to take a vacation, his activities can be audited and any suspicious behavior will be more likely to be noticed and detected because he is not there to prevent its discovery.

5. **B** Merely deleting a file or an e-mail from a hard drive doesn't necessarily delete the data. Many OSs use a special recovery method to enable you to recover deleted files easily. When a file is deleted, it usually still exists in its original location; only the locator for the file in the hard drive directory has been removed. To ensure complete destruction of data on magnetic media, it should be overwritten.

6. **D** A company has a responsibility to adopt and implement a policy for protecting the privacy of personally identifiable information, such as credit card or banking information, login credentials, or any data that can be used to specifically identify a user.

7. **A** Through mandatory security-training courses for new employees, you ensure they're aware of and understand all company security policies. If new employees receive only a manual, you have no assurance they'll read it.

8. **C** By shredding a document, you ensure no one can piece the document together again. Documents thrown into the trash or recycle bins can be easily recovered.

9. **D** An Unclassified document can be accessed by, or distributed to, anyone within or outside the company or organization. The document contains information that isn't confidential or proprietary in nature and is not damaging to company security.

10. **B** As a security precaution, network diagrams shouldn't be generally published because the information can be used maliciously by a hacker, giving him or her a roadmap of the company's network, including IP addresses of the most critical network devices and servers.

About the CD-ROM

Mike Meyers' Certification Passport CD-ROM Instructions

The CD-ROM included with this book comes complete with MasterExam (a practice exam that is a simulation of the actual Security+ exam), the electronic version of the book, and Session #1 of LearnKey's online training. The software is easy to install on any Windows 2000/XP/Vista computer and must be installed to access the MasterExam feature. You may, however, browse the electronic book directly from the CD without installation. To register for LearnKey's online training and a second bonus MasterExam, simply click the Online Training link on the main page and follow the directions to the free online registration.

System Requirements

The software requires Windows 2000 or higher, Internet Explorer 6.0 or above, and 20 MB of hard disk space for full installation. The electronic book requires Adobe Reader. To access the online training from LearnKey, you must have Windows Media Player 9 or higher and Adobe Flash Player 9 or higher installed on your system.

Installing and Running MasterExam

If your computer CD-ROM drive is configured to auto-run, the CD-ROM will automatically start up upon inserting the disc. From the opening screen, you can install MasterExam by clicking the MasterExam button. This will begin the installation process and create a LearnKey program group. To run MasterExam, choose Start | All Programs | LearnKey | MasterExam. If the auto-run feature did not launch the CD, browse to the CD and click the LaunchTraining.exe icon.

MasterExam

MasterExam provides a simulation of the actual exam. The number of questions, the type of questions, and the time allowed are intended to be an accurate representation of the exam environment. You have the option to take an open-book exam, which offers hints, references, and answers; a closed-book exam; or the timed MasterExam simulation.

When you launch MasterExam, a digital clock display will appear at the lower-right corner of your screen. The clock will continue to count down to zero unless you choose to end the exam before the time expires.

Electronic Book

The entire contents of the Study Guide are provided in Adobe's Portable Document Format (PDF). Adobe Reader software is included on the CD.

Help

A help file is provided through the help button on the main page in the lower-left corner. Individual help features are also available through MasterExam and LearnKey's online training.

Removing Installation(s)

MasterExam is installed on your hard drive. If you want to remove the MasterExam program, choose Start | All Programs | LearnKey | Uninstall, and then choose the program.

Technical Support

For questions regarding the technical content of the electronic book or MasterExam, please visit www.mhprofessional.com or e-mail customer.service@mcgraw-hill.com. For customers outside the 50 United States, e-mail international_cs@mcgraw-hill.com.

LearnKey Technical Support

For technical problems with the software (installation, operation, removing installations, and so on), and for questions regarding LearnKey online training content, please visit www.learnkey.com, e-mail techsupport@learnkey.com, or call toll-free 800-482-8244.

Career Flight Path

CompTIA's Security+ certification is an international, vendor-neutral certification that validates knowledge for industry-wide security principles and best practices. The recommendation is for the exam candidate to have at least two years of networking experience with an emphasis on security.

The Security+ exam is organized into six domain areas:

- **Systems Security (21 percent)**   Includes topics such as software and hardware security threats, OS hardening, application security, specific security applications and tools, and software virtualization.

- **Network Infrastructure (20 percent)**   Includes topics such as network ports and protocols, network design, network security tools, network device vulnerabilities, transmission media vulnerabilities, and wireless security.

- **Access Control (17 percent)**   Includes topics such as access control methods and models, security groups and roles, file and print permissions, logical access control, authentication, remote access, and physical access security.

- **Assessments and Audits (15 percent)**   Includes topics such as risk and vulnerability assessments, monitoring tools and methodologies, logging, and auditing.

- **Cryptography (15 percent)**   Includes topics such as general cryptography concepts, hashing, encryption algorithms and protocols, public key cryptography, Public Key Infrastructure (PKI), and certificate management.

- **Organizational Security (12 percent)**   Includes topics such as redundancy planning, disaster recovery, incident response, organizational policies, environmental controls, and social engineering.

Recommended Prerequisites

CompTIA recommends that the candidate have the knowledge and skills equivalent of those tested for in the CompTIA Network+ certification. The CompTIA Network+ exam is a vendor-neutral certification exam that is targeted at networking professionals with at least nine months of experience in network support or administration.

The CompTIA Network+ certification consists of one exam:

- Network+ Exam: N10-003 (2007 Edition)

Security+ and Beyond

The CompTIA Security+ certification consists of one exam. Once you're certified, you're certified for life. Security+ is an excellent exam that lets you prove your knowledge about basic network security. Security+ is also a great stepping stone for more advanced security certification, such as the Certified Information System Security Professional (CISSP) certification.

The CISSP certification consists of 10 domain areas:

- Access Control
- Application Security
- Business Continuity and Disaster Recovery Planning
- Cryptography
- Information Security and Risk Management
- Legal, Regulations, Compliance, and Investigations
- Operations Security
- Physical (Environmental) Security
- Security Architecture and Design
- Telecommunications and Network Security

For more information on the CISSP certification, please visit www.isc2.org.

Getting the Latest Information on Security+

Security+ is a great place to start your network security professional career. To find out the latest information about the Security+ exam, please visit www.comptia.org.

Index